INTERNATIONAL AIR TRAFFIC CONTROL

Management of the World's Airspace

Night time "lift-off". A Boeing 747 departs Heathrow international for New York.

INTERNATIONAL AIR TRAFFIC CONTROL

Management of the World's Airspace

by

ARNOLD FIELD OBE

PERGAMON PRESS

OXFORD · NEW YORK · TORONTO · SYDNEY · PARIS · FRANKFURT

U.K.	Pergamon Press Ltd., Headington Hill Hall, Oxford OX3 0BW, England
U.S.A	Pergamon Press Inc., Maxwell House, Fairview Park, Elmsford, New York 10523, U.S.A.
CANADA	Pergamon Press Canada Ltd., Suite 104, 150 Consumers Road, Willowdale, Ontario M2J 1P9, Canada
AUSTRALIA	Pergamon Press (Aust.) Pty. Ltd., P.O. Box 544, Potts Point, N.S.W. 2011, Australia
FRANCE	Pergamon Press SARL, 24 rue des Ecoles, 75240 Paris, Cedex 05, France
FEDERAL REPUBLIC OF GERMANY	Pergamon Press GmbH, Hammerweg 6, D-6242 Kronberg-Taunus, Federal Republic of Germany

First edition 1985

Library of Congress Cataloging in Publication Data
Field, Arnold.
International air traffic control.
Rev. ed. of: The control of air traffic. c1980.
Includes index.
1. Air traffic control. I. Field, Arnold. Control of air traffic. II. Title.
TL725.3.T7F53 1984   629.136'6   84-9200

British Library Cataloguing in Publication Data
Field, Arnold
International air traffic control.
2nd ed.
1. Air traffic control
I. Title
629.136'6   TL725.3.T7

ISBN 0-08-031312-4

Printed in Great Britain by A. Wheaton & Co. Ltd., Exeter

Foreword

H. HARRI HENSCHLER,
President International Federation of Air Traffic Controllers' Associations

Very few people who have been involved in the international civil aviation community in any capacity will be unfamiliar with the name of Arnold Field, his involvement and his long-standing efforts to improve the safety and efficiency of the world-wide air traffic control system.

In both the United Kingdom and the international context Arnold Field has contributed to the rationalisation of air traffic control. Through his elected offices in the International Federation of Air Traffic Controllers' Associations, The British Guild of Air Traffic Control Officers, and his subsequent involvement in IFATCA's Technical Standing Committee, Mr. Field actively worked towards a greater understanding of the Profession of Air Traffic Control, and towards its proper recognition.

Arnold Field's present book will be of great interest to members of the air traffic control profession world-wide. It addresses and explains all systems existing at present, from the sophisticated, computerised, radar-based to the very basic 'manual' control concept where separation of aircraft is achieved through the 'three-dimensional picture' in the controller's mind using controller-computed times on hand-written flight progress strips.

The inclusion of the historical development of international air traffic control gives a fascinating picture of 'where we have started and how we have progressed' and the look at electronic systems now being developed and tested, ground-based and airborne, gives an indication of 'where we are going and how we will get there'.

'International Air Traffic Control' will undoubtedly become a much-read and appreciated work within the controller community. However, it is of equal interest to anyone in aviation circles, and to those laymen who have pondered the question why it is that flying, apart from being the fastest means of reaching one's destination is, at the same time, the safest way to travel.

This book allows the non-air traffic controller a fascinating look, in easily read language, at a profession practiced by a comparatively small number of dedicated individuals and it will further the recognition and improve the understanding of the effort by air traffic controllers, working in a great variety of technical environments, to consistently provide the safest and most efficient possible air traffic control.

Safety and expediency in aviation, nationally and internationally, are the shared goals of all who are part of the aviation community. Mr. Field's book offers another one of his contributions towards achieving these aims, and there is no question that it will be widely read with interest and appreciated with satisfied curiosity.

Preface

Air Marshal Sir Ivor Broom KCB, CBE, DSO, DFC, AFC

Arnold Field gained an enviable reputation as a professional air traffic controller during the 35 years or so in which he was closely associated with the evolution of air traffic control from the simple red and green signalling lamp to today's highly sophisticated radar control systems. He was President of the International Federation of Air Traffic Controllers for two years and has served on many international air traffic control committees. Since his retirement from one of the key positions in the United Kingdom's National Air Traffic Services he has gained an equally respected reputation as a writer on air traffic control subjects. His articles will be found in many professional journals and he keeps abreast of development by being a consultant to a major British electronics group.

His first book on air traffic control was published in 1980. It was written primarily for the layman and it gave a fascinating insight into the United Kingdom's air traffic control system. This book has been written for a much wider audience and the systems and principles he describes have a world-wide application. It will have a special appeal to those who fly or who are involved in the manufacture of equipment for air traffic control systems, but will appeal also to the layman. I know of no other such book which attempts to describe every aspect of air traffic control in such readable language.

His description of present-day ATC systems starts at the point where an airline or private pilot advises the ATC organisation of where he wishes to go at a given time. He then deals with each phase of the control procedures which start whilst the passengers are boarding the aircraft and are not complete until the aircraft's engines have been stopped at the destination.

Radar is very much a mystery to many people. Without getting too technical he describes how it works and the benefits it has brought to safety in the air – and also can bring to aircraft on the ground at busy airports in very poor visibility. What information does the radar provide for the controller? How does the controller use that information to separate aircraft? It's all here in this book. He then looks into the near future in this rapidly changing radar environment and mentions developments in ground/air data links and collision-avoidance systems available to the pilot, which will eventually complement the ground controller in some countries.

The United Kingdom prides itself on having a national air traffic service for both civil and military aircraft. He lifts the veil on the methods used to co-ordinate the movement of civil and military aircraft which so often wish to fly in the same airspace at the same time. He is an ardent supporter of close collaboration between civil and military aviation authorities – not only for safety reasons, but also to ensure the most economic use of national resources. Procedures which suit one country may not suit another country, but some of the principles and ideas he annunciates in this book certainly have world-wide application.

Author's Introductory Note

My previous book, "The Control of Air Traffic", which was published in 1980, dealt primarily with the manner in which air traffic is controlled in the United Kingdom and although the principles explained are internationally applicable, the written content did not expressly address itself to a world-wide market. However, the success of this first edition and the fact that the management of the airspace is indeed a world problem, has prompted me to write a second book, intended for application to an international audience.

In this regard the text, format and presentation has undergone change and reference has been made, where appropriate to the international standards and recommended practices of the International Civil Aviation Organisation (ICAO).

Also I have taken the opportunity to extend the content to include a number of additional subjects, which not only add to the scope of the book, but some of which introduce new techniques and avionic equipments which are still in the formulative stage. Therefore, I hope their inclusion will add to the interest of readers in observing their application to air traffic control and airspace management in the years that lie ahead.

The list of additional subjects are:—

Airspace Management
The application of Automation to Air Traffic Control
The Basic Principles of Primary Radar and Secondary Radar
The Development of the Use of Radio Telephony
A list of the R/T phraseologies currently in International use (1984)
Threat Alert and Airborne Collision Avoidance Systems
Micro Wave Landing Systems (MLS)
Monopulse SSR and SSR Mode 'S'
The Structure and Organisation of the International Civil Aviation Organisation

For those readers who are particularly concerned with military aviation, I have expanded the chapters which are related to the co-ordination of military and civil air traffic, and have added a further chapter, which complements that concerned with the flight of a civil aircraft in which I have described the military air traffic operations associated with the flight of a military aircraft and in which I have described as many of these functions as possible. The flight described, represents current techniques and procedures and is given as an example of the application of the subject matter, discussed in the related text which precedes it.

Additionally, as the aviation world and its associated avionics industry is inevitably littered with confusing acronyms and abbreviations, I have taken the opportunity to include a 'Glossary of Terms' and an 'Index of Abbreviations'. These lists are by no means complete, but

Author's Introductory Note

I have endeavoured to select the majority of those which have a direct relationship with air traffic control. Throughout the book I have endeavoured to spell out these abbreviations wherever possible, but occasions do arise where brevity is essential, therefore I hope these two lists, which I have included, will assist in dispelling the annoyance which can occur when a reader is faced with an abbreviation with no corresponding explanation. The procedures, rules and regulations quoted are accurate at the time of publication but as aviation and its associated technology operates in a continually changing environment, readers should refer to the relevant official publications in regard to any application of the subject matter.

It should also be recognised that the equipments associated with Air Traffic Control are extremely complex and the regulations pertaining to the application of the Rules of the Air equally so; therefore in a document of this nature it is only possible to deal with these complexities as a primary introduction to the basic requirements essential to the exercise of Air Traffic Control.

I hope that the manner in which I have structured this book will enable those persons engaged in or associated with the aviation profession and aviation enthusiasts, even if they for the moment, are only armchair travellers, to obtain an appreciation of the manner in which civil and military air traffic control operates and how the world's airspace is managed to assist in the safety of those who fly.

In carrying out this task I am indebted to Mr. Alan Steel, Publishing Director, Pergamon Press, Ltd., and Catherine Shephard, Publishing Manager for their generous advice and guidance.

Throughout this book the author has followed the terminology and spelling adopted by the International Civil Aviation Organisation (ICAO) and published in PANS–RAC Doc. 4444 (Rules of the Air and Air Traffic Services) and the relevant annexes to the Convention.

Acknowledgements

In the writing of this book I have had to rely upon the assistance and advice of organisations and individuals. This has been particularly important to ensure that the technical content, at the level of writing, is correct, and the procedures, rules and regulations and their application which I have described, equally so.

In particular I am indebted to:—

The International Civil Aviation Organisation (ICAO) for their assistance in providing information on their structure and organisation and permission to quote from their documentation.

The United Kingdom Civil Aviation Authority
Anne Noonan for her help with descriptive material.
John Dancer for his help with R/T phraseology
Edge Green for his assistance with present day operating procedures.
Derek Morgan for providing assistance from the College of Air Traffic Control (NATS)

Military Air Traffic Operations of the U.K. National Air Traffic Services
Air Commodore G. McA. Bacon RAF for providing access to his staff.
Air Commodore M. Harvey RAF for advising and commenting upon the military air traffic control content of the book.
W/Cdr. D. A. Emery RAF for providing the original draft of the military air traffic operation.

Plessey Electronics Systems Ltd.
Mrs. Sue Wright and her staff for advice and support in the practical problems of pre-publication.
Mr. Danny Winter for his advice and scrutiny of the technical content of the description of navigational aids and radar.
Mr. Ron Pearce for his assistance in describing Microwave Landing Systems.
Mr. Jerry Fearnehough for his assistance in the description of Threat Alert and Collision Avoidance Systems.
Mr. Morris Gardner for his advice and assistance in relation to ATC Display Systems.
Mr. Ian Atkinson for providing practical information on the requirements of authorities in the more remote regions of the aviation world.

Cossor Electronics Ltd.
Mr. Nigel Ross for his assistance in providing information on Monopulse SSR and SSR Mode S.

Racal Avionics Ltd.
Mr. Bill Thompson for his assistance in providing information on Airport Surface Movements Indicator Systems.

Acknowledgements

Litchstreet Electronics Inc. (New York)
Mr. George Litchford for permitting me to explain his system for airborne threat alert and collision avoidance (AIRCAS).

International Aerospace Consultants
Air Marshal Sir Ivor Broom K.C.B., C.B.E., D.S.O., D.F.C., A.F.C. for his constructive and most helpful comments on my final draft.

Eton Publishing Ltd.
Mr. Derek Baker for his consideration and co-operation in making possible the publication of the first edition.

Commuter World
Mr. Don Parry Editor, and previously British Airways aircrew, for his enthusiasm and advice on the type of information of value and guidance to pilots.

And finally to my Secretary, Mrs. Hazel Girling, for the speed, accuracy and unfailing good humour with which she typed innumerable drafts of my dreadful long-hand script.

Contents

Contents

Contents

List of Figures

Page   *Page*

1

Introduction

The objective of this book is to try to convey in readable form, how the tens of thousands of aircraft, who share the world's airspace at any particular moment in time, do so, with such a high record of safety. From the experience gained in the compilation of my previous book I have therefore endeavoured to achieve this objective by not only increasing its content, but also by improving and extending the narrative, in those areas where I consider explanation will be of benefit to the reader.

For example, it is reasonably easy to visualise the operation of an aerodrome, for it is possible to see it; even the control tower is readily recognisable as a symbol of some form of organisation. At night-time aircraft approaching to land at a busy airport can be recognised from their landing lights, neatly spaced like a string of pearls, out to the periphery of vision. But how did they arrive there, so tidily spaced apart? What happens when departing aircraft disappear from view, heading for one of the world's aerial highways? They fade from sight and cannot be registered by human vision, and yet the occupants of these vehicles, designed to move us from one point of the earth's surface to another, must be cocooned in their own small parcel of airspace and be separated one from another, to ensure that the aircraft, the crew and its passengers

arrive safely at either London or Baltimore. To try, therefore, to convey the principles of the air traffic control system which makes this desirable objective possible, I shall endeavour to describe in a stage-by-stage narrative, supported by diagrams, how the organisation operates in the discharge of its task of the safe, expeditious and orderly flow of air traffic.

Air traffic control is an essential element of the communications structure which supports air transportation. It is, in fact, a 'service', the prime objective of which is to provide for the safety of those who fly for profit or pleasure in the air, or in defence of the realm. Its closely followed secondary objective is to carry out this task, as expeditiously as possible, to meet the objectives of its customers. In this regard it has to recognise the varying requirements of all of the users of the air such as commercial passenger transports, military defence and communications aircraft and executive and private aviation. In this context the performance characteristics of the aircraft for which it is required to provide this service, can vary from the light executive aircraft which may have a cruising speed of say 160 knots to the wide-bodied jet transport cruising at 500 knots or supersonic transport (SST) and fighter aircraft flying at Mach 1 plus (speed of sound). Additionally these aircraft, even in the field of

1

civil aviation, can vary in their climb and descent performances, from rates of 500 feet per minute up to rates in excess of 5000 feet per minute.

The problem is further compounded by the fact that busy international airports often sustain landing and departure rates in excess of one a minute and the airports themselves are invariably situated within busy terminal areas and in close proximity to airports of similar capability. Furthermore, by their very nature these airports are often sited near the junction of air routes serving other destinations. Military aerodromes also provide their own specific problems, in that, invariably, tracks to be followed by aircraft bound for or from training and operational areas often conflict with the route networks and terminal areas which serve air transport movements.

The technique of applying a service of safety and expedition to these air movements is one of separation in three dimensions: one of time, one of geographical position and one of height – added to which is the complication of continuing movement, both in direction over the earth's surface and in climb and descent. I recognise that the mathematical purist will contest the statement of three dimensions, but it is essential, in the context in which this word is used, to recognise that a controller, even when looking at a modern radar display, is presented with a flat plate. Height cannot be observed, except in sophisticated systems, where even then it has to be read as a symbol alongside the aircraft's radar response. There are indeed many parts of the world where radar cover does not exist at all or is impractical to provide, and in these circumstances a controller has to build up from pieces of paper (flight progress strips) a moving mind picture of the air traffic for which he is responsible. He therefore has to recognise, although he cannot see it, a further dimension, other than that presented to him on his displays. Doubtless advances in technology will one day make this

explanation superfluous but at present an observable 3D display of moving air traffic is not a practical proposition.

To return, however, to the methods which are used to separate aircraft, these are basically, 'vertically' using height separation, 'longitudinally' using time or distance separation or 'laterally' using geographical or horizontal separation. In effect these separations can be regarded as parcels of air which are wrapped around each aircraft and the art of controlling is to ensure that these parcels of air are never infringed one by the other. A phrase was coined many years ago, of which I claim to be the author, that this art can aptly be referred to as playing three-dimensional chess at high speed. It was true then; it is even more so today.

As the separation of one aircraft from another forms the very foundation of air traffic control, I have placed it as the first chapter in this book. I apologise in advance for the fact that it is not a subject for an inspiring narrative, but until the time arrives when we travel by thought transference the basic principles of separation will hold good, even though the values applied to them in height, time and distance may diminish. It is therefore vital that their importance be understood at the very commencement of this work.

The application of these separations between aircraft requires that the controller has available to him not only the regulated airspace in which to perform his task, but technical facilities to enable him to put them into effect. These facilities can range from the humble telephone and a radio telephony set, to sophisticated electronics such as processed radar displays and automation techniques. The level of sophistication varies with the task to be performed, which can range from, for example, a small aerodrome which is concerned only with controlling aircraft within its air traffic zone to a busy international airport with its associated control zone or to an air traffic control centre whose responsibilities extend over national and international air routes. To assist in an understanding of this application of air traffic control I have, in the first part of this book, introduced under separate chapters the procedures, facilities and functions which, when assimilated, will, I trust, provide an appreciation of the manner in which an air traffic control system operates. These fundamental elements have been broadly divided as follows:

Separation standards
Airspace requirements
Radio navigation aids
Radio telephony
Radar
Flight data
Aerodrome control
Approach control
Area control
Automation techniques

Having explained these elements under their separate headings I have endeavoured to convey in narrative form, some idea of the environment within which air traffic control operates, and having done so I have then illustrated, by example, how these various elements combine together to provide a service. Because I am conversant with the United Kingdom I have used this as a setting for my examples. I wish, however, to emphasise that irrespective of the natural instinct to explain that with which one is familiar, the principles contained in the narrative apply on a world-wide basis, subject only to local interpretation and rule-making.

Finally, in looking towards future developments, I have included a chapter on airborne collision-avoidance systems, and SSR Mode 'S', whose arrival on the aviation scene will doubtless cause considerable international debate. As both of these developments, as they mature, will have an impact upon ATC procedures, I considered it would be of value to provide information upon them, even though I

can only speculate, in general terms, upon their interface with ATC systems.

The latter part of the book is devoted to the co-ordination of civil and military air traffic, not only because I have had professional experience in seeking equitable solutions to this problem, but also because, as I travel around the world, I find it increasingly necessary to try to advise upon the necessity to recognise the differing requirements of these two types of traffic and to seek solutions which permit airspace to be shared, rather than sterilised. I have therefore sought to explain what are the differing requirements of military aircraft, and have detailed the air traffic services which are provided by military air traffic operations and, in particular, the methods which are employed to provide for the co-ordination of civil and military air traffic, where interaction could otherwise result in delay or denigration of safe operation. I have also provided a detailed example, in which I have tried to show as many of these co-ordinations as possible, and in this regard I wish to express my appreciation of military air traffic operations of the Royal Air Force, who were extremely co-operative and equally concerned that readers should be aware of the service which they provide to ensure the safety not only of military aircraft, but also of civilian aircraft accepting their services, or which are concerned with the joint co-ordination procedures.

It is appreciated that the procedures I have described, and the example of operation and of an organisational structure, refer to the United Kingdom, and in totality represents but one method of achieving the co-ordination of civil and military air traffic. However, as with the basic principles of the control of air traffic, so the problems expounded in this part of the book are common on a world-wide basis; it is only the solutions themselves which may differ.

In considering these problems and their solutions on an international basis, I have endeavoured to write this book in such a manner that

3

the basic principles of the control of air traffic, both civil and military, are capable of intepretation and application, irrespective of the numbers of aircraft to which ATC services require to be applied or of the geographical location of particular ATC units. In this regard it has to be accepted that large differences will arise between, for example, the sophisticated procedures and technical support facilities which are essential to cater for the traffic volume and complexity of the New York terminal area and the relatively light volume of air traffic and limited facilities necessary at a location such as Kano in Nigeria near the border of Niger and the vastness of the Sahara desert. However, both of these geographical locations have the same prime factor, the safety of air traffic, but it is then sensibly a matter of logical development how far it is necessary to employ the procedural and avionics developments which I have explained in this book to assist in the process of supporting the safe and expeditious flow of air traffic in these differing circumstances.

It is, however, of interest to speculate upon how the control of air traffic will develop from this 'Orwellian year' of 1984, into and beyond the 21st century. There are, I consider, certain elements which can be identified as common factors on a world-wide basis. Foremost amongst these is the fact that even though a navigation system should be developed in the future which permits aircraft to operate independently of any reliance upon surface ground-based aids, the requirements of those aircraft, irrespective of their civil or military operation, would be to proceed on as direct a route as possible from their departure point to destination or to a target area, as appropriate. Therefore, national and international route structures will remain a feature of any future ATC systems, and it is only the methods of separating the aircraft which will change. Even, for example, should airborne collision-avoidance systems advance to a stage where

they could be incorporated into an overall control function, it is difficult to envisage their independent operation in busy terminal areas, where the objective of each inbound aircraft is a minute (in relative scale) piece of concrete, the access to which is impeded by other arriving, departing and overflying aircraft, the flight profiles and routes of which are invariably in conflict one with the other. Therefore, regulation and separation of air traffic into and out of these route structures will require the existence of a ground-based ATC system very similar in context to that described in the following chapters of this book. The material future changes are, it is considered, more likely to lie in the realms of the technical facilities, particularly in avionics, which are available both to the controller and the pilot. In this regard, radar, both primary and secondary – which gives the controller the ability to see what is physically happening in the unseen skies around him – will undoubtedly remain the most important of these facilities. The availability of radar in this context is as important to the small aerodrome handling only two aircraft, one of which may be heading towards the hills to the complete ignorance of both parties, as it is to a high-density traffic area. Internationally the use of radar for air traffic control purposes has tended to develop empirically, and ICAO has yet to make any pronouncement upon when radar is considered essential for air traffic control purposes, other than the density of air traffic. It is, however, considered that this availability of ground-based radar at most of the world's aerodromes which provide air traffic services cannot be long delayed. It is the advent of secondary surveillance radar (SSR) which opens up vast horizons for future exploitation; for not only does it enable intelligence on an aircraft's identity and height and flight profile to be communicated to the ground organisation automatically, but it can also be used as a data communications channel between the aircraft and ground-based computers, for the relay of both control and flight management messages. This facility, in conjunction with the use of computers, presents a very thought-provoking advance in ATC techniques. Its implications are as equally applicable to those authorities who are at present still emerging as world aviation contenders, as they are to the established authorities. The lessons to be learned for their future use by ATC authorities is to approach the application of these techniques on a step-by-step build-up basis; a philosophy which I have endeavoured to outline later in the book for both manufacturers and users alike.

In the future there will also be greater and greater pressure for all-weather operations, that is the ability to take off and land aircraft irrespective of the prevailing weather. In this regard recent events have tragically underlined the need to provide, to both controllers and pilots, assistance from surface movement guidance systems, in those conditions where the unaided human eye is no longer capable of physically seeing the way ahead. Such facilities do, of course, already exist and doubtless their availability will in the future be a requirement at those major aerodromes where all-weather operations are to be permitted.

In the foregoing I have outlined some of the problems and their postulated solutions which will have a bearing on the development of world-wide ATC systems. It is my personal view, however, that in the immediate future we require a period of consolidation to get to understand, and to be able to apply competently, the avionics wonders which have been developed extremely rapidly over the past decade.

In the chapters of the book which follow I have endeavoured to spell out the basic principles of the control of civil and military air traffic as they apply on a world-wide basis to all ATC units, whether large international airports and military aerodromes or small aerodromes in the more remote parts of the world. I have also described the procedures, techniques and facilities which are available and in use at the world's busier locations, and in doing so have described all of the advanced avionics which appear in these chapters. I hope that, having read this book, readers will have at least an appreciation of how aircraft are controlled throughout this range of activity and whilst I have perforce to leave you at 1984, I hope that my explanations of present-day technology may assist controllers, pilots, aviation authorities and avionics manufacturers to see the way ahead with more clarity than I have been able to convey in this introduction. I would ask you to bear in mind, however, that technology alone cannot provide the solution to future events; the man, the controller and the pilot, must remain firmly in the loop and in 'control'.

2

Separation Standards

Introduction

The art of controlling air traffic is based upon a set of rules which have been devised to ensure the safe separation of one aircraft from another, throughout the duration of their flight from the point of departure to destination.

The application of separation between aircraft can and does vary according to the type of airspace through which the aircraft is flying and the navigational and air traffic control facilities which are available to the pilot. However, in this book we are concerned primarily with explaining how aircraft are controlled, which are flying in those airspaces within which an 'air traffic service' is provided. In general terms this covers the air traffic which flies in and out of the majority of civil and military aerodromes and along the world's air routes. To clarify this statement I will explain later how the airspace is managed and what are the rules which apply to these airspaces.

The rules for separating aircraft are known as 'separation standards', they are internationally agreed by the member states of the International Civil Aviation Organisation (ICAO) for world-wide application. The separation standards themselves are minima, and where a state is unable for any reason to comply with these minima, it is required to file what is termed a 'difference'. This 'difference'

is then notified on a world-wide basis, to enable pilots to be aware of any deviations from standard practices. The separation standards have two broad divisions:

(1) vertical separation – that is the separation vertically of aircraft by thousands of feet; and
(2) horizontal separation – of which there are three types, namely: lateral separation, longitudinal separation, and radar separation

Before explaining these separations in detail it is essential to recognise the fact that the air traffic control system is generally based upon the fact that navigational responsibility is vested within the aircraft and the 'system' does not normally assume navigational responsibility except in those instances where the controller has a better quality of aircraft position data than is available to the pilot. It is true to say, however, that with the increased use of ground radar by air traffic control there has been an increased requirement for controllers to assume some navigational responsibility and in these instances the navigational instructions required to initiate and maintain a correct flight path are determined and issued by the controller. I will be dealing with the use of radar by air traffic control in some detail at later stages in the book, for undoubtedly the advent of radar and its use in air traffic control systems has been a significant development in regard to the separation of air traffic. However, irrespective of this development it is fundamental to have a sound appreciation of the separation standards which form the basic foundations of the method of allocating blocks of airspace to individual aircraft, to ensure that no two aircraft are in the same place at the same time. In this regard it is worthwhile reflecting one moment upon the fact that the air traffic to which these separations are being applied are in continuous movement not only in regard to their flight paths over the earth's surface, but also by their very nature are required to climb and descend. The application of these separations to aircraft is indeed, as mentioned earlier, a highly professional art of three-dimensional aerial chess enacted at exceptionally high speed.

Because aviation takes on many forms, from club flying and passenger-carrying to military deployment, the separation standards which I shall describe do not necessarily apply to all of these flying activities. As a general guide, however, separation standards must be applied to the following categories:

(1) IFR flights in controlled airspace;
(2) IFR flights in special rules airspace;
(3) flights in special rules airspace in the upper air space;
(4) IFR flights participating in the air traffic advisory service;
(5) IFR flights and special VFR flights;
(6) flights operating on special VFR clearances;
(7) IFR flights outside controlled airspace receiving an approach control service.

As the application of these categories may, however, vary from state to state, pilots of aircraft wishing to enter the airspace of a neighbouring state would acquaint themselves with any 'differences' which had been notified to the ICAO by that state and also with the rules of the air, pertinent to the particular geographical area. This procedure is, however, normally taken care of by the issue of international notices to airmen (NOTAMS) and from the information available at the aeronautical information services (AIS) briefing units, established by the larger airline operators and/or aerodrome owners.

I now propose to describe the basic separations which are required to be applied to these categories of flight. The separations I shall describe are based upon a set of standards which have been agreed and published for international use by ICAO. The contracting states of ICAO, then use the publication as a basis for their own national instructions, and it is these national instructions, such as the *Manual of Air Traffic Services* and the *Air Navigation Order and Regulations,* of a particular state, which contains the interpretation of these international agreements, such as the standards for separating aircraft (see chapter 12, which explains the structure and organisation of ICAO).

The more important of these internationally agreed separation standards are:

Vertical separation

This is the simplest of the separations to describe, in that if an aircraft has less than the separation subsequently described, vertical separation must be applied as follows:

> 1000 feet up to flight level 290;
> 2000 feet above flight level 290.

The reason for the increase in vertical separation above flight level 290 (approximately 29,000 feet) is due to the inherent inaccuracies of altimeters at these heights. It is a precautionary measure which will undoubtedly be resolved by future advances in instrumentation.

As the term 'flight level' will again be referred to, it might be as well to explain briefly why it is used instead of thousands of feet. The altimeters of aircraft measure height from zero in accordance with a pressure setting fed into the instrument by the pilot. For example, when an aircraft is landing or taking off from an aerodrome the pilot requires his altimeter to register zero when he is on the surface of the aerodrome, therefore the pressure which he will feed into his altimeter to register zero is the barometric pressure of that aerodrome, called the QFE. However, away from the aerodrome, due to changes in climatic conditions, a variety of pressures can be in force. To ensure uniformity of height separation it is therefore necessary to set a standard pressure for a specific region of the aircraft's flight. The geographical extent of the regions is agreed between air traffic control and the Meteorological Office and the resulting areas are known as altimeter setting regions. The Meteorological Office advice air traffic control of the pressure values throughout a particular region and it is the lowest of these pressure values which is then expressed as the regional QNH. Aircraft are instructed by air traffic control to change to the QNH on departure from the aerodrome and conversely to change to the QFE on arrival at the aerodrome. During the progress of an aircraft's flight it is probable that it could proceed through a number of QNH regions, requiring adjustments to the pressure setting of the altimeter. In order to avoid continuous changes a common pressure value (datum) known as the standard pressure setting using a value of 1013.2 millibars is introduced, and heights are then expressed as flight levels. The change from QNH to the standard pressure setting takes place on instructions from air traffic control. The height at which this change takes place, is dependent upon local geographical conditions, and therefore will of course vary in different parts of the world. Published information for these areas is, however, available to pilots, thus enabling them to be aware of the pending altimeter pressure setting change procedures, prior to the instruction

given by ATC to initiate the change. There is a complex procedure which ensures that a 1000 feet vertical separation will always exist between the QNH value and the standard setting, and that adequate clearance from terrain exists, but the object of the use of all of these pressure setting values is to ensure that at all times a minimum of 1000 feet vertical separation exists between aircraft at a specific point in space and time.

Horizontal separation

As stated in the introduction there are three types of horizontal separation; they are: lateral separation, longitudinal separation and radar separation.

Lateral separation

The determination of separation minima is based upon the usable accuracy of whatever designated system of navigation is being used, plus a reasonable pilotage allowance for the normal conduct of a flight, plus a further buffer. The usable accuracy is assessable from a combination of the ground equipment, the airborne equipment and instrument components.

An example of the application of lateral separation is termed *track separation*. This would typically be used where the concerned aircraft were navigating using VOR (very high frequency omnidirectional range), DME (distance measuring equipment) or TACAN (tactical airborne navigation). However, where the measured distance values are being used, each aircraft must be using the same 'on-track' VOR/DME/TACAN facility; that is, the aircraft must be flying towards or away from the same navigational aid. The track separation is established by requiring aircraft to fly on specified tracks which are separated by a minimum amount. The minimum separation between aircraft in this example is as shown in red at

LATERAL SEPARATION

Track Separation

Track separation shall be established by requiring aircraft to fly on specified tracks which are separated by a minimum amount appropriate to the navigation aid employed. Aircraft must be within the protection range and altitude of a VOR or the service range of an NDB as shown in the COM section of the Air Pilot. The minimum separation between aircraft is shown in red in the diagrams below.

(a) Using a VOR and associated DME/TACAN station. Both aircraft must have reported established on radials at least 20° apart.

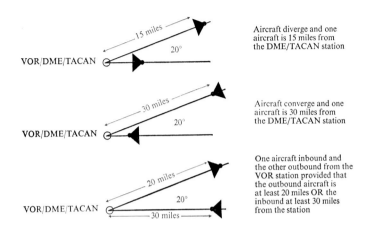

Aircraft diverge and one aircraft is 15 miles from the DME/TACAN station

Aircraft converge and one aircraft is 30 miles from the DME/TACAN station

One aircraft inbound and the other outbound from the VOR station provided that the outbound aircraft is at least 20 miles OR the inbound at least 30 miles from the station

(b) Using VOR radials; when one aircraft is a time equivalent of 15 miles or 4 minutes (whichever is the greater) from the VOR and both aircraft have reported established on radials which diverge by 20° or more.

Aircraft diverging

(c) Using VOR radials; both aircraft must have passed a VOR on tracks diverging by 45° or more and have reported established on the relevant radials.

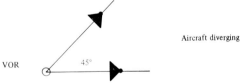

Aircraft diverging

(d) Using specified tracks from an NDB; when one aircraft is the time equivalent of 15 miles or 4 minutes (whichever is the greater) from an NDB and both aircraft have reported established on tracks which diverge by 30° or more.

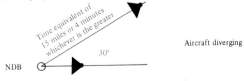

Aircraft diverging

If a pilot reports that he suspects the accuracy of the NDB indications this separation shall not be used.

FIGURE 1. Lateral separation
(Diagrams Courtesy U.K./CAA.)

Figure 1 (a). Further examples of track separation are shown at Figure 1 (b), (c) and (d), the minimum that can be used being shown in red.

There is a further form of lateral separation known as *geographical separation*. The requirements for the application of this form of separation are as follows:

(a) geographical separation must be positively indicated by position reports over different geographical locations as determined visually or by reference to a navigational aid; and

(2) it must be constant or increasing.

Longitudinal separation – time and distance

There are two distinct methods of providing separation in the longitudinal dimension. One is to use 'time' separation between aircraft and the other is to use 'distance' separation between aircraft. The application of the techniques concerned with this type of separation depends to a large degree upon the quality of the information which is available to the controller at his display. For example, the information on aircraft position reports, where aircraft may be flying over sparsely populated land areas such as the Sahara or sea areas such as the South Atlantic, can be very limited, in comparison with the quality and frequency of information received in respect of aircraft flying over the land mass of North America and Europe. In the former case ground-based aids to assist pilots in navigation can be very sparse, whereas in the latter case a proliferation of navigation aids permits frequent determination of position. Time separation is therefore on a sliding scale dependent upon the intelligence available to the controller. It can vary from 3 minutes where aircraft are departing from the same aerodrome and following the same route, providing the preceding aircraft is at least 40 knots faster, to 15 minutes where aircraft are following the same track and determination of position is infrequent. I should mention that over areas such as the North and South Atlantic and the South Pacific oceans the separation distances can be as great as 30 minutes, but doubtless future satellite navigation and onboard navigational systems will materially improve this situation.

Before commencing to give some examples of this type of separation I feel it would be worthwhile explaining the technique which the controller employs. It can probably best be described as an airspace sampling process, where certain points on the earth's surface are used as key points. These key points are usually ground-based navigational facilities such as a VOR (very high frequency omnidirectional range) or an NDB (non-directional beacon). By determining the estimated time of passage of each aircraft, over or near these key selected points, a display is generated to the controller portraying the estimated time relationship of all of the concerned aircraft. This future time relationship is revised from the past history of the aircraft's flight and from actual position reports relayed to him. The displayed picture which the controller builds up, usually in the form of a 'flight progress board' is dependent also upon the accuracy of the aircraft's position information and the frequency of its reporting. From this amalgam of information the controller is then able to make a calculated judgement regarding what type of 'time' separation to apply, or whether or not he has to opt for a different type of separation, such as vertical.

Time separation is also a vital factor in climbing or descending one aircraft through the level of another. It is governed by a similar set of rules, the vital factor being that of when the levels are actually crossed. The time separation in this instance is either 5 minutes or 10 minutes at level change, dependent upon the quality of the information.

Aircraft crossing tracks at the same level are

also based on time separation. In this instance it is either 10 minutes or 15 minutes, dependent once again upon the quality of the information.

As aircraft by their very nature spend their existence climbing and descending and plying their business on a spider's web of routes, it is, I hope, apparent that this art of the application of standard separations by the controller is extremely demanding and requires a high degree of skill and training. Whilst the advent of radar has materially assisted this mental art, nevertheless the majority of the world's en-route airspace still requires to be controlled in the manner described.

I think it will be appreciated, from what I have said, that there are many permutations to the application of time separation. How-ever, whilst it is not necessary to explain or illustrate all of these. I have included in Figure 2 examples of those I have previously described. The illustrations I have selected have been taken from the ICAO document entitled 'Rules of the Air and Air Traffic Ser-vices' (Doc. 4444). My reason for so doing is that ICAO is the international forum for agreeing the safety separation standards and as such they are applicable on a world-wide basis.

FIGURE 2. Longitudinal Separation based on Time. Aircraft at the same cruising level
AIRCRAFT FLYING ON THE SAME TRACK

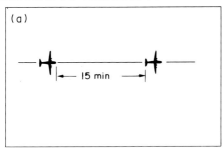
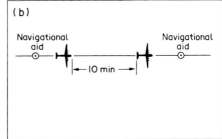

(a) fifteen minutes (see Fig. 2(a)); or
(b) ten minutes, if navigational aids permit frequent determination of position and speed (see Fig. 2(b)); or

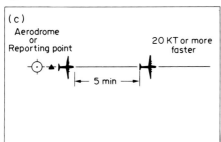
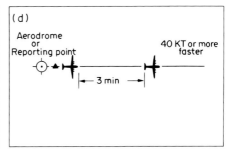

(c) five minutes in the following cases, provided that in each case the preceding aircraft is maintaining a true airspeed of 20 knots or more faster than the succeeding aircraft (see Fig. 2(c)):
    (i) between aircraft that have departed from the same aerodrome,
    (ii) between en-route aircraft that have reported over the same exact reporting point,
    (iii) between departing and en-route aircraft after the en-route aircraft has reported over a fix that is so located in relation to the departure point as to ensure that five-minute separation can be established at the point the departing aircraft will join the air route; or
(d) three minutes in the cases listed under (c) provided that in each case the preceding aircraft is maintaining a true airspeed of 40 knots or more fastsr than the succeeding aircraft (see Fig. 2(d)).

Separation Standards

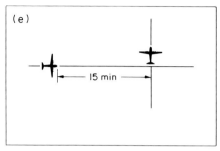 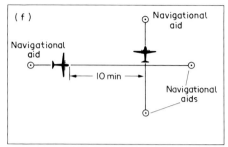

(a) fifteen minutes (see Fig 2(e)); or
(b) ten minutes if navigational aids permit frequent determination of position and speed (see Fig. 2(f)).

AIRCRAFT CLIMBING OR DESCENDING

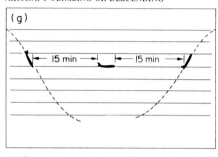 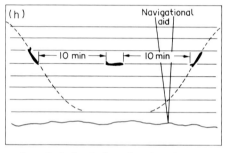

Traffic on the same track. When an aircraft will pass through the level of another aircraft on the same track, the following minimum longitudinal separation shall be provided:
(a) fifteen minutes at the time the level is crossed (see Fig 2(g)); or
(b) ten minutes at the same time the level is crossed, provided that such separation is authorized only where navigational aids permit frequent determination of position and speed (see Fig. 2(h)); or

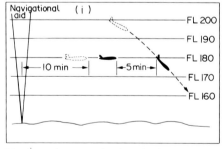 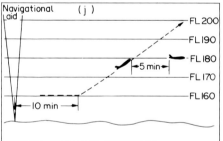

(c) five minutes at the time the level is crossed, provided that the level change is commenced within ten minutes of the time the second aircraft has reported over an exact reporting point (see Figs. 2(i) and Fig. 2(j).

Note.—To facilitate application of the procedure where a considerable change of level is involved, a descending aircraft may be cleared to some convenient level above the lower aircraft, or a climbing aircraft to some convenient level below the higher aircraft, to permit a further check on the separation that will obtain when the level is crossed.

FIGURE 2 (Cont.,).   Lateral separation

12

TRAFFIC ON CROSSING TRACKS

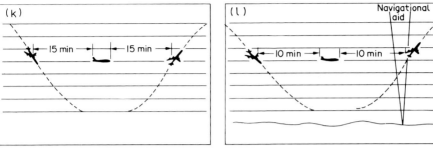

(a) fifteen minutes at the time the levels are crossed (see Fig. 2(k)); or
(b) ten minutes if navigational aids permit frequent determination of position and speed (see Fig. 2.(l)).

FIGURE 2 (Cont.,). Longitudinal separation

(Diagrams courtesy ICAO)

Radar separation

The separation standards previously described form the basis of what is termed a procedural air traffic control system. Such a system relies primarily upon the fact that if a pilot says he is certain of his position, the controller must accept this statement and arrange for the separation of other air traffic, based upon this premise. If, however, the pilot should be mistaken or the navigational aids he is using are inaccurate then the separation between the concerned aircraft may be prejudiced. It is for this reason that the separations described have built-in buffers, the result of which means that large volumes of airspace must be sterilised to ensure safety. The availability of radar to the controller, however, materially alters the situation, for by providing the controller with a means of confirming the pilot's report, not only can the safety level of the separation service be improved but also the economic and flexible use of the airspace be materially improved.

ICAO in its rules of the air and air traffic services, when referring to the reduction of separation minima says:

The separation minima may be reduced as determined by the appropriate ATS au-

thorities and after prior consultation with the aircraft operator – when, in association with rapid and reliable communication facilities, radar-derived information of an aircraft's position is available to the appropriate air traffic control unit.

In its guidance material in relation to the application of radar separation ICAO makes the following statement:

The radar separation which can safely be applied in practice by a particular radar controller, using a particular radar equipment, on a particular day, at a particular time, on a particular sector, under particular traffic conditions and when controlling particular aircraft, can only be assessed by the radar controller himself using the prescribed minima as a starting point.

I have included reference to these two statements to indicate the very considerable care which is entered into before any reduction in the standards of separation between aircraft can be implemented. They may sound much like the type of official language which is often used to maintain a *status quo*, but their intention is very clearly to underline the caution which must always be exercised where the safety of human life is concerned.

Having said that, the general interpretation of radar separation is:

> 5 nautical miles minima except that 3 nautical miles minima may be used in respect of aircraft being controlled by approach control, provided aircraft being so separated are within 40 nautical miles of the antenna and not above a certain height (usually flight level 200 – approximately 20,000 feet)

Comment

In this chapter I have dealt with the general separations which apply to aircraft; there are, however, a number of variations which I have not mentioned, such as the separation of 1 minute in respect of aircraft departing from the same aerodrome and whose tracks diverge from 45 degrees after take-off or the 'track' and 'composite separations' used on the North Atlantic routes. I hope I have, however, been able to convey something of the basic fundamentals of air safety in relation to the separating of one aircraft from another. If any reader wishes to delve deeper into the subject, further material is available in ICAO Doc. 4444 – RAC/501/ 11, Rules of the Air and Air Traffic Services, or in the *Manual of Air Traffic Services* for the concerned state. Finally I should like to add that the controllers who practise this profession have to be trained and licensed in all aspects of its operation and are required to obtain ratings and validations. In a similar manner to pilots, they require to be pronounced medically fit to exercise this responsibility and require also to be re-validated in any aspect of their duties which they have not practised in any period exceeding 90 days.

3

The Management
of the Airspace

Introduction

Having described in the previous paragraphs the general rules which are used by air traffic controllers to separate aircraft, it is now essential to describe how the airspace is managed to make the application of these rules possible. However, before commencing to explain the various types of airspace and how it is organised, it might well be of assistance to outline briefly the historical background to airspace management.

In the years immediately preceding the Second World War the increasing use of the air as a practical means of rapid transportation was already beginning to require the provision of regulations to provide for safety in the air and on the ground. A form of air traffic control was also being pioneered, but certainly in Europe, this was largely restricted to a type of positive control which was limited to within the immediate vicinity of an aerodrome, with an advisory information service, largely conducted by wireless telegraphy, outside this area. This generalisation is in no way intended to belittle the efforts of the stalwart band of gentlemen who laid the foundations of the present-day sophisticated 'systems'. It would indeed be in-

teresting to place on record their endeavours in some other forum. It is possibly worth recording that in the United Kingdom it was a Department of the then Air Ministry, who were responsible for both the airside and groundside of aviation safety, and who then commenced to build the foundations of the ATC systems of the present day.

It was in fact the cessation of hostilities which acted as a catalyst to concentrate minds upon the need to provide air traffic control services, based upon both the experience which had been gained pre-war and the experience of the handling of large concentrations of aircraft by the Armed Services. The reason for the urgency was, quite simply, that aircraft had not only undergone rapid development in design and performance characteristics, but had demonstrated their vast potential in the movement of goods and persons. This potential was readily recognised in support of the occupying forces and of the growing needs of commerce.

Although the example of the awareness to act is quoted as Western Europe, the problem was also recognised internationally, and in 1944 an international meeting was held in Chicago (U.S.A.) where the Provisional International Civil Aviation Organisation was formed (PICAO) and the Chicago Convention was ratified as a basis for the development of international standards and practices for aviation – it was indeed this body that gave as its interpretation of air traffic control, a phrase which still obtains today; that is: 'The safe, orderly and expeditious flow of air traffic.'

It was, however, to be several years before the deliberations of this organisation would be able to impact upon the fast-growing aviation scene and therefore states had of necessity to seek some short-term solutions for themselves. It was indeed reasonably easy to provide an air traffic control service within the immediate vicinity of aerodromes and to declare the airspace 'air traffic zones' to which rules could be applied. These rules required aircraft to make contact on R/T or W/T for an air traffic control clearance, or by prior permission obtain authority to enter and leave in accordance with visual flight rules. It was also possible, as was the case with the London area, to encompass several aerodromes within a parent control zone. In the case of London the first of these zones, known as the Metropolitan Control Zone, was a circle of 25 nautical miles radius centred on Westminster Bridge with a prohibited area of 3 nautical miles from the bridge itself. Having drawn up the original map myself I was never quite certain why we had to have this prohibited zone, but possibly it was to protect our MPs from the sight of such forward progress.

It has to be remembered that pilots of aircraft, being unfettered at that time in regard to routes to be followed to destination aerodromes, had quite naturally set as direct a course as possible immediately after take-off. They had therefore by force of circumstances established a series of aerial highways linking the capitals of Europe and the Mediterranean states. In accepting the situation that aircraft would, however, enter and leave the control zone at recognised points on the periphery of the circle, it was then reasonably logical to site as near as possible geographically, ground-based navigational aids, which at this stage of development were non-directional beacons (NDB), at these locations. Pilots of aircraft were thus, by using these beacons, able to establish their position in relation to the earth's surface and to report to the controlling authority the time which they estimated to be at the facility and then subsequently their actual time over it. From this information air traffic control were then able to allocate height and times at which the aircraft could be cleared to a particular NDB. The theory was very simple, in that aircraft outbound from aerodromes within the zone were cleared not above 3000 feet and those inbound, not below 4000 feet. Therefore provided the inbound aircraft was not descended below 4000 feet until it reached the holding facility of the aerodrome of intended landing, no conflict existed between departing and arriving traffic within the zone itself. It should be remembered also that, at this time in aviation development, 500 feet was the accepted vertical separation between aircraft, which therefore permitted a reasonably high permutation of level allocation.

Readers with a personal knowledge of these times will, I know, realise that the dictates of brevity have obliged me to omit a number of the innovations which occurred prior to the installation of the NDBs, of the truly pioneering efforts of the aerodrome controllers in sorting out arriving and departing traffic, and of the area controllers and telecommunications officers who had to battle away with static-filled W/T, in order to get their instructions across to the sometimes wayward pioneers of the air. I appreciate that the temptation to write history is very strong, but I have to limit it to my purpose, that of leading into the management of the airspace.

The problem, however, was that in the airspace outside these control zones and aerodrome traffic zones no system existed to be able to provide an air traffic service for the majority of the en-route phase of an aircraft's flight. Each state had its own flight information region (FIR) which covered the entire airspace of a state up to internationally agreed contiguous boundaries. Within these FIRs there existed, as it still does today, a very simple flight safety rule, known as the quadrantal height rule, which operates in respect of all aircraft flying above 3000 feet. The rule requires that aircraft flying in specified quadrants of the compass (360°) should fly at either even levels, or even levels plus 500 feet, if in the opposite quadrant, or odd levels or odd levels plus 500 feet in the reciprocal quadrant. As you will see, the rule provides for a very rough form of separation for aircraft in level flight, in that either approaching head-on or crossing quadrants a theoretical separation of 500 feet vertically should exist between the concerned aircraft.

This then was the general world-wide situation in regard to airspace regulation at that point in aviation development. There was, however, one notable exception – that was North America and in particular the United States. The U.S.A., because of its geographical position and of the need to communicate over long distances, had not only fostered the use of aircraft as a method of transport but had developed a system of airways to protect and regulate the flight of aircraft between departure points and destinations. These 'airways', which were the first of the present world network of aerial highways, were 10 miles wide and extended from approximately 3000 feet to 10,000 feet above ground level. The method employed to ensure that pilots of aircraft could locate and navigate along these airways was by the positioning on the ground of a facility known as a radio range. The radio range radiated four legs on a published radio frequency and transmitted the Morse letter 'A' on one side and the Morse letter 'N' on the other. By positioning the legs of the range along the route of the airway, the pilot, by knowing the geographical position of the range and its frequency and by receipt of its either 'A' or 'N' characteristic, was then able to navigate himself from range to range along his predetermined route and also be able to pass, by radio telephony, a position report over the range and give a calculated estimate for the next range. In this information, and by the application of rules relating to flight in the airspace encompassed by these airways, lay the beginnings of the application of an air traffic service to aircraft in the airspace away from the aerodromes. It is interesting to observe that communications by air traffic controllers with aircraft in those days was by relaying messages by telephone to the aircraft's company for broadcast on their own discrete company radio, or through an operator physically sited at the radio range site.

Once again it is tempting to write history, but certainly on the American scene I would not have the temerity to try. I wish, however, to make mention of one of the great pioneers of air traffic control in the U.S.A., the late Glen Gilbert, whose book on air traffic control explains most vividly those early days of a system which has since been copied world-wide. I myself was fortunate enough, with a colleague Len Winter, to be seconded in 1949 to the then Civil Aviation Authority (CAA) in the U.S.A. to study the system and then qualify as an en-route controller at the Chicago Air Traffic Control Centre, and on my return to introduce the first of the European airways which ran from a place called Woodley near Reading to Strumble Head on the Welsh Coast, code-named, and still today – 'Green Airway One'.

Thus then was airspace management commenced, and Figure 3 is a diagram which may convey some impression of the complex manner in which events have progressed since those early days. The diagram shows the upper air routes, which are generally aligned with the relevant airways. It may be of interest to observe at the upper left of the chart UG1 (upper air route Green One) which faithfully follows its older brother, Green Airway One, immediately below it.

Rules of the air

Having described, in the introduction, the background to the management of the airspace, I wish now to explain how the airspace is organised to achieve the objective of a safe, expeditious and orderly flow of air traffic.

To channel the flow of air traffic and to obtain the necessary degree of orderliness to apply separation standards between aircraft it is essential to establish a system of airspaces sufficient to protect an aircraft's flight path from take-off to touch-down, and then to apply rules regarding the use of these airspaces which are designed to provide for the safety of all those who fly within them. These rules are known as 'rules of the air' and their origins and general interpretation are set out in Annex 2 of the Convention of the International Civil Aviation Organisation.

In regard to the international use of these rules it is interesting to note that they apply to the aircraft itself. In practical terms this means that these rules will be obeyed by any aircraft bearing the nationality and registration of any contracting state of ICAO, wherever they may be and provided the rules do not conflict with the rules of any state which has jurisdiction over the territory being overflown. This latter point is important, for it is possible for a variety of reasons that a particular state may have to place a different interpretation on a specific rule. States themselves in fact, as I previously stated, produce their own legislation based on these rules, such as for example, in the U.K. 'The Air Navigation Order', and therefore operators of aircraft are able to acquaint themselves with any differences in interpretation, prior to undertaking flights into or over the concerned territories.

However, whatever the interpretation of a particular rule may be, the objective is common, and that is to ensure the enforcement, by law if necessary of their application, which is to ensure the safety of national and international flight.

As mentioned earlier each state has its own flight information region contiguous with its bordering states, and it is within these FIRs that the various categories of controlled airspaces are contained. As will doubtless be appreciated from a sight of Figure 3, it is obvious that a great deal of co-operation and co-ordination has to take place between these various states to ensure that not only the rules applicable to the airspaces, but also their physical layout, do not conflict one with the other.

The rules of the air cover, of course, many aspects of an aircraft's flight, but from the point of view of the air traffic control service the most important is the rule requiring an air traffic control 'clearance' to be obtained prior to operating a controlled flight. In simple terms this means that no aircraft is allowed to enter controlled airspace without having been given a clearance (instruction) to do so by the air traffic control authority responsible for that airspace. There are some exceptions, in various parts of the world, where flight in accordance with visual flight rules (VFR) is permitted. This rule permits an aircraft to be flown visually in accordance with a set minimum standard of weather conditions and here responsibility for avoidance of collision is vested in the pilot. However, due to the restricted design of modern cockpits in regard to visual look-out and high closing speeds, often of 1000 kts plus, many states, the United Kingdom in particular, apply instrument flight rule (IFR) conditions to their controlled airspaces, irrespective of the weather conditions.

It is these designated airspaces which permit air traffic control to be able to apply the separation standards mentioned in earlier paragraphs. I should now like to explain in rather

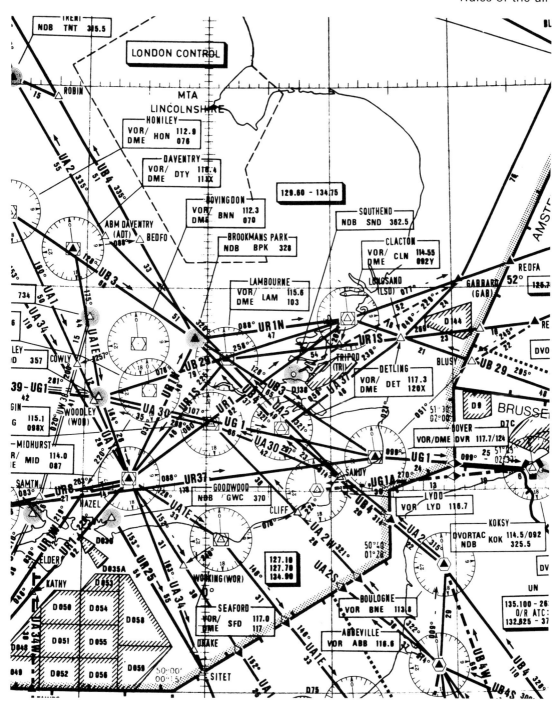

FIGURE 3. A section of the Upper Air Space Navigation Chart for North West Europe, showing the Upper Air Routes and their associated navigation aids.

graphs. I should now like to explain in rather more detail how the airspace is managed, starting from an aerodrome and working outwards to the en-route phase of flight.

Control zones

Control zones are established at busy aerodromes, usually within a terminal area complex, and they extend from ground level to 2500 ft or a level appropriate to the base of the surrounding terminal area. Their purpose is to protect the flight paths of aircraft arriving from the protection of the terminal area or departing into it.

Terminal areas

Terminal areas are established around one or more busy aerodromes and extend usually from 2500 feet or the top of the concerned control zone/s to a height of approximately flight level 245 (the base of the upper airspace which can vary from state to state) and the area extends laterally to connect with the system of airways serving the terminal area complex. Their purpose is to protect the flight paths of aircraft leaving the airways system to land at an aerodrome in the terminal, or alternatively the flight paths of aircraft departing the terminal for an en-route airway. Their vertical extent is to enable protection to be given to the flight paths of aircraft which may be overflying the terminal to other destinations served by the internal or international airways system.

Airways

Airways are established to connect the main areas of population within a particular geographical area and to link up with the major cities of adjacent states. They are usually a minimum of 10 nm wide and generally have a variable base between 3000 feet and flight level 55, and with some exceptions extend vertically

up to flight level 245, the base of the upper airspace. Their purpose is to protect the flight paths of aircraft which are flying en-route between destinations served by the airways network, or to a specified point of departure from the system.

Upper airspace

The airspace above flight level 245 or such other level as determined by a particular state and extending up to flight level 660 is designated a special rules area, and within this area there are upper air routes. The majority of these routes are contiguous with the airways network below that level. The purpose of this airspace is to protect the flight paths of aircraft flying not only on the network of air routes, but also in any part of this particular airspace. In general, however, the majority of aircraft, either civil or military, which are operating in accordance with civil procedures conform to the air-route network. The base at which the upper airspace commences can vary between states, as also can the procedural rules. The foregoing does, however, represent a general interpretation of the intent of this airspace. The international accepted term for this airspace, within which exists the Upper Air Routes and Special Rules Airspace is the Upper Flight Information Region (UIR).

Flight information regions

The airspace outside the control zones, terminal areas, airways and special rules areas, but within which these areas are contained, is designated the flight information region. It is not protected airspace and aircraft are free to fly without being subject to control procedures, provided they comply with a set of simple rules for flight in instrument conditions and avoid the air traffic (circuit) zones of aerodromes which do not have protected airspace.

It is appreciated that it may seem rather ambiguous, in a book which is dealing with the control of air traffic, to accept that the majority of the world's airspace which is occupied by these flight information regions, is uncontrolled. There are, however, very sound reasons why, at this stage in aviation development, it is neither practical, nor even possible to apply control procedures to those aircraft who elect to fly in areas outside controlled and special rules airspaces. However to assist readers in a further understanding, I have included a paragraph on the flight information services in the FIRs at Chapter 7 of the book ('The Provision of Air Traffic Services').

Special rules airspace

Within the flight information region there are additionally a number of areas to which special rules apply, such as military training areas, relatively busy aerodromes, danger areas, etc. The rules which apply to these airspaces are designed to protect aircraft within the airspace itself from those aircraft which may be in free flight in the FIR and also to enable such aircraft to use the airspace if they so wish, in accordance with these special rules. The rules themselves vary considerably, but pilots wishing to plan flights in the FIR would refer to the aeronautical information publication (AIP) of the concerned state in which all such information should be detailed.

To assist in a further understanding of the previous paragraphs on airspace management I have included the following diagrams: Figure 4, which shows the vertical division of the airspace; Figure 5, which is an artist's impression of the main configuration of civil controlled airspace in the United Kingdom and Figure 6, a diagrammatic display of airspace usage.

The progressive establishment of the air traffic services

The progressive establishment of air traffic services based upon the management of the airspace can therefore be briefly summarised as follows.

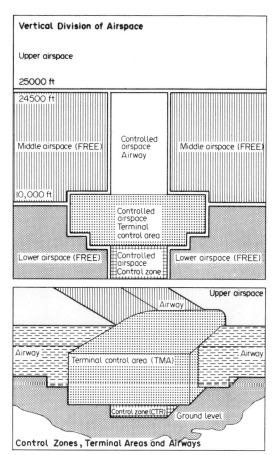

FIGURE 4. Vertical division of the airspace

Where, at an aerodrome which is being used only for operation in accordance with visual flight rules, the amount of air traffic reaches a point where the pilots cannot be reasonably expected to decide the correct action necessary to ensure their own safety, a control tower facility should be established to provide an aerodrome control service. The service should be provided by qualified air traffic control personnel and be restricted to aerodrome traffic and within a reasonable distance of the aerodrome. Where visual flight rule traffic only is controlled, the designation of controlled airspace is not necessary.

21

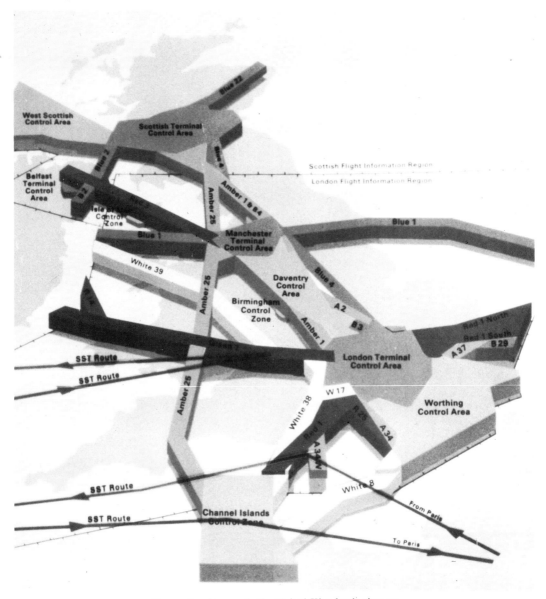

FIGURE 5.   Airways in the United Kingdom's airspace

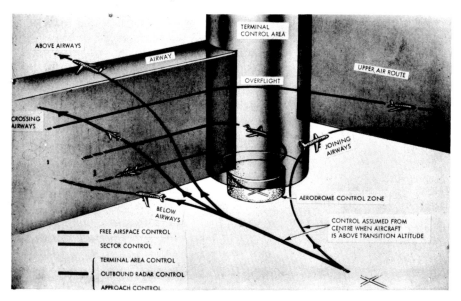

FIGURE 6. Diagrammatic display of airspace usage

When, in further development of the aerodrome, it is decided to also handle aircraft operating in accordance with instrument flight rules (IFR) it then becomes necessary to protect this traffic by extending control to them and by placing restrictions on those flights which are permitted to continue to operate in accordance with visual flight rules (VFR). To protect the flight paths of these IFR aircraft during the departure, arrival or holding phase of flight it is necessary to establish controlled airspace, usually in the form of a *control zone*.

As air activity increases, and where it becomes necessary to provide air traffic control services over an area beyond the vicinity of the aerodrome, additional controlled airspace in the form of a *control area* should be established to supplement the control zone. Usually this increase in controlled airspace is in the form of a *terminal area*. This has the advantage that as the base of the terminal area need only be low enough to encompass the flight paths of aircraft outside the confines of the control zone, VFR flights can continue to operate beneath the terminal area, outside the control zone.

When the amount of air traffic flowing between two or more aerodromes so necessitates, control should then be extended to cover the en-route portion of the flight between the respective terminal areas or control zones. This linking of controlled airspaces is normally in the form of the establishment of *airways*.

The management of the airspace relative to the co-ordination of civil and military air traffic

Whilst later in this book I shall be dealing with the co-ordination of civil and military air traffic, I should like to spend a short time to explain why I consider an understanding of the management of the world's airspace is also vital to the efficient co-ordination of this traffic.

As previously stated, to obtain order and security in the air – in particular in areas of high traffic density – it is essential to apply a variety of rules. It is equally essential to create controlled airspaces within which these rules can be applied. However, controlled airspace

23

cannot be designated for the sole purpose of enforcing rules, but must be related to the provision of an air traffic control service. These services will vary according to the specific aerial activity within a particular area, and the application of these services and the establishment of these restricted areas apply to all air users, both civil and military.

Additionally, the term 'restricted airspace' covers a variety of airspaces, such as danger areas, military training areas, military exercise areas, tanker refuelling areas, etc – all essential for the protection of military aerial activity. In these types of airspaces an air traffic service is not necessarily a pre-requisite of their establishment, and their existence can vary from permanent to existence by prior notification. However, the objective remains the same: to manage the airspace in such a manner that aerial activity of both types of flying obtain maximum security of flight. Not surprisingly the generic term which has been accepted on a world-wide basis to embrace this activity is 'airspace management'.

The sensible application of the management of the world's airspace by civil and military aviation authorities, is vital not only for the safety of aircraft flight but also for the economic use of airspace which, whilst the contenders for its use get more numerous, stubbornly refuses itself to get any bigger. In this regard, therefore, it seems reasonable to suggest that a general appreciation of the progressive establishment of air traffic services and of the types of controlled airspaces may assist in a more informed understanding of the application of this type of 'management'.

In particular the efficient operation of an air defence system demands a close liaison between civil and military air traffic control agencies. This co-ordination of the use of the airspace not only assists in the safe operation of both types of flying but also enables the military agencies to more easily isolate, identify and intercept possible hostile targets. Ad-

ditionally, through co-ordination the vital task of military training can be accomplished with the minimum interference.

Internationally the problems which arise through the expansion of both civil and military aviation have been recognised by the International Civil Aviation Organisation, which has recommended that air traffic service authorities shall establish and maintain close co-operation with military authorities responsible for activities that may affect flights of civil aircraft.

In practical terms, whilst it is not possible to propound a world-wide solution, it is suggested that fundamental to any organisation is the fact that the airspace within which both of these types of aerial activity are required to operate is managed in such a manner that co-ordination can be limited to those areas where a conflict could arise in respect of the use of the airspace.

As explained earlier, to assist in the management of the airspace, and primarily for the protection of civil air traffic, over the years there has been built up a system of control zones and control areas to protect major airports, together with airways to protect the major routes between airports. Such airspace is generally subject to agreement between all airspace users, and both military and civil aircraft may only fly in these areas with ATC permission. However, the creation of these controlled airspaces can be, and often are, at variance with the military requirement for freedom of the airspace to carry out their tactical role.

Simply stated, in this context the problem of the use of the airspace is that civil operators demand the rigid application of separation standards between aircraft, and the protection by law of much of the airspace in which they fly, and therefore by implication, acceptance of the control of their flight paths by a ground organisation. From a military point of view, the adherence to predetermined flight paths, and the application of stringent separation rules, negate the role for which they exist, which is one of freedom of movement and tactical flexibility.

The tasks facing military aviation are many and varied, and most of them do not fall readily into the fairly rigid concept of control as practised in a civil capacity. However, the service pilot is as much concerned for the safety of himself and his aircraft as is his civilian counterpart; therefore it is sensible to recognise that where a differing requirement may exist for the use of airspace, co-operation and co-ordination offer the best compromise towards promoting both the safety and flexibility of both types of flying.

In practical terms the amount of the world's airspace which is 'managed' in the sense of 'controlled airspace' is relatively small in relation to that available for flight. It is, however, a fact of life that, small as it may be, its existence is often geographically in conflict with military interests. Therefore, as stated earlier, the priority for co-ordination rests at the interface where – for either operational, training or en-route flight – it is essential for military aircraft to penetrate these controlled airspaces.

The methods by which this co-ordination can be achieved are many and various, and their application should be dependent upon the operational problems in a specific area. They can range from 'radar slots' to procedural clearances, and control can be exercised by military or civil controllers, or jointly by both.

It is wise and flexible to first recognise the problem and then apply the method. Suffice it to observe that in many of the world's most congested airspaces, both terminal and en-route, co-ordination of civil and military air traffic results in the safety of both types of flying with the minimum of interference to their differing roles.

Essential, however, to the success of this type of co-ordination of air traffic is the acceptance by those in command of the need to effectively manage the airspace for the benefit of all air users and of the existence of an administrative organisation to bring this about. What this organisation should be, is a matter for individual states, and whilst examples exist of how this can be done, there is no necessity, nor is it desirable, to postulate a world-wide solution. What is common, however, are the problems themselves, and it is in this particular aspect that an exchange of operational experience can be of material assistance.

How this management of the airspace can be approached by military authorities in order to achieve the co-ordination of military and civil air traffic and to provide for the flexible use of the airspace, is discussed later in the book, in Chapters 12 to 15. These chapters deal specifically with the problems associated with the co-ordination of these two types of air traffic and postulate solutions aimed at achieving the foregoing objectives.

4

Navigation and Communication Aids

Introduction

In previous paragraphs I have made mention of the fact that navigational aids are required not only to enable the pilot of an aircraft to determine his position in relation to the earth's surface, but also to delineate the routes, airways and airspaces within which air traffic services are provided, and finally to enable him to align his aircraft with the runway in use, and effect a landing at the aerodrome of destination.

Navigational aids come within two broad definitions – 'ground-based' which, as their name implies, are installations on the earth's surface whose geographical position is known and published, and 'airborne', which relates to the equipment carried in an aircraft, which enables the pilot to interrogate and obtain information from the ground-based installations.

There is a third category, called 'on-board' navigation systems, which enables the aircraft to be navigated without recourse to ground-based aids, such as satellite navigation and inertial navigation (INS) but it is not my intention to deal with these systems at this stage. Informed readers will also be aware that 'dead reckoning navigation' and 'astral navigation'

are still widely used in many of the world's airspaces, that are without adequate ground-based cover. Navigation, as these readers will know, is a very wide and complex subject, best dealt with in the many learned books which have been published; therefore my explanations will be limited to those aids which are generally in use in air traffic systems. In this regard, however, I wish to reiterate a point which I made earlier, which is that, responsibility for the navigation of an aircraft is vested in the pilot-in-command, and only exceptionally – as for example, when an aircraft is being 'directed' by a radar controller – is this responsibility temporarily transferred.

Radar could also be generally regarded as an aid to navigation, and, of course, it is widely used in modern air transport and military aircraft in a variety of airborne roles. From an air traffic control point of view, which is the aspect I shall be discussing, its role is primarily that of assisting in expediting the flow of air traffic. Because of its importance in this regard I will deal with the principles of radar and how it is used later in the book.

Additional facilities are, however, required for both pilots and controllers to enable them to carry out their allotted tasks, and in general terms these are known as 'communication aids'. They embrace radio telephony for communication between the air and the ground, telephone networks for rapid communication between controllers and for use as data links, and teleprinter networks for the passing of routine messages and the latest of these communications devices, secondary surveillance radar (SSR Mode 'S'), which I shall be describing later, and which is to be used as a data link between the aircraft and the ground, without the need to use a radio telephony speech circuit. Computers are also becoming increasingly used as a rapid method of communication, but because they have a special role in their application to air traffic control I propose to deal with this subject separately under the heading of automation.

Having therefore previously explained the separation standards which a controller employs, and the management of the airspace which makes the application of these separations possible, I now propose to explain, against this background, the major facilities which the controller has at his disposal to enable this task to be discharged. I should like to emphasise that not all of the facilities I shall describe are essential at every locality, for much depends upon the level of traffic and also the specific environment of a particular area. Also whilst the basic requirements for navigation and communication will remain fundamental to any system, it is undoubtedly true that the rapid development of technology, particularly in the field of avionics, could well outdate the methods by which these standards are achieved today.

Navigation aids

It is considered it would be helpful to give an explanation of the role of navigation aids in present air traffic control systems and to describe how the efficiency of these aids contribute towards the safety and expedition of aircraft into and out of the airport environment. You are aware of the airways or en-route networks previously described, which act as links between the major centres of aviation interest and which form the basis of the air traffic control systems outside the immediate environments of terminal areas. These routes rely for their delineation upon the existence of ground-based navigational aids of sufficient accuracy and in sufficient quantity not only to ensure that the aircraft using these airways remain within the confines of the airspace but are also sufficiently accurate for the aircraft to be able to determine its position within a tolerance which will permit air traffic control to use this information for the purpose of separating traffic one from another in time sequence and for confirming or correcting other planned applications of separation standards. It is, then, these navigational aids which mark out the routes and act as three-dimensional traffic lights at which the airborne position of the aircraft can be checked and also at which they can be 'held' if necessary, to regulate the traffic flow on a particular route or at a conflux of routes such as a terminal area.

DVOR/DME

The use of navigational aids for this purpose has progressed from the radio range and its associated fan markers supplemented by M/F non-directional beacons, as described earlier, to the present-day VHF omnidirectional range (VOR) which operates in conjunction with distance measuring equipment (DME). This latter equipment enables the pilot of an aircraft to determine how far away he is from the geographical position of a VOR on a specific radial of that facility. The VOR itself has for some 30 years been the ICAO international short-range navigational aid, and consists of a ground beacon which transmits a signal from which an airborne receiver can determine the aircraft's bearing from the beacon. It thus provides a simple means of flying radial paths either from or towards the ground station. More recently the use of airborne navigation computers combined with VOR and DME enables the aircraft to fly desired paths, other than the direct radials, thus providing an area navigation capability.

Doppler VOR (DVOR), so called since the well-known doppler principle is used in generating the ground beacon signals, has considerably improved the VOR system performance since such beacons have much greater immunity from multi-path propagation effects. (A photograph of a typical DVOR installation is shown in Figure 7.)

Multipath effects describe a situation where both direct and indirect signals occur, causing noticeable variations in course indications. Large built-up areas close to the beacon, or mountainous terrain between the beacon and aircraft, are sources of this particular problem, largely overcome by DVOR. These navigational aids, however, are what is known as 'point source aids'; that is, they are physically located on the earth's surface and aircraft using their radiated signals will eventually arrive at the same spot on the earth's surface. An exception to this is, as previously explained, the carriage and use of distance measuring equipment (DME) which together with VOR, permits an aircraft to be navigated, if desirable, using its on-board computers, on a course parallel to the physical position of the associated ground aid. It follows that if all aircraft using an ATC system were capable of lateral tracking, and if the navigational aid in use possessed a high degree of accuracy, it would be possible to separate aircraft on lateral tracks at the same height or level instead of in a line-astern configuration, which is primarily the case at present. This capability within a system is called area navigation. There have been several attempts to establish a practical method of operation, of which, possibly the Decca Navi-

gator is an outstanding example. However, I am certain readers will appreciate that to be effective such a system requires all concerned aircraft to have the same standard of navigational capability. It is undoubtedly the way ahead in which to obtain the economic and flexible use of the airspace, and future advances in aviation technology will hopefully supply an answer to this problem.

Closer to the environment of the airport, navigational aids of the types previously described play a vital role in the efficient operation of the terminal area surrounding the airport complex. For example, in considering the arrival phase of an aircraft's flight it is a well-known fact that the vagaries of weather, and the requirements to meet passenger demands, inevitably result from time to time in the fact that arriving traffic exceeds the capacity of particular airports to accept aircraft without incurring the penalty of a delay in the landing interval. As a result a continuous descent from cruising level followed by a straight-in approach cannot always be achieved, and therefore the use of the navigational aid must be resorted to, to enable aircraft to hold their positions in a very accurate configuration whilst awaiting their turn to approach the runway in an orderly sequence for landing. The advances in technology previously described permit the safe holding or stacking of aircraft in busy terminal areas, for not only must an aircraft be able to hold its position in space within a tightly prescribed airspace but the controlling authorities must have sufficient confidence in the ground-based aid and the airborne equipment, to accept this fact. The accuracy with which aircraft are able to position themselves in these holding patterns also facilitates the movement of transiting or departing aircraft by enabling them to by-pass the holding facility, often at the same level and whilst using a form of lateral separation. This type of separation is applied in the firm knowledge that the navigational aids being used per-

FIGURE 7. Doppler VHF omnidirectional range (DVOR). The photograph shows the DVOR installation at Ibsley (U.K.), which is a navigational reporting point on Red Airway One. In the centre of the counterpoise, which is 30 metres in diameter, can be seen the 'carrier' antenna, which is surrounded by a ring of 50 'sideband' antennas. The signal is commutated around these 50 'sideband' antenna and when combined with the 'carrier' provides the directional information for use by the pilot.

(Photo. Courtesy Plessey Radar)

mit air traffic control to assume the concerned aircraft will be confined to the airspace allotted to them.

Under these circumstances these navigational aids also perform the vital function of containing reservoirs of air traffic for the approach controllers of the concerned airports to sequence into an orderly flow, onto the extended centre line of the runway in use. The volume and complexity of traffic will vary from one location to another but in the busier environments it is not unusual to have four or more holding positions in use at any one time, acting as reservoirs of traffic for landing onto a single runway.

Instrument Landing System (ILS)

The complex nature of this sequencing operation and its vital role in maintaining full utilisation of the runways will be described in detail later. Possibly, however the most exacting of the navigational aids is the instrument landing system (ILS) which enables the aircraft to locate accurately the extended centre line of the runway, and the correct descent path. The presentation of the ILS to the pilot in the cockpit of his aircraft is a cross-pointer instrument which indicates to him whether or not he has to fly left or right or up or down. Thus the pilot is able to navigate his aircraft in both azimuth and elevation to a point at which he can commit the aircraft to an approach to land. This aid to landing is subject to many variables and can be categorised in relation to its accuracy and integrity up to certain limits from the threshold of the runway and along the runway. Similarly so can the aircraft, according to its type and the equipment it carries, and there are such features as the dominant obstruction allowance, particular to specific locations, and the decision height, which is laid down by the airline operator. At this point, as its name implies, a decision to land or abort the approach has to be made by the pilot in com-

mand. A great deal of technological development has taken place over recent years to try to aid the safe operation of aircraft in this aspect of one of the most critical phases of its flight. In simple terms the ILS has two primary elements. One, the localizer, operating at VHF, is situated on the extended runway centre line beyond the stop end, and the other, the glide path, operating at UHF, is situated to the side of the runway about 1000 feet from the runway threshold. They both operate in a similar way, except that the localizer provides guidance in the azimuth plane, and the glide path in the elevation plane. The basic principle is that the aerial systems radiate signals in two overlapping beams, each identified by a different audio frequency, 90 Hz and 150 Hz. The intersection of these beams is made to contain the plane of the runway centre line, or the plane of the glide path angle. Thus the course line in azimuth or elevation is defined by equality of the 90 Hz and 150 Hz signals, and either side of the defined path one predominates over the other. Over a small sector about the course-line, approximately $\pm 5°$ the rate of the two tones changes, in direct proportion to the angle, and this deviation signal is displayed to the pilot on a conventional cross-pointer meter. The same signal can also be fed to the 'auto-pilot', providing the capability of automatic approaches. This operation is usually carried out once the aircraft is established on the ILS at approximately 8/9 miles from the runway threshold and is standard practice amongst many of the world's airlines. It is an automatic approach and not an automatic landing, and in this type of operation a pilot still requires sufficient forward visibility to carry out the 'flare' manoeuvre, in other words the final landing of the aircraft has to be carried out visually. However, in the future these ILS signals will be combined with the radio altimeter to control the flare manoeuvre, and so the automatic approach capability will be extended to complete automatic landing. In this condition the approach from the 8/9 nm point, to about 1/4 nm from touchdown, will be controlled by the flight control system (FCS), receiving inputs from the glide-path and the localiser. From the 1/4 nm point inwards, the aircraft, will use its own radio altimeter, and localiser only. The diagram at figure 8 illustrates a typical standard ILS approach and on the right hand side portrays the type of instrumentation the pilot would see in his cockpit.

Microwave landing system (MLS)

Before proceeding to discuss the next subject of radio telephony, I consider it would be of value to devote a few paragraphs to the microwave landing system (MLS). I do so not only because of its topicality, but also because MLS has been adopted internationally, to succeed the present generation of instrument landing systems (ILS) and you will appreciate from the previous paragraph the vital importance of this facility, particularly in regard to all-weather operations and fully automatic landings.

ILS was first adopted by ICAO as the standard aid to approach and landing in 1949. Since that date the system has evolved to a point where the quality of guidance, reliability and integrity are sufficient to permit full Category III (automatic landing) operations as a matter of routine. However, the ability of an ILS to achieve and maintain any category of service is highly dependent upon external factors such as the presence in the vicinity of the installations of buildings and undulating terrain. This dependence upon siting, and the limitation that the equipment provides only a single approach path to the runway, has meant there have been virtually no advances in performance since the introduction of the first Category III compatible equipment in the late 1960s.

There therefore existed a requirement for a new generation of equipment which would improve upon the sensitivity to siting, stability of performance and the provision of more than one line of approach to the runway (multipath).

In 1978, after almost 3 years of international debate, the ICAO All-Weather Operations Panel decided to adopt the U.S.A./Australian time reference scanning beam (TRSB) technique as the new standard aid to approach and landing. After debate within this panel, the standards and recommended practices for MLS based upon the TRSB techniques were approved in 1981 and these subsequently became effective in 1983. This process may seem rather lengthy and laborious, but many safety aspects were involved as also were many states and avionics industries, who often had conflicting views on the technology to be employed. For readers who are interested, Chapter 12 (the International Civil Aviation Organisation, ICAO) details the organisation and consultative machinery which is necessary to persuade 151 separate sovereign states to debate, adopt, and accept such a decision.

For the technically minded it would also, I feel, be of interest for me to outline in general terms what operating principles for MLS developed from this lengthy process, they are as follows.

MLS provides position information comprising azimuth angle, elevation angle, range and various ground-to-air data, over a wide sector of the approach. The basic ground equipment configuration includes approach azimuth equipment, approach elevation equipment, means for transmitting basic data and distance measuring equipment (preferably of the precision type, DME/P), all with associated monitoring, remote control and indicator equipment. Expanded configurations can include back azimuth equipment, flare elevation equipment and means for transmitting auxiliary data words.

Angle and data functions can use any one of 200 channels in the frequency band 5030 MHz to 5091 MHz and are radiated with sufficient power to provide coverage to at least 20 nm. Approach azimuth guidance must extend to at least ±40° of the extended runway centreline, of which a minimum of ±10° must be proportional guidance. Proportional elevation guidance must be provided over at least 0.9° to 7.5° above the horizontal, with up to 15° recommended. The MLS angle guidance signals are characterised by the transmission from each ground function of a narrow beam of vertically polarised, unmodulated, microwave radiation, which is scanned across the guidance sector alternately in TO and FRO directions, with linear velocity. The elapsed time between successive TO and FRO transits of the beam past the aircraft enables the angle of the aircraft to be calculated with reference to the zero degree reference angle.

Guidance and data functions are transmitted in a time division multiplexed format on a single-channel frequency, and each function is preceded by a unique error-protected identity code. To provide protection from synchronous interference the timing interval between repetitive transmissions of any one function is varied within the format by inserting blocks of basic or auxiliary data transmissions. In addition to its identification, each function is preceded by a preamble transmission which is radiated throughout the guidance sector coverage. For azimuth guidance signals a number of additional signals are radiated immediately following the function preamble, and include:

(1) a Morse code runway identification signal;
(2) an antenna select signal, to enable the airborne installation to determine which antenna (in the case of aircraft with multiple antennas) is receiving the best signal;
(3) a rear out of cover indication (OCI) signal, which is radiated into a sector behind the azimuth equipment;
(4) a left OCI signal, similar to (3) above but

radiated into a sector to one side of the azimuth equipment;
(5) a right OCI signal, similar to (4) above but radiated into a sector to the other side of the azimuth equipment.

Accuracy and signal quality of guidance from any configuration of the MLS must be suitable for Category III, regardless of the approved operational category of the airfield or aircraft. The accuracy is defined in terms of parameters which affect the aircraft flight control systems, namely path following error (PFE) and control motion noise (CMN). PFE contains any bias/alignment error and those low-frequency error terms which an aircraft can follow, designated path following noise (PFN) (analogous to beam bends in ILS). CMN contains noise errors with frequencies that the aircraft cannot follow, but which can cause control surface motion affecting flyability.

In practical terms, however, what do these operating principles confer upon the aerodrome owner and the user? Nearly all predictions of the year 2000 and beyond indicate the requirement for more widespread availability of precision approaches and an increase in Category III operations at major airports. The 200 channels available with MLS will permit up to five times the population density presently available with ILS. The relative independence of MLS from site effects is highly complementary to this increased channel capacity; not only does it ensure the highest quality guidance in bad weather at sites made difficult by buildings and/or terrain, but it affords the possibility of providing precision approaches at airfields not suitable for ILS.

It is this insensitivity to site conditions which will benefit the major airport operator because, subject to availability of other relevant facilities of the required standard such as lighting, Category III operational capability can be virtually guaranteed.

The wide-angle guidance both in azimuth

32

and elevation opens up new possibilities for curved and segmented approaches. This facility offers the potential to remove a number of site-specific restrictions. Hong Kong's Kai Tak Airport Runway 13 with its dog-leg approach is an example of a site where such facilities might be well used.

Further benefits are expected to accrue from the availability of alternative approach patterns in noise-abatement procedures and in permitting the interleaving of aircraft flying at different speeds.

By virtue of the basic use of digital techniques, MLS is inherently more stable and easier to maintain than ILS. Not only will this reduce direct maintenance costs, but it also offers potential for reducing the number of flight checks, a major element in all navaid running costs. A parallel might be drawn here with the doppler VOR described earlier which, typically, is flight-checked once very 5 years as compared with once every 90 days for a conventional VOR.

Viewed overall these economic factors, in conjunction with the technical factors, put instrumented approaches within the reach of many more airfield operators.

However, because many of the world's aerodromes are equipped with ILS installations and the aircraft which use these aerodromes carry expensive electronic equipment compatible with these installations, there has to be an international transition plan for the introduction of MLS. This transition plan at the time of writing is, that up to the year 1990 ILS is the *standard* aid and is protected as such until the year 1995; in this period MLS is an *optional* aid. In the period 1990 to 1995 ILS remains the *standard* aid but MLS is *recommended*. In the period 1995 to 2000 MLS becomes the *standard* aid and ILS becomes *optional*. In the period 2000 to 2005 MLS remains the *standard* aid, protected until at least 2005 and ILS is *withdrawn*. Figures 9a and 9b clearly demonstrate the wide angle of guidance to the runway

which is made possible with the MLS system (Figure 9B).

Radio telephony

At the present stage of development of air traffic control all of the aids at a controller's disposal finally result in the use of a speech circuit to issue an executive instruction to the pilot of an aircraft for the safeguarding of his flight. It is generally standard practice for a controller at an operating position to have his own R/T circuit, discreet to himself and the pilot of aircraft within the airspace for which he is responsible. The frequencies used are normally in the VHF/UHF band for aerodrome and airways control, and for communication over long distances, such as for example the North Atlantic, H/F speech is used. New techniques, such as the development of satellite communication, could of course materially alter long-distance speech communication.

To obtain some measure of the complexities of speech communication it is of interest to note that at a busy air traffic unit, for example, an air traffic control centre, there can be 80/100 separate R/T channels working at any one time. As safety is paramount in the control of air traffic all of the R/T speech circuits, and increasingly, the telephone circuits, are continuously recorded. The purpose of these recordings is to enable the concerned authorities to try to build up a picture of the events surrounding an accident or an incident. Fortunately accidents are rare but incidents may occur for a variety of reasons and an intelligent understanding concerning the circumstances surrounding a particular incident can prudently result in remedial action to prevent a future occurrence. In this regard, whilst I have not yet dealt with the subject of radar, it may be of interest to note that many aviation authorities, of which the U.K. is one, are also introducing the recording of radar data. However, in the future even the use of the spoken word to relay executive instructions to safeguard

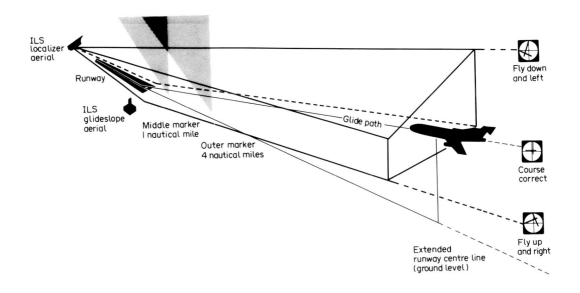

FIGURE 8. The instrument landing system (ILS)

the flight of an aircraft may well be supplemented, or even superseded, for part of an aircraft's flight by the use of new techniques involving the use of secondary radar as an air/ground data transfer system. However, as communication between the air and the ground is paramount, whatever method is used it is considered it would be of interest for readers to have an understanding of the manner in which we have arrived at our present methods of direct verbal communication and of the language which is used in international communications.

The development of radio telephony in international aeronautical communications

In the early days of the development of aviation no requirement existed for communication between the aircraft and a ground station. Flying was carried out within sight of the ground or water, and information required by a pilot was mainly visual. For example, navigation was carried out by the observation of well-known landmarks and the direction of landing at an aerodrome was judged either from visual observation of a windsock or a white letter T displayed in a signals square. The approach to land was also by visual communication. A green lamp signal was an all clear and a red lamp signal advised the pilot to make another visual circuit before attempting to land. In extremes, when a red lamp signal had not been observed, the firing of a red Verey light usually achieved the objective.

As the numbers of aircraft began to increase and the carriage of passengers began to become a practical method of transport, the need arose for a method of communication between the air and the ground which had a greater range of understanding, and would provide a safer means of passing intelligence, than was possible by visual means alone.

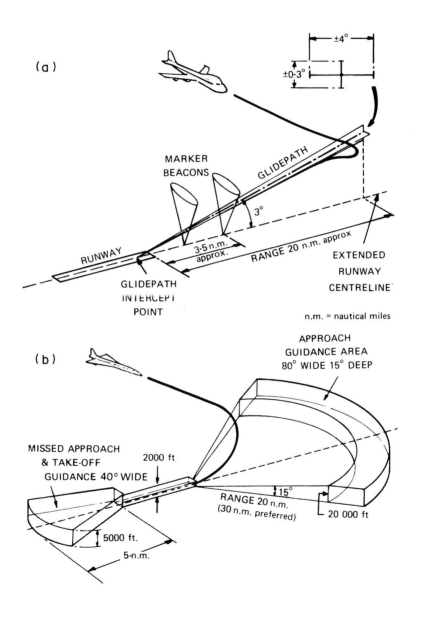

±4°

±0·3°

(a)

MARKER
BEACONS

GLIDEPATH

3°

RUNWAY

3·5 n.m.
approx.

RANGE 20 n.m. approx

EXTENDED
RUNWAY
CENTRELINE

GLIDEPATH
INTERCEPT
POINT

n.m. = nautical miles

APPROACH
GUIDANCE AREA
80° WIDE 15° DEEP

(b)

MISSED APPROACH
& TAKE-OFF
GUIDANCE 40° WIDE

2000 ft.

RANGE 20 n.m.
(30 n.m. preferred)

15°

20 000 ft

5000 ft.

5·n.m.

FIGURES 9a, 9b. Comparative diagrams ILS–MLS

The first of these methods was the use of wireless telegraphy, which required the carriage in the aircraft of a wireless operator and similarly wireless operators on the ground, at the various locations concerned with communication with particular flights. Messages were passed between the aircraft and the ground using the Morse code. Letters of the alphabet were formed by using a series of dots and dashes, following the long-established practice used by seaborne vessels. The letters so formed used an international grouping known as the 'Q' code. They were usually in groups of three letters and their decode was in accordance with an internationally agreed format. The decode had the virtue that the written interpretation could be expressed in any language, provided the translation conformed to the agreed decode.

The 'Q' code employed a wide range of aviation expressions and the addition of the letters IMI to a transmitted code or group of codes indicated they were interrogative, thus the same code group could be used for question and answer. For example, an aircraft which required a course to fly to reach a specific location, would transmit the following message to a particular W/T ground station, *'QDM IMI'*, which when decoded meant:

> Will you indicate the magnetic heading for me to steer towards you with no wind.

An example reply would be in the form *QDM 090 1030* – which decoded meant:

> The magnetic heading for you to steer to reach me with no wind was 090 degrees at 1030 hours.

This then was a relatively simple and unambiguous method of international communication, albeit with a somewhat limited vocabulary.

Two major events, however, in the development of aviation have combined to outdate wireless telegraphy, and the Q code, as an effective method of communication, other than for use over very long distances, which are at present beyond the range of the frequencies used for voice transmissions, or in some of the more remote parts of the world. The two events are:

(1) the speed of the vehicle being communicated with (the aircraft); and
(2) the dramatic increase in the numbers involved.

To try to put this rapid expansion into some sort of perspective, from a 'need to communicate' point of view, it would, I think, assist to refer briefly to the development of aviation as stated in the 'Introductory' remarks.

Prior to the advent of the Second World War, aviation in Europe was very much in its formulative stage. From a civil point of view air traffic, as a means of communication, was not only expensive but was still being undertaken in a pioneering spirit, and from a military aspect the use of aircraft in a defensive and offensive role, as a major weapon of war, had still to be proved, despite the lessons of aerial bombardment learnt in the Spanish Civil War. Only on the continent of North America had the potential of the use of aircraft as a rapid means of communication advanced to a stage where regulation of aircraft flights prompted the need for intervention by a ground organisation to assist in the safety and economy of operations.

The events of the Second World War, however, led to a dramatic exploitation of the use of aircraft, not only as a defensive and offensive weapon, but also as a means of rapid transportation. Following the cessation of hostilities this expansion continued, particularly in the role of civilian passenger-carrying aircraft, which became used increasingly for commerce and also for pleasure purposes.

Equally rapid was the expansion in the sophistication and performance characteristics of both civil and military aircraft, resulting in the fact that today the mix of air traffic varies from the light executive aircraft cruising at 160 knots to the wide-bodied jet transport cruising at 500 knots, and supersonic transport and fighter aircraft flying at Mach 1 plus. Additionally, these aircraft, even in the field of civil aviation, can vary in the climb and descent performance from rates of 500 feet per minute to rates in excess of 5000 feet per minute.

To try to give some idea of the number of aircraft involved in this equation, for example, at the present time the London Air Traffic Control Centre handles more than 3500 aircraft movements a day, over half of which are climbing and descending in the congested airspace around London. Heathrow Airport, the busiest international airport in the world, is used by 70 different airlines and for the greater part of the day has at least one aircraft landing or taking off every minute. Even on the broad waters of the North Atlantic Ocean some 500 aircraft cross each day to and from the North American continent.

To channel this flow of air traffic, and to obtain the necessary degree of orderliness to separate them one from another, requires the application of the complex set of rules and procedures previously described. It is not the purpose of this paragraph to spell out the complicated art of controlling air traffic which is dealt with throughout the book, but to refer to it only in the context of the need to 'communicate' for at present, as stated earlier, all of the sophisticated aids at an air traffic control officer's disposal finally result in the use of a *speech* circuit to issue an executive instruction to the pilot of an aircraft, for the safeguarding of his flight.

It was therefore the urgent need for direct speech between the pilot and the controller, rather than through a wireless operator, which resulted in the use of radio telephony for voice communications and the abandonment of wireless telegraphy and the 'Q' Code, other than in those areas to which I have previously referred.

It was, however, clear that as aviation had progressed beyond national boundaries, was rapidly developing both economically and geographically on a world-wide basis, and was by its very nature dependent upon the highest level of safety, any speech to be used had to be unambiguous and clearly understood by the mix of nationalities who could be present in any particular airspace at any specific time. A further inexorable factor in speech understanding was that aviation was happening, was rapidly expanding, and would not wait upon lengthy world-wide debate of well-intentioned sectional interests.

In recognition of the fact that the growth of aviation would promote a wide variety of problems, in addition to international communication, a Convention on International Civil Aviation was held in Chicago (U.S.A.) in 1944. As a result of this meeting of world-wide aviation interests an organisation was established, called the Provisional International Civil Aviation Organisation (PICAO). Later, following the ratification of the Convention, the organisation became the International Civil Aviation Organisation (ICAO) and today has a world-wide membership ranging from the U.S.A. to the U.S.S.R. and from Iceland to Japan.

The organisation works by consent through committees, and it is a matter for the concerned participating states to adopt the deliberations of these committees, by inclusion of them in their national operating manuals, or, if appropriate in air legislation (see Chapter 12 'The International Civil Aviation Organisation').

It was then this body, ICAO, who applied itself to the task of introducing for aviation a world-wide method of standard speech communication, to be adopted in all airspaces used by international flights. In doing so three main factors had to be recognised:
(1) the language used had to be common;
(2) the pronuciation of words had to be common;
(3) a set of phraseologies had to be compiled to cover as many as possible of the stan-

dard communications essential to control the flights of aircraft, taking off, en-route, landing, and moving on the surface of aerodromes.

In regard to the language to be used it is possibly an historic accident that a form of English provided the basis of the standard phraseologies. It has to be remembered however, that the U.S.A. even before 1945 had, due to its economic growth and great geographical distances, promoted the use of aviation as a means of rapid transport, and in doing so, had not only developed the techniques for the control of air traffic, but had been using voice communication via a network of company radio frequencies for the issue of control instructions over long distances. Also amongst the greater part of the world's nations who were emerging as potential aviation users, the English language was undoubtedly the one most commonly understood. It was therefore possibly a case of common sense and expediency rather than design which resulted in the use of English.

With regard to pronunciation and word spelling, an alphabet was devised which was designed, as far as possible, to cater for the difficulties experienced by speakers other than native English. For example, the word 'hotel' loses its aspirate and is pronounced 'otel'. Another example is the word 'Quebec' which when pronounced in accordance with the phonetic alphabet becomes 'Kehbeck'. Thus a genuine attempt was made to try to cater for difficulties in pronuciation in those areas where known problems existed.

The standard phraseologies themselves were designed to be as simple as possible within the constraints of a very technical subject, and had to be particularly phrased to try to eliminate any ambiguity. In this regard they have to be submitted to continuing review, not only to prevent any liability to misinterpretation, but also to keep pace with the changing situation resulting from technological growth. An essential element of this common usage language is this continuing

review, and for aviation purposes this is carried out by one of the working groups of ICAO which comprises foreign nationals and representative of the users; that is the pilots and the air traffic control officers.

The success of this use of a common method of communication for world-wide aeronautical purposes, can it is suggested, be attributed to four main causes.

(1) *The need to safeguard human life* – the closing speeds of modern aircraft can be likened to the velocity of a bullet out of a rifle, approximately 1000 miles an hour. Therefore when this is related to the three-dimensional spider's web of air traffic, which was described earlier, it will be readily apparent that there must be, as far as is reasonably possible, no ambiguity in the verbal messages which are exchanged between the ground and the air.

(2) *The economic factor* – the rapid expansion, in particular of commercial aviation, would undoubtedly have been severely inhibited in its growth without the existence of a ground organisation capable of ensuring the safety and expedition of air movements. A basic requirement of such an organisation is the capability to relay, rapidly, intelligence in written and verbal form, across the boundaries of separate languages.

(3) *The lack of sectional interests* – it is tactfully suggested that a well-intentioned concern for the preservation of the grammatical structure of a particular language often inhibits the development of a common method of communication. The urgency of the requirement to provide a solution for the safety and expedition of world-wide aviation meant that sectional academic interests, and champions of particular languages, became a secondary consideration.

(4) *The use of an existing language* – by general consent it was decided to use an existing language as the basis for aviation communications. Historically and geographi-

cally a form of English was the language most commonly in use on an international basis, and therefore urgency and common sense conspired to confirm its application.

It is considered that the success of the adoption of a common international language for aviation, was due to the will to succeed, abetted by the fact that safety of human life and commercial expediency were paramount to the bustling growth of air transport and the fact that a permanent international body, the International Civil Aviation Organisation, was in existence, for debate on agreement by consent.

As stated earlier, new methods of communication, particularly between the air and the ground, will doubtless be advanced with the advent of modern technology. However, whatever form these may take, it is considered vital that the principle of a world-wide standard format, and the symbols and phrases to be used, follow a similar forum of international agreement, as has been the case with radio telephony.

For the interest of readers, I have included as Table 1 the present internationally agreed phonetic alphabet. Following the letters of the alphabet are the words to be used, when it is required to transmit individual letters; for example, the callsign of an aircraft. Following the words is the method in which the words are to be pronounced, and in this regard the underlining indicates the syllables which require emphasis. Finally I have included the 'Morse code' equivalent of the letters of the alphabet. Additionally, for those readers who may have a requirement for a more detailed knowledge of R/T speech, and also because of the international importance of the use of standard phraseologies, I have reproduced as an appendix, with the kind permission of the United Kingdom's Civil Aviation Authority, an extract from their *Manual of Air Traffic Services*. This extract sets out not only the standard phraseologies to be used, to ensure uniformity of communication between a variety of nationalities, but also the speech technique to be used to obtain the correct enunciation of words. Also it is fortunate that the International Civil Aviation Organisation (ICAO) has just completed its review of standard phraseologies to bring them into line with the developments which have occurred in recent years, both in the air and on the ground. The information contained in the appendix is therefore, up to date at the time of going to Press (1985) and should remain so for several years ahead.

Telephony

The humble telephone is so well known, and used, as an instrument of communication, that its existence is taken for granted and the penalties of its non-availability only recognised on the relatively rare occasions when it is out of service. In a social sense these occasions can result in annoyance, and in a business and professional sense lead to irritation and frustration. For air traffic control, however, the telephone represents a vital operational piece of equipment, without which the controller would be unable to carry out his tasks, for whilst computers are increasingly being used to automate a number of routine tasks, speech circuits remain the primary means of the co-ordination of aircraft movements between the various elements of the ground organisation. Co-ordination in particular requires instant communication between the parties concerned. These can range from communication between the aerodrome and approach controllers, to contact between domestic air traffic control centres and those of a neighbouring state or, as is the case with the North Atlantic, between the controllers in the United Kingdom and those in New York or Gander in Newfoundland. The objective of co-ordination, in air traffic control terms, is to ensure that intelligence on the exact situation of a particular aircraft is passed to the next controlling agency, ahead of the physical appearance of the concerned aircraft in the airspace for which the receiving controlling agency is responsible, and also that any change

TABLE 1 *Pronunciation of letters and the Morse code. The underlined syllables are emphasised.*

Letter	Word	Pronunciation in English	Morse code
A	Alfa	AL FAH	· —
B	Bravo	BRAH VOH	— · · ·
C	Charlie	CHAR LEE	— · — ·
D	Delta	DELL TAH	— · ·
E	Echo	ECK OH	·
F	Foxtrot	FOKS TROT	· · — ·
G	Golf	GOLF	— — ·
H	Hotel	HOH TELL	· · · ·
I	India	IN DEE AH	· ·
J	Juliett	JEW LEE ETT	· — — —
K	Kilo	KEY LOH	— · —
L	Lima	LEE MAH	· — · ·
M	Mike	MIKE	— —
N	November	NO VEM BER	— ·
O	Oscar	OSS CAH	— — —
P	Papa	PAH PAH	· — — ·
Q	Quebec	KEH BECK	— — · —
R	Romeo	ROW ME OH	· — ·
S	Sierra	SEE AIR RAH	· · ·
T	Tango	TANG GO	—
U	Uniform	YOU NEE FORM	· · —
V	Victor	VIK TAH	· · · —
W	Whiskey	WISS KEY	· — —
X	Xray	ECKS RAY	— · · —
Y	Yankee	YANG KEY	— · — —
Z	Zulu	ZOO LOO	— — · ·

in that intelligence is passed immediately to that receiving agency. It follows therefore that not only must direct telephone circuits exist, wherever possible between the agencies concerned with the control of an aircraft's flight, but also that a high degree of serviceability must prevail and additionally, alternative circuit routeings be pre-planned to provide against any unforeseen failure of a direct or indirect circuit.

From the previous section on radio telephony (air/ground) it will be obvious that a controller is required to speak on both telephone and R/T circuits. However, whilst an 'alert' to an incoming telephone call, or the initiation of an outgoing call, does not demand continuous monitoring of these circuits, quite a different situation prevails in regard to radio telephony (R/T). A controller is required to continuously monitor the R/T frequency or frequencies which are in use for controlling air

traffic. Whilst at the smaller air traffic units with light traffic, or exceptionally at busier locations where traffic may be light in the night-watch hours, it is possible to use loudspeakers; such a situation is not tenable at the larger air traffic units or where there is a medium to heavy volume of air traffic.

Without stating the many reasons why this should be so, it will, of course, be clear to readers, from the previous paragraph, that it is not unusual, for example at busy air traffic control centres, to have up to 100 separate R/T frequencies in operation; the resulting cacophony of sound generated by loudspeakers in such a situation, could not, of course, even be contemplated.

At these busier units, therefore, to enable the controllers to carry out their tasks with a minimum of physical interruption, they are provided with light-weight headsets. These headsets are so designed that speech on radio-telephony is received in one ear and telephone speech in the other. To provide for transmission, either over the R/T or on the telephone, a boom microphone is mounted on the headset, adjustable to individual requirements. The boom employs two microphones mounted back-to-back, one acting as the speech circuit and the other acting ingeniously as a noise-cancelling device.

The microphone itself is dual-purpose, in that when the controller depresses his key, associated with the R/T circuit he has selected, transmissions go out over the air, and then it acts in exactly the same way as a telephone when he selects a circuit on his telephone panel.

Quite apart from relieving the controller of the tedious task of picking up and setting down separate instruments for the R/T and telephone, the contribution of this type of listening and transmitting device to the over-all noise level is enormous. For those of you who may have visited one of the world's air traffic control centres, at which there can be 100-plus operating positions, I am certain you must have been impressed by the relatively low noise level which exists, when recalling the continuous speech which is being transmitted and received on the R/T and telephone circuits, as the combined air traffic control staffs go about their tasks of co-ordinating and controlling air traffic.

Aeronautical fixed telecommunications network (AFTN)

A further vital element in the communication of information is the world-wide aeronautical fixed telecommunications network (AFTN). As its name implies, it operates on a world-wide basis through a network of relay stations, positioned on the earth's surface, although in extreme cases use can be made of an airborne aircraft, as a mobile platform for relaying a message, and doubtless communication via satellite will form part of future networks.

Its use is governed internationally by agree ments within ICAO in exactly the same way as the rules of the air, previously described. These agreements result, amongst many other things, in the application of standard formats for the transmission of messages and, of equal importance, a category of priorities associated with such messages. Whilst I shall be describing in detail, later, the role of an aircraft's 'flight plan' this particular subject provides an excellent opportunity to describe how the AFTN is used in this particular instance. If, for example, we take the flight of an aircraft from London (Heathrow) Airport to Sydney, Australia, the pilot or his representative is required to file a flight plan ahead of the proposed departure of the flight. The flight plan is required to be addressed not only to his destination airport (Sydney) but also to the air traffic control agencies (ATCCs) of the states through whose airspace the aircraft will pass on the route to its destination. The message, when transmitted, contains groups of characters, which, when related to the standard format, are readily transposable by the recipients. The operator who initiates the messages uses a keyboard similar to that of a typewriter, with a back-roll copy to check the correctness of the message content. In the example quoted the originator of the message would address it in the first instance to a message-switching centre, where on arrival the message would be reproduced as a punched tape. This tape is then fed either manually or automatically into a central processor which then initiates copies of the message (flight plan) to all of the addresses nominated by the originator of the flight plan. The AFTN system thus provides a rapid and efficient method of the communication of information, particularly over long distances and to a multiplicity of addressees.

I should like to emphasise that the example I have illustrated is just one of the many services provided by this network which, as I remarked, forms a vital link in the communications chain which is concerned with aircraft safety.

5
Radar

Introduction

In explaining the facilities which a controller has at his disposal, we now come to the most significant advance in technology which, although it had its origins in the Second World War, was not exploited as a 'tool' of air traffic control until the late 1950s, and in fact its major impact as an aid to the separation of aircraft did not really materialise until the mid 1960s. I refer to the advent of radar, both 'primary' and 'secondary'.

The use of radar as a means of assisting aircraft to land, had, however, been pioneered in the United Kingdom by the Royal Air Force, since the first of the ground approach control (GCA) sets arrived in this country from the U.S.A. in 1942 accompanied by its mentors, Dr Alvarez and Dr Comstock. In fact, prior to the development of the instrument landing system (ILS) referred to in the earlier chapter, the talkdown controller, as he became popularly known, was a key member of the approach control team at many international civil airports, and it was indeed a very famous sight to see the two GCA caravans moving from one runway to another, whenever a change of wind also dictated a change of runway. To pay tribute to this past band of stalwart talkdown controllers and technicians, I should mention that at that stage of develop-

ment the GCA trucks, which were prime movers, had to be very precisely positioned alongside the runway in use. Working inside the operational truck, which was very small indeed, took place in almost total darkness and controlling was conducted from two cathode ray tubes, each 6 inches only in diameter. One tube was used for a 360° surveillance of the immediate vicinity of the aerodrome and was used by the director to locate the aircraft and feed it into the azimuth and elevation funnel of the talkdown controller's display. The talkdown controller was assisted by a 'tracker' whose task was to servo the two aerials (azimuth and elevation) onto the aircraft's response, and then the controller, who was able to view the aircraft's response in glide angle and displacement from the runway centre-line through an ingenious arrangement of silvered mirrors, literally did talk the aircraft down onto the runway. In the early days of aviation expansion all of the staffs of these GCA trucks did a magnificent job, and I count myself fortunate to have been amongst them. We did not, of course, in those days concern ourselves overmuch with the 'Factories, Shops and Railway Premises Act'. Later developments, however, enabled the runway guidance elements (azimuth/elevation) of the GCA to be remoted to the approach control rooms, where it became known as 'precision approach radar' and where it remained as an operational facility at many international airports including London (Heathrow) until the early 1970s. There are in fact, some airports, including Hong Kong (Kai Tak) where PAR is still available, and ground controlled approaches still remain very much an operational feature of many military aerodromes.

The use of radar, to assist in the separation of aircraft took some time to develop, however, and because of its importance in this regard, and its present and future role in automated air traffic control systems, I propose to explain very briefly the basic principles of primary and secondary radar. I do so because I find, strange though it seems to me, many people, even amongst those directly concerned with aviation, who find it hard to visualise what a controller's display of radar data looks like, and how the information is generated. I must, however, emphasise that my description is a very simple explanation of a highly technical subject, for which I apologise in advance to my learned professional colleagues, but I trust it will help in a greater appreciation of the Pandora's Box of technology, which it has opened up to almost limitless application.

The basic principles of radar

The term 'Radar' was derived from an acronym of the phrase 'radio detection and ranging'. It can better be described as the art of detecting by means of radio echoes, the presence of objects and of determining their direction and range. It is based upon the principle that electromagnetic energy, which is propagated from a transmitter at the speed of light, can be directed onto a reflecting object – for example, an aircraft – and that the distance of the object can be calculated by measuring the time a pulse of the radio energy took to travel to the object and back again. Further that by using an antenna, which produces and collects

a narrow beam of energy, similar to a searchlight and rotating this beam through 360°, the direction from which this energy is being reflected can also be determined. This reflected energy, when accepted by the 'receiver', is first decoded and then amplified and turned into a signal which can be observed by a radar operator. The received signal is usually referred to as a 'blip' and the display upon which it is observed by the operator is known as a cathode ray tube (CRT). To enable the operator to have a plan position view the front of the CRT, which looks similar to that of a television set, is used as a plan position indicator (PPI).

Therefore for the purposes of this elementary explanation a radar set consists of:
(1) a *transmitter* which produces the radio energy pulses (Figure 10a);
(2) an *antenna* which radiates the energy and collects the echo (Figure 10a);
(3) a *receiver* which decodes the reflected energy (Figure 10a) *Note:* most antennas act as both the radiators and collectors of energy. The transmitter itself allows enough time for the reflected echoes to return to the antenna, before the next pulse is sent. This 'time' is in the order of a millisecond.
(4) an *amplifier* and processor which amplifies the energy (signal) and separates it from clutter and transforms it into video form (Figure 10a); and
(5) An *indicator* (cathode ray tube on which the returned signal can be displayed; (Figure 10b).

These are then the basic elements of a radar set, but readers will wish to be aware of at least some of the complexities, many of which have still to be solved even with the aid of modern technology. For example, radar signals returning to a receiver are often mixed with unwanted signals other than those reflected from aircraft. These unwanted signals are generally known as 'clutter'. They are caused by buildings within the vicinity of the antenna, high ground, weather, and in particular rain drop-

Radar

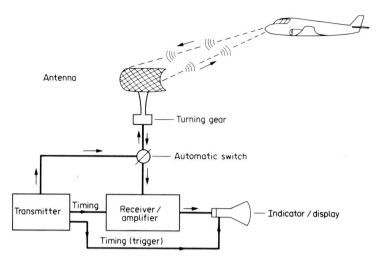

FIGURE 10a. Block diagram of a radar set

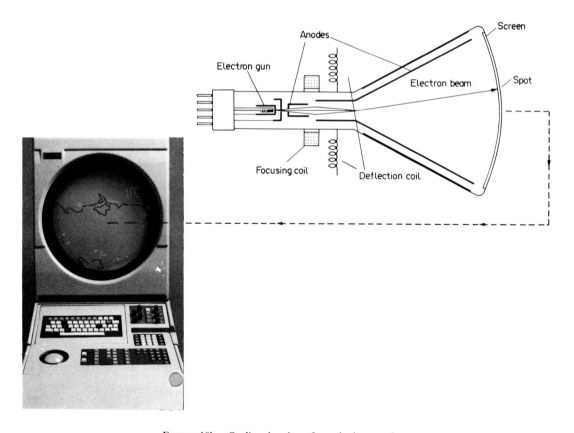

FIGURE 10b. Outline drawing of a cathode ray tube

44

lets. A particular phenomenon is the effect of temperature creating a radio duct, resulting in mirror images of targets from a longer distance being shown at a shorter range; these are popularly known as 'angels'. Much of this unwanted 'clutter' can, however, be suppressed by sophisticated processing of the returning signals within the radar. The range at which a target can be detected depends upon a number of parameters, of which the power output of the transmitter, the frequency of the signal, the gain of the antenna and the quality of the receiver are most important. The radar set generates bursts of radio energy, known as pulses, and it is the frequency at which these pulses occur, known as the pulse recurrence frequency (PRF), allied to the power output, which characterises the radar. Many readers will no doubt have heard of the terms 'X band', 'S band', 'L band' to describe the different frequencies of operation. In very general terms:

(1) *J and KU Band* represent very short microwaves and would be used in equipment such as ground surface movement detection (e.g. aircraft and vehicles moving on the surface of an aerodrome, where very high definition is required). This frequency, however, suffers high attenuation in rain and is therefore a short-range device.

(2) *X Band* represents short microwaves and is used in precision approach radar (PAR) and marine systems, where good definition is needed and only medium range.

(3) *S Band* represents medium microwaves and would be used in equipment such as terminal and approach control radars (e.g. for the sequencing of arriving and departing aircraft, where it represents a compromise between good definition and medium range).

(4) *L Band* represents long microwaves and would be used in equipment such as area or en-route radar (e.g. for the control of aircraft over long distance such as airways, where long range and immunity from weather are more important than high definition).

Radar signals are 'line of sight', which means that the further away an aircraft is from the transmitting antenna, the higher it must fly to remain within radar cover. Also the shape and size of the antennas are extremely critical to the task the radar is required to perform, and to the desired vertical and longitudinal coverage.

These then are some of the factors which have to be taken into consideration both by the manufacturers and users of radar.

Through the courtesy of one of these manufacturers, Plessey Radar Ltd, Figure 11 shows a modern radar antenna, which operates on 'S' band frequencies, and would be typically used for approach and terminal area radar control purposes. Mounted on top of the primary radar antenna is a secondary surveillance radar (SSR) antenna, which is a subject discussed later in this chapter.

It is emphasised, however, that the foregoing is a very abbreviated and simplified explanation indeed of the properties of radar, and a reader or student who wishes greater knowledge is advised to read the many excellent textbooks on radar theory.

Radar displays

The purpose of the radar is to provide the radar operator with an indicator or display upon which the information made available by the radar system can be interpreted by him as easily as possible. The best known of these displays is called the plan position indicator (PPI), which in effect is a radar map of the area of coverage. The radar antenna represents the centre of the map and the radar echoes or 'blips' appear as bright spots of light on the surface of the display. Whilst radar displays

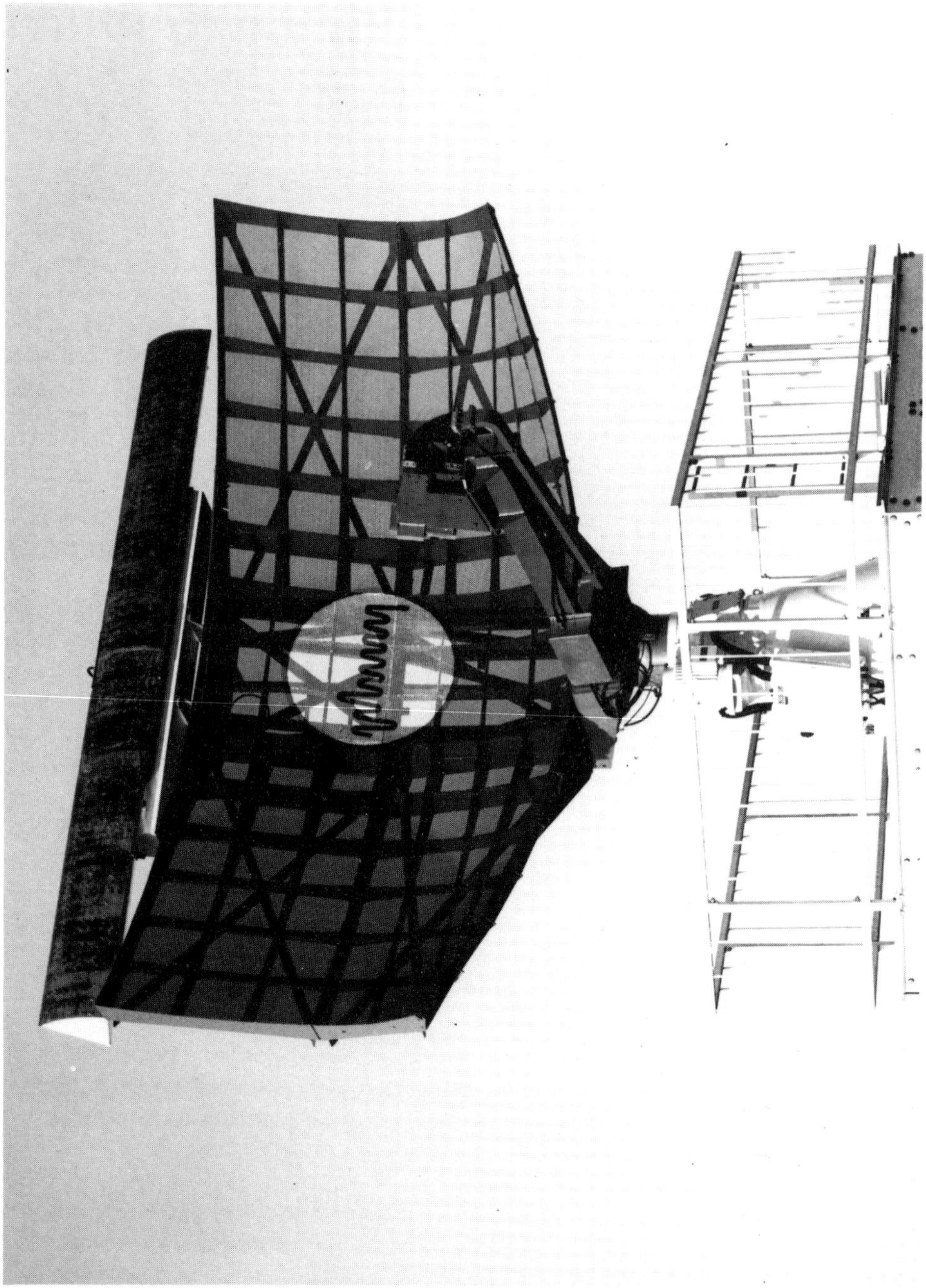

FIGURE 11. A modern primary radar antenna with on-mounted secondary surveillance radar (SSR). This antenna is typical of a modern Approach Terminal Area Radar. The short antenna mounted on top on the main antenna is the Secondary Surveillance Radar, and in this configuration has certain advantages, including the use of the same turning gear as the parent antenna.

(Photograph Courtesy Plessey Radar Ltd)

have today reached a highly sophisticated stage using digitised/computerised techniques, it is considered it would be of more general interest at this level of introduction to use as an example the standard form of display based upon the cathode ray tube (CRT) (Figure 10b).

The cathode ray tube, which is also used in domestic television sets, is a device which produces electrons in the form of a stream, from a source called an 'electron gun'. This stream of electrons can be controlled in such a manner that the information derived from the radar can be displayed on the screen. The stream of electrons is first focused into a narrow beam which appears as a bright spot on the face of the tube and can then be moved about by the use of deflection coils, and therefore made to follow the movement of the antenna. The gun can be switched off to simulate those areas where there are no signals, and then switched on again when an echo is received, so indicating its position on the tube. The inside surface of the face of the tube is usually coated with phosphorus, permitting sufficient 'afterglow' to permit the most recent position of the spot to persist for a short time, and thus show the track of the aircraft. This will, however, be accomplished in the future by the use of digital memory techniques.

The plan position indicator uses a cathode ray tube to provide a plan view of the reflected responses from aircraft. This plan view is obtained, as was explained earlier, from a knowledge of the range and bearing information sent from the antenna. As the antenna is continuously rotated it is possible to introduce onto the display range circles which illuminate on every sweep of the antenna. This sweep around the tube face is known as the 'time base' (Figure 12).

It is then possible to introduce, onto the display, bearing mark lines, which enable the radar operator to determine the bearing of the echo from the antenna (Figure 13), also a map outline known as a video map which can show

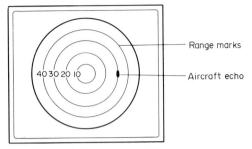

Aircraft echo is indicated at a range of 30 nautical miles

FIGURE 12.   Plan position indicator

features such as coastlines or the position of airways, airports and navigational aids. Thus the radar operator is able to establish the precise position of the target aircraft, and having carried out an identification procedure, direct the aircraft to any position within the coverage of his radar. A more detailed description of the facilities which are available on a modern radar display console, is given in Chapter 8, 'Automation and Air Traffic Control', in the section dealing with 'The display of radar-derived data'.

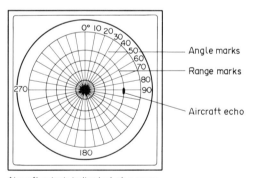

Aircraft echo is indicated at a range of 30 nautical miles on a bearing of 090°

FIGURE 13.   Plan position indicator with range and bearing marks

The basic principles of secondary surveillance radar (SSR)

Fascinating as primary radar may be, it is the

advent of secondary surveillance radar (SSR) that has escalated the techniques for the processing of radar data and the application of computer technology, towards the development of automated air traffic control systems. In fact, from the point of view of controlling air traffic the introduction of SSR has been the most significant advance since the application of primary radar.

As stated earlier, primary radar works by reflection, from an aircraft, of radio pulses transmitted by a radar station on the ground. From this reflection can be detected the direction from which it returned and the time taken to return. The returning echo is, however, extremely weak, and requires considerable boosting and refining before it can be processed through to the radar display. The greater the range of the aircraft the higher the transmitted power must be, to try to achieve as many strikes (pulses) upon the aircraft as possible.

There are, however, penalties associated with increases in power output, which are rather complex to detail in this explanation, but whilst there exist some very good counters to these penalties, high-technology solutions are equally highly priced. Even so, primary radar alone is no longer able to satisfy the requirements of modern ATC systems, which must have instantly available information that is both accurate and reliable. This requirement is able to be satisfied by the fact that the aircraft itself is able to co-operate with the ground-based radar system. That is, it can carry its own airborne equipment, known as a 'transponder', which is capable of communicating with the ground-based SSR system.

The 'transponder' is one of the well-known 'black boxes' which is carried in the aircraft and operates in much the same way as the war-time IFF (identification friend or foe), but now gives more information to the controller. The

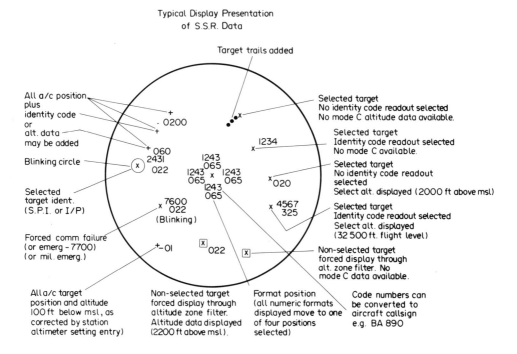

FIGURE 14. Display of presentation of SSR data

transponder is activated by pairs of pulses transmitted by a ground interrogator, and its reaction is to transmit a 'train' of pulses on a different radio frequency to the SSR interrogator receiver on the ground.

Because the transponder is not relying upon reflected energy from the aircraft to provide a radar echo, but is making a full-blooded reply itself, this enables the transmitters on the ground to be of lower power and employ simpler and cheaper technology and also ensure a certainty of signal return, unaffected by weather or other clutter factors.

Also the returning train of pulses from the aircraft can be coded to contain data pertinent to that specific aircraft such as, for example, the identity of the aircraft and the height at which it is flying. This factor gives the SSR receiver and its computer processor the ability to separate and identify different targets in a manner that the primary radar cannot do, and then be able to compute additional information such as the speed of the aircraft and its flight attitude, all without recourse to any radio telephony speech with the pilot, other than an initial request to select a special group of code numerals on his SSR select panel in the cockpit. Figure 14 provides some idea of the type of information which can be presented on radar displays, where SSR is being used, either singly or in conjunction with primary radar.

I will be dealing with the application of automation later in the book, under which heading I will endeavour to explain how the information derived from SSR forms the basis of modern ATC systems. However, to give an idea of the vast difference between primary radar only, and primary plus secondary, I have included two figures. Figure 15 shows a typical primary display of aircraft targets. It is interesting to note that in the early days of the application of radar the standard method of achieving identification was to request the pilot to make a 90° turn from his present course, hold it for 1 minute and then make a further 90°

turn, back onto his original course. To confirm that the radar response was in fact the concerned aircraft, both turns had to be observed by the radar controller who then, using a chinagraph pencil, marked the face of his display with the aircraft's identity and continued to plot its course on the display. It is easy to imagine that pilots were none too keen to follow this tedious manoeuvre, and it is only surprising to recall that so many did so, to assist in the development of ATC techniques. As a complete contrast Figure 16 shows a modern digitised radar display, upon which appears not only the outlines of the geographical area under radar surveillance but also, alongside the aircraft's radar response, its identity and the height at which it is flying. There were of course many stages of development before ATC arrived at these techniques, but it is a truly remarkable development by any standards.

The role of radar in air traffic control

Before leaving the subject, and although I will be dealing with its detailed application later, it might be worthwhile to consider the role of radar in the control of air traffic.

In the section dealing with 'Separation standards' I mentioned radar separations, and in regard to their application it is essential to recognise the two following fundamental principles.

(1) radar is primarily used by air traffic control to reduce the separation between aircraft and by so doing enable more air traffic to be controlled in a given airspace; and

(2) there has to be in existence a basic ATC system which can be readily employed in the event of the failure of the radar element or part thereof.

In general terms the operational role of an approach/terminal area radar can be described as the provision of a service for:

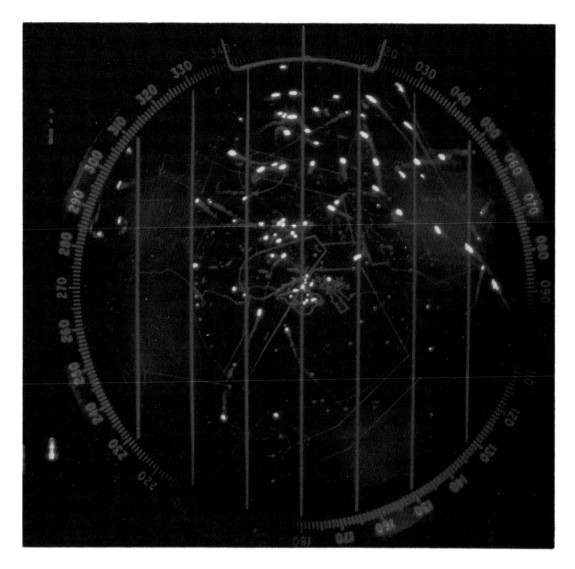

FIGURE 15.   A primary radar display This is a display of primary radar responses from aircraft and demonstrates the difficulty of identifying the aircraft to which the responses belong. A problem which has been largely overcome by the use of Secondary Surveillance Radar (SSR)

(Photograph Courtesy Plessey Radar Ltd)

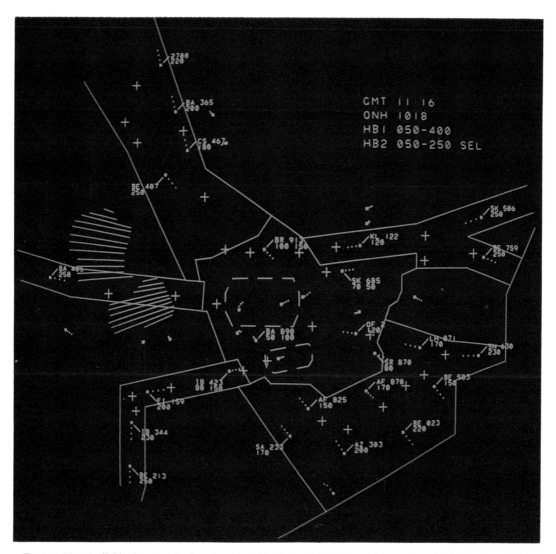

FIGURE 16. A digitised radar display showing SSR data. This picture of a modern digitised radar display indicates the clarity of the aircraft targets alongside which can be seen their identity and height. This information has been obtained from the use of SSR techniques. The dots which are observable behind the aircraft symbols are known as 'trail dots' and enable the controllers to assess the history of the particular aircraft's previous flight path.

(Photo courtesy Plessey Radar Ltd)

(1) the control of air traffic overflying or transitting the approach terminal area;

(2) the guidance and sequencing of arriving traffic, either onto a pilot-interpreted instrument landing system or a precision approach radar (PAR);

(6) the sequencing of aircraft departing from the aerodrome until either handed over to an area control centre, or until clear of the approach/terminal area, or until control is transferred to a military air traffic air defence authority;

(4) the provision of an approach control service to one or more adjacent aerodromes;

(5) the provision of a radar advisory service, where this is required, within the area of radar cover.

To carry out these tasks, not only is an area of primary radar cover of approximately 60 nautical miles up to a height of 30,000/45,000 feet required, but also the radar must have the capability to detect responses from aircraft through 'fixed' and 'moving' clutter returns.

As mentioned previously 'fixed' clutter is produced from energy sent out by the transmitter, which is then reflected back to the receiver, by stationary objects such as airport buildings within the immediate vicinity of the aerial head, or high ground which penetrates the envelope of the transmitted power. 'Moving' clutter is usually produced by weather, such as the reflection of energy from rain droplets.

It is vital for the safe control of air traffic, where radar separation is being provided, that the radar sensor which is being used for this purpose has the ability to continue to detect the responses from aircraft targets through these areas of clutter returns. Of equal importance is the capability of the radar to be able to discriminate between aircraft targets, throughout the range of the primary radar cover, claimed by a manufacturer. For, apart from the variety of speed ranges of modern aircraft, their radar reflecting area can vary from a wide-bodied passenger aircraft to a light private aircraft, or in a military sense from a heavy air transport to a supersonic fighter aircraft. But whatever the size of the target aircraft may be, it is the responsibility of air traffic control, when providing a radar service, to ensure the safety of that aircraft in relation to all other air users within the area of responsibility of the particular authority. To do so the radar controller requires continuous and precise target information and the elimination of as much of the unwanted interference as modern technology can provide.

Secondary surveillance radar (SSR/IFF) does, of course, materially assist in the resolution of these problems, but provision still has to be made for good solid primary radar cover, in the approach/terminal area environment, for a variety of reasons, including those occasions where the carriage of transponders may not yet be a legal requirement, or where from a military point of view the radar is required to operate in a hostile or semi-hostile environment.

It has to be accepted, however, that most modern air traffic control systems, both civil and military, rely heavily upon the fact that the air traffic for which they are responsible is co-operative; that is to say, that the aircraft are fitted with an airborne transponder. In fact many states now require aircraft flying at or above certain heights to carry a serviceable transponder as mandatory equipment for receiving an air traffic control service.

The foregoing principles apply equally to area radar control, that is the airspace outside the approach and terminal areas, which contain the airways and air routes. The primary radar, however, needs a much greater power output to achieve the desired range and height. It is nonetheless interesting to observe in this regard that, apart from the understandable military requirement of long-range primary radar cover, civil air traffic control authorities are likely in future systems, to rely upon the extended cover provided by SSR to cater for their area radar requirements. For example, the quoted range of primary radar cover which I gave for an approach/terminal area radar of 60 nautical miles, would be extended to between 120 and 150 nautical miles with the addition of an associated SSR installation; therefore, as modern ATC systems are becoming increasingly dependent upon the carriage by aircraft of SSR transponders, it seems sensible and economic to take advantage of the increased range of cover, which is provided by this facility.

In my Preface I made mention of the fact that the control of air traffic is operating in a continually changing environment, and readers may find that this paragraph on radar underlines that statement more than any other.

6

Flight Planning and Flight Data

Introduction

The prior notification, by the pilot of an aircraft, of the details of a proposed flight, has two basic purposes.

(1) that should he desire to, or be required to, receive an air traffic service, prior information is essential for the provision of that service; and

(2) in the event of an accident or incident the information contained in this notification is vital to the success of the search and rescue services (SAR).

This notification of the pilot's intentions can either be *'booking-out'* if he does not wish to, or is not required to, receive an air traffic service, or the filing of a *'flight plan'*, which is a mandatory requirement for certain types of flight. Apart from this mandatory requirement pilots can still file a flight plan, and are certainly advised to do so, if intending to fly more than 10 nautical miles from the coast, or over sparsely populated or mountainous terrain. The difference between 'booking-out' and filing a 'flight plan' is that with a flight plan all of the information it contains is passed to the air traffic services units concerned with the route

of the flight, whereas the information contained in the booking-out procedure remains at the aerodrome of departure.

As, however, we are concerned with explaining the provision of air traffic services, it is those categories of flight, which are required to submit a flight plan which are our concern.

I should make the point, before proceeding to detail what a flight plan is and how it is used, that a pilot who has not filed a flight plan at his departure aerodrome can still file an airborne flight plan, provided he gives adequate warning and passes the required information to the concerned air traffic services unit (ATSU).

The flight plan

The application of air traffic control is dependent upon a knowledge of the aircraft's present position and the intentions of the pilot-in-command. A vital factor in the provision of this service, and one from which all subsequent data acquired during the course of an aircraft's flight corrects or amends, is the filing of a flight plan.

The flight plan is an internationally agreed document, which, for ease of transmission and understanding on a world-wide basis, is prepared in a standard format. The types of flights which are required to submit flight plans are also agreed internationally and are set out in ICAO rules of the air (Annex 2). As a general guide however, the requirement can be described as follows:

A flight plan shall be submitted prior to operating:

(1) any flight, or portion thereof, to be provided with an air traffic control service;
(2) any instrument flight rule (IFR) flight, within advisory airspace;
(3) any flight within or into designated areas, or along designated routes, when so required by the appropriate ATS authority, to facilitate the provision of flight information, alerting and search and rescue services;
(4) any flight across international borders.

These rules may vary somewhat in interpretation by the contracting states of ICAO when translated into a particular state's air navigation orders (ANO), but my experience is that these variations are minor in nature and the intent of the ICAO rules are applied worldwide.

I should like to underline the fact that the wording says 'prior to operating'. As I have previously stated ATC requires to have prior information of a pilot's intentions, therefore the submission of a flight plan before the departure of an aircraft is required to take place at least 30 minutes prior to the estimated departure time (ETD) of the concerned aircraft. In fact some states, of which the United Kingdom is one, require 1 hour's notification, if the aircraft's flight is operating into or through that country's complex route network.

I shall be dealing at a later stage with the application of automation, but as it will occur to readers, particularly those who fly by scheduled airlines, that many of these flights are repetitive in nature and operate on a published timetable, the filing of a flight plan for each flight would be a very cumbersome process. To assist in this administrative requirement many states have adopted a procedure whereby, if the flight has a high degree of stability and operates at the same time/s of day(s) of consecutive weeks and on at least ten occasions without change of details, then a single repetitive plan can be filed. There is a further procedure which provides for the amendment of such flight plans and for the notification of the change of details to the other states which are concerned with that particular flight. One of the advantages of this method of flight planning is that, where a computer is being used to assist the air traffic services, the information can be placed in what is termed the 'bulk store' and the computer programmed to bring the relevant details forward at a predetermined time.

I should now like to explain the details which a pilot or his representative is required to insert on the flight plan. they are:

(1) aircraft identification;
(2) SSR data (code etc.);
(3) the type of flight rules under which the pilot proposes to operate;
(4) type of flight (e.g. scheduled/general aviation/military);
(5) the aircraft type;
(6) the aircraft's callsign;
(7) the aerodrome of departure;
(8) the estimated time at the FIR boundaries;
(9) the aircraft's cruising speed;
(10) the desired flight levels;
(11) the proposed route of flight;
(12) the aerodrome of destination;
(13) the alternate aerodromes;
(14) other information pertinent to the flight such as the aircraft's endurance, the number of passengers, the type of survival equipment carried.

Figure 17, which has been reproduced with the kind permission of ICAO, is a completed copy of a flight plan, depicting a flight from Rotterdam (EHRD) to Lisbon (LPPT). In the paragraph dealing with the teleprinter network I mentioned that it is through this system that flight plans are addressed to all the ATC authorities concerned with the conduct of a specific flight. The route followed by this aircraft takes it through the airspaces controlled by Amsterdam (EHAM), Brussels (EBBB), Paris (LFFF), Biarritz (LFBZ) and Madrid (LECM) and you will note that all of these units are addressees of the message. I should mention that the four-figure codes which are used are the international designators of the telecommunications network, usually in this instance, aerodromes and air traffic control centres.

Before leaving the subject of the flight plan I mentioned that it was also possible to file an airborne flight plan. This situation usually occurs where an aircraft, in flight, wishes to cross or join an airway or penetrate controlled airspace for the purpose of transitting or landing at an aerodrome within the confines of that airspace. Also, in some parts of the world aircraft are permitted to fly in some designated airspaces, in accordance with visual flight rules (VFR); however, due to either traffic density or adverse weather conditions a pilot can decide to change the nature of his flight and seek the protection of an air traffic service. In these circumstances the pilot is required to give minimum notice, usually not less than 10 minutes, of a request for an air traffic clearance. The information which the pilot is required to pass to the ATC authority is in the form of an abbreviated flight plan and the content will depend upon the traffic circumstances existing at the material time and the complexity of the routeing desired by the pilot.

Flight data

The word 'Data' is relatively new in dictionary terminology but as far as its use in our particular aspect of aviation is concerned, it means the gathering of intelligence, in regard to the flight of an aircraft, both prior to and during the course of that flight. It is the gathering of this intelligence and the actions based upon it that forms the fabric of a system whereby control can be exercised. In this context there are two basic forms of 'data', 'radar data' and 'flight data'.

From the earlier paragraph on radar, readers will be aware of the manner in which intelligence is gathered, by both primary and secondary radar, and then presented to the controller on his display. This intelligence is known as radar data. However, radar data alone would be almost incomprehensible to the controller without the existence of flight data, to enable him to interpret the information presented to him on his radar display. At this point in the development of air traffic control systems it is also necessary to draw attention to the fact that many parts of the world, and even parts of sophisticated systems, do not enjoy the benefit of radar coverage, but nonetheless, an efficient and safe ATC system must operate within these areas. It does so because of the presence of the flight data which exists as a basic foundation of any system.

Whilst I shall be detailing later the various air traffic services which are the responsibility of air traffic control, they can for the purpose of this chapter of the book be broad-banded as follows:

(1) aerodrome control;
(2) approach control;
(3) terminal area and area control.

To underline the importance of flight data, I wish to point out that it is only the first of these, 'aerodrome control', where the controller physically sees the aircraft he is controlling. In all other aspects of the services he provides, the controller has to 'imagine' the aircraft he is responsible for, by building up a mind picture of the air situation under his control and from this mind picture, assisted by a flow of data from various sources, determine a course of

FLIGHT PLAN
PLAN DE VOL

PRIORITY INDICATOR Indicateur de priorité *FF*	ADDRESSEE(S) INDICATOR(S) Indicateur(s) de destinataire	*EHAM ZQ* *EBBB ZQ* *LFFF ZQ* *LFBB ZQ* *LECM ZQ* *LPPT ZQ* *LPPT ZT*	《≡
FILING TIME Heure de dépôt *230856*	ORIGINATOR INDICATOR Indicateur d'origine	*EHRDZP*	《≡

SPECIFIC IDENTIFICATION OF ADDRESSEE(S) AND/OR ORIGINATOR
Identification précise du (des) destinataire(s) et/ou de l'expediteur

3 DESCRIPTION Description	7 AIRCRAFT IDENTIFICATION AND SSR DATA Identification de l'aéronef et données SSR		8 FLIGHT RULES AND TYPE OF FLIGHT Règles de vol et type de vol	
《≡ (FPL	— *SY402/A5120*	—	*IS*	《≡

9 NUMBER AND TYPE OF AIRCRAFT AND WAKE TURBULENCE CATEGORY Nombre d'aéronets et type, et catégorie de turbulence de sillage		10 EQUIPMENT/Equipement COM/NAV/APP_____ SSR _____		
— *S210/M*		—	*S*	*/4*	《≡

13 AERODROME OF DEPARTURE AND TIME Aérodrome de départ et heure	FIR BOUNDARIES AND ESTIMATED TIMES Limites de FIR et heures prévues
— *EHRD 0940*	→ *EBBB 0950* *LFFF 1007* *LFBB 1115*
LECM 1205 *LPPT 1331*	《≡

15 ROUTE

CRUISING SPEED / Vitesse de croisiere LEVEL / Niveau

— *0360 F290* → *A6* *UA6* *DEN/0440 F290* *UA5*

RBT *UB19* *DXM* *UR10* *RB* *DCT* *41N005W* *DCT*

CCV/0340 F100 *UR24* *R24*

《≡

17 AERODROME OF DESTINATION AND TIME Aérodrome de destination et heure	ALTERNATE AERODROME(S) Aérodrome(s) de dégagement	
— *LPPT 1411*	→ *LEMD*	《≡

18 OTHER INFORMATION Renseignements divers	
— *REG/CPALD*	
	)《≡

NOT TO BE TRANSMITTED IN FPL MESSAGES
A NE PAS TRANSMETTRE DANS LES MESSAGES DE PLAN DE VOL

19 S U P P L E M E N T A R Y I N F O R M A T I O N Renseignements complementaires		
ENDURANCE Autonomie	PERSONS ON BOARD Personnes à bord	EMERGENCY AND SURVIVAL EQUIPMENT Equipement de secours et de survivance
— FUEL/*0620*	→ POB/*135*	→ RDO/*121.5* → *243*

EQUIPMENT Equipement	LIFE JACKETS Gilets de sauvetage		FREQUENCY Fréquence
POLAR→ DESERT → MARITIME → JUNGLE → JACKETS → LIGHT → FLUORESCEIN →			

DINGHIES Canots	COLOUR Couleur	NUMBER Nombre	TOTAL CAPACITY Capacité totale	OTHER EQUIPMENT Equipement divers
DINGHIES → COVER	*YELLOW*	*5*	*150*	→ RMK/

	Name of pilot-in-command Nom du pilote commandant de bord	
)《≡ *MAIER*		

FIGURE 17. Example of a completed flight plan

action to ensure the safe operation of the concerned aircraft.

The main source of flight data, which enables the controller to commence the build up this mind picture, is that which is obtained in the first instance from the submission of the aircraft's flight plan. From the previous section you will remember that whilst the majority of flight plans are filed prior to an aircraft's departure, occasions can arise where a request to file a flight plan to obtain an air traffic control clearance can be made whilst an aircraft is in flight. However, whichever method is used the purpose is to permit the controller to have sufficient data upon the aircraft to enable him to issue an air traffic control clearance, and to use this data to form a display of air traffic, sufficient for him to visualise the aircraft which are under his control, and from this information predict their forward movement in time and space.

At present the universal method of achieving this mind picture is to transpose the received flight data onto a 'flight progress strip'. The flight progress strip is literally a strip of paper which, when slid into a holder, can be used as a very elementary but highly efficient method of the display of aircraft information, in time, height and geographical position. Figure 18 shows the layout and content of a typical flight progress strip. The manner in which these flight progress strips are displayed to the controller depends to a large degree upon the tasks which are performed by the concerned air traffic control facility. For example, at a busy air traffic control centre, flight progress boards would be used, upon which the flight progress strips can be displayed under geographical headings, which are usually related to an en-route reporting point, thus conveying to the controller a plan view layout of his area of responsibility. Alternatively an approach control unit, which has a much smaller area of responsibility, would only need a simple display, with the flight progress strips sequenced

under the heading of the holding facilities (stacks) serving the airport. Even air traffic control systems, which are radar-based, still provide the controller with flight progress strips, not only to assist him in his planning tasks but also to provide a basis for the procedural control of air traffic in the event of a radar failure. The versatility of computers does, of course, promote the prospect that the information displayed on a flight progress strip, and the updating of this information, can be performed by these machines and the results displayed to the controller on a visual display unit (VDU). However, the economy of operation of a flight progress strip display, and its self-evident understanding by a trained controller, makes it difficult to replace, and whilst it has yet to be satisfactorily demonstrated that a VDU is an effective replacement, doubtless time and technological advance will provide acceptable solutions. But for the present, the humble flight progress strips carry on at the majority of ATS units as the primary means of providing the controller with flight data, on those aircraft either under his control or pending acceptance of control by him.

I shall, as I stated earlier, be dealing with the application of automation to air traffic control in a later chapter, but before leaving the subject of flight plans and flight data, I consider it would be of value to examine how computers are being used to process this information, not only as a foundation for the application of automation but also to assist air traffic control in the performance of a task which previously required the laborious presentation of data by hand.

Computer-assisted flight data processing (FDP)

Introduction

At the smaller air traffic control units the manual preparation of flight progress strips and

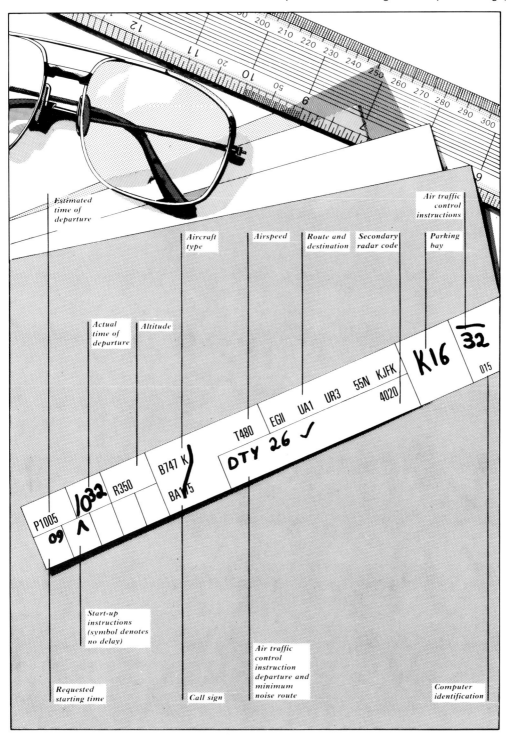

FIGURE 18.   The flight progress strip

59

their update is still viable and would not warrant the introduction of computer techniques, either on cost or safety grounds. At the larger units, however, such as air traffic control centres, which have a considerable requirement for the exchange of data both internally and externally, these new techniques can produce a considerable benefit. To illustrate the problem which confronts personnel at busy ATC units in the manual preparation of flight progress strips, Figure 19 shows the overflight times of a variety of different types of aircraft on a direct track from Paris to Copenhagen, and although the generations of aircraft illustrated have changed somewhat since I prepared this diagram, the wide range of speed differences are equally applicable to aircraft which are operating on today's route networks. In any event these techniques are essential to the future application of automation, providing as they do a 'memory' data base of active and passive flight data. It is therefore this aspect of the use of computer techniques which I wish to explain in more detail at this stage, for without an effective and efficient flight data base the application of automation would be akin to trying to build a house without foundations.

The computers which are at present in use throughout the world for this purpose are almost as diverse as the types of radar installations, but provided they conform to acceptable standards of reliability and performance, choice is a matter of personal preference. What does seem regrettable, however, is that in the evolutionary process different computer languages have been permitted to develop. It is therefore not uncommon to have a situation where two computers carrying out allied tasks, which require them to communicate, are obliged to do so through an expensive intermediary which converts one language to another. The lapse in commonality has not gone unnoticed by ICAO, and doubtless a common computer language will emerge from their deliberations.

However, irrespective of the type of computer or the language which is used, the basic principles for the processing of flight data are a constant factor even though detailed procedures for input and updating will vary on a world-wide application. The accepted term for this operation is, not surprisingly, 'flight data processing' (FDP), and can be simply described as 'that function which is related to the use of computers, concerned with the input of flight plans, their amendment, the production of flight progress strips and/or electronic data display (EDD) messages, and any update information which is relevant to these data'.

Before proceeding further I wish to reiterate the point which I made at the commencement of this chapter, which is that in respect of the majority of services applied by the controller he cannot physically 'see' the aircraft he is controlling. In this regard it is considered important to recognise the fundamental role of a flight data display, particularly when it is used in conjunction with a radar display. The flight data display is a 'planning' tool. It displays advance information to the controller, it is currently updated from the radar data, and is also used to display a 'planned' air traffic solution ahead of the radar data observed on the controller's radar display. Whilst the role of the flight data display will vary, dependent upon the task of a specific ATC unit (either military or civil), it is nonetheless an integral part of the overall operation of the ATC function. It is appreciated that the display itself can vary from a scribbled note on a piece of paper to an amalgam of electronic data and flight progress strips, but whatever form the display takes the basis of its origin and credibility lies in having access to data other than those immediately available from a radar display. These data are in fact a compound of radar information, computer, telephonic, and teleprinter information, and even verbal messages passed to the controller outside this information network.

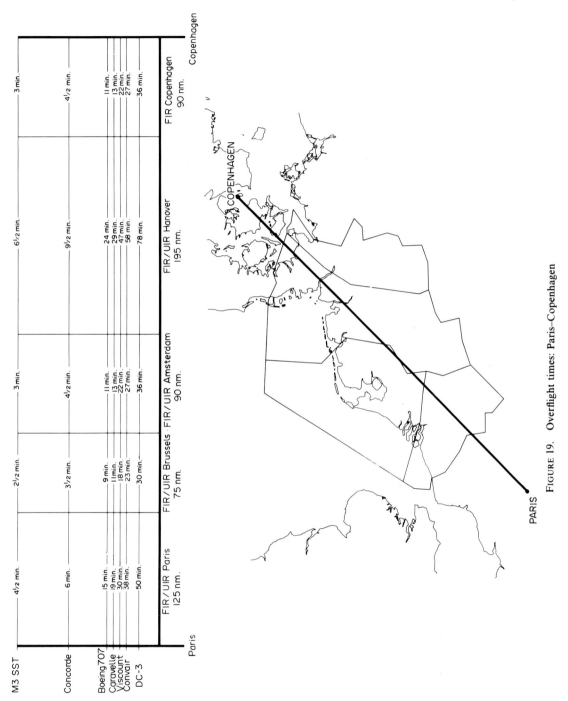

FIGURE 19. Overflight times: Paris–Copenhagen

Having said that, I should now like to give a brief explanation of the role of the computer as a device to assist in the processing and presentation of flight data.

The computer's role in flight data processing

The computers which are at present in use at many ATC locations for flight data processing can provide information either in the form of a printed flight progress strip, as symbols on a radar display, or on a separate electronic data display. They possess facilities for the alteration of these data and for the transfer of information between locations within an air traffic control unit and between geographically separated units within the same state. The majority of this equipment also possesses the capability of 'linking' with other computers, either domestic or with those of adjacent states, which are being used for a similar purpose.

Because safety is paramount to air traffic control, and therefore as a corollary the integrity and reliability of equipment equally so, it is not unusual, where dependence is being placed upon computers to provide an integral part of a data display system, to find a 'triplex' system in operation. Such a system comprises three computers, two of which would be 'on-line' at any one time, with the third acting as a back-up. The philosophy is that if a fault develops in one computer, the second can immediately take over all of the functions of the first, and the third, the back-up, can be brought 'on-line'. Additionally, some sophisticated systems employ a 'simplex', which is a single computer system for use in research and the development of 'software' programs.

In general terms the computer can be regarded as being in two main parts:

(1) *part 1* – which contains all permanent functions and instructions which can be re-

62

garded as common features in all ATC locations; and

(2) *part 2* – which contains features which are unique to the environment and requirements of a particular location.

The input of flight plan data

The flight plan data which are input into the computer can be generally regarded as being contained in two main facilities: the 'core' store, which is a name derived from the magnetised rings used in early computers and the 'disc' store, which uses magnetic discs, from which data can be 'picked up', in much the same way as a tape-recorder is used, and without removing the stored data from the disc. For example, details of flights which are scheduled to take place regularly over long periods are stored on a disc until they are required, at which time they are automatically transferred to the core store and can be used in the production of flight progress strips, and to build 'data' blocks on the radar displays. Flight plans which are not on the disc are input directly to the core store by means of a variety of input equipments. These flight plans can be input either as 'pending' or a 'proposed' flight or with an indication that the aircraft is 'in-flight' or 'live'. This would, of course, be the case where, as explained earlier, an aircraft had submitted a flight-plan when airborne. Since, however, the computer stores flight plan data for a considerable time after it has been input, 'pending' flight plans are activated by the input to the computer of an airborne time or a 'live' time given by the aircraft in relation to a known position report. This data, both pending and live, can be amended, throughout the time they remain in the core store.

In more detail, therefore, there are two main methods of the input of flight plan data into the computer.

(1) Stored flight plans

As mentioned earlier in the paragraph on flight plans, details in respect of scheduled flights that will take place regularly over long periods can be filed as a single or repetitive flight plan and entered into the computer's 'bulk store file'. This file is normally renewed twice a year and between these times, permanent amendments or deletions are made, to keep these files up to date. The computer is then programmed to ensure that, at a predetermined time on any day when a specific flight is to take place, the flight plan details are automatically transferred from the bulk store file to the core store. At a further predetermined time, prior to the time at which the concerned flight plan indicates that the flight is expected to depart from the aerodrome, or to arrive over its first reporting point within a specific air traffic control unit's area of responsibility, the computer prints out a flight progress strip at each of the ATC operational positions which require advance warning of the flight. These strips are called 'warning strips' and the time indicated on them is intended to alert the controller to the fact that a flight is pending and is awaiting an air traffic control clearance. Later, an input to the computer is made of an 'activation message'. This message results either from the input of an aerodrome departure time, or a 'joining time' if the aircraft has filed an airborne flight plan, or an update message if the control of the aircraft is being transferred from an adjacent ATC unit. As a result of this message the flight plan in the computer is made active and, as programmed, flight progress strips are then printed by output devices to all of the concerned ATC operational positions, including strips for all of the points at which the aircraft is required to report. The information printed on the flight progress strips includes the clock times which the computer has estimated that the aircraft will be over the particular 'reporting' points on its proposed route of flight. These estimates are arrived at from computer calculations which are based upon the clock time information given in the 'activation' message.

Readers with a knowledge of computer technology will realise that a great deal more is involved at this stage in the software routines, such as the profile the aircraft is following and the wind vectors and velocities which it is experiencing. It is my intention to refer to these aspects in the later sections on 'automation', and therefore for assistance in ease of understanding of the flow of data I am deliberately keeping this paragraph on computers reasonably simplistic.

(2) Manually input flight plans

Flight plans which are not retained in the bulk store file are usually received either by telephone or via the aeronautical fixed teleprinter network (AFTN) which I described earlier. At the larger ATC units it is usual to have a separate position for their receipt, known as the 'flight plan reception section'. The section will normally be provided with a teleprinter station linked to the AFTN, telephone facilities sufficient for its task, and an input device for access to the computer. The details which are required by the computer format are extracted by an operator from either the AFTN message or a telephone call, and a clock time is added to the input message, to indicate to both the controller and the computer that the flight is pending. Thereafter as in the case of bulk stored flight plans 'warning strips' are printed for the manually input flight plans and at a later stage the flight is 'activated', to produce either an 'update' message or a 'live' flight progress strip.

Computer input and output devices

There are many ingenious devices which are related to the interface between the ATC system and the computer, ranging from 'light-pens' and 'rolling balls' to a typewriter keyboard. However, for the purpose of the subject under discussion I wish to restrict our considerations to the simpler of those devices, which are usually associated with flight data processing. With all of these input devices it is, however, necessary to bear in mind that each of them has the capability for a manual check before the computer is virtually ordered to execute the contents of a message. There is a very salutary reason for this manual check for, whilst the human mind will refuse to accept some information which is manifestly nonsense, within the context of the task being performed, the computer, unless it has been programmed with multi-safeguards, will endeavour to accept the information, even though its only response is 'corrupt message'.

In this context therefore, in regard to the computer interface, the following are amongst the standard input devices.

(1) Alpha-numeric keyboard (ANK)

The alpha-numeric keyboard is, in many respects, similar to a typewriter keyboard, except that the input keys are arranged in an order which corresponds to their usage within an ATC environment. A single key can have many functions dependent upon the software routines which have been built into the computer program. The 'read-out' panel for an input message prior to the activation of the 'execute' key, would normally be associated with an electronic data display. It is the type of input equipment usually sited at operational ATC positions.

(2) The touchwire display (TWD)

The touchwire display, as its name implies, is activated as a computer interface by the operator touching, by hand, a set of wires. The wires are approximately $\frac{1}{2}$ inch long and are positioned in parallel lines, usually three deep,

at the lower portion of an electronic data display. Each wire when touched performs a function similar to the keyboard (ANK) previously described, and in a similar manner wires can be devoted to specific functions. Additionally these functions can be dedicated to the manner in which the display and its keyboard can be used to access different parts of the computer program. However, as we are at present only concerned with its flight data role, the display above the touchwires in this instance is used for traffic information and as a 'read-out' panel, prior to operating the computer 'execute' wire.

(3) Input/output typewriter

This is the facility which is normally used at flight plan reception. It has a keyboard similar to that of an ordinary typewriter and a built-in back roll, upon which appears the message which has been composed for input to the computer, as a check before execution, and also to display any send-back message, generated by the computer itself.

Output equipment

The main output device at present in use for flight data processing is a flight strip printer. These strip printers are positioned at, or adjacent to, the air traffic control positions which are concerned with the receipt of flight data. They produce the flight progress strips and subsequent update messages which form the basis of the controller's traffic display. This is a subject which, from previous reading, you will have gathered is an absolutely vital element in enabling the controller to discharge his responsibilities.

The alternative to the strip printer, is to use the computer to generate the same information which is given on the flight progress strip, but in character form, on an electronic data display. At the time of writing this method is still in the formulative stage but, as mentioned earlier, it will doubtless eventually evolve to supersede the printed strip.

Operation of a computer-assisted flight data processing system

Previously in this chapter I remarked upon the versatility of computers, and one of these obvious features is the ability to be able to access them from different geographical locations, away from the central processor's home base. For example ATC at London's Heathrow airport can input to, and receive information from, the parent computer at the London air traffic control centre situated at West Drayton some 5 miles away. Even further away Manchester sub-centre and Manchester airport some 150 nautical miles distant have similar access. These are, of course, relatively short distances, but are given to convey the versatility of the computer interface, where the distance apart of the terminals is virtually unlimited provided access between the two components is available through a communications link.

To provide a more practical illustration of how the processing of flight data occurs, under operational conditions, and how the various ATC elements interface with the computer I considered it would be of value to provide, by brief example, the procedures which operate within the United Kingdom to discharge this function. I am using actual locations for this purpose, for I am of the opinion that the examples which follow, although their geographical situation may not be familiar to all readers, will nonetheless convey a practical impression of the relatively complex 'software', with which a computer has to be programmed in order to carry out the reasonably simple manual task of the preparation of flight progress strips. The example also underline the fact that, to provide a viable alternative to the manual task, a computer programmer must

have a detailed knowledge of the concerned ATC system, prior to the commencement of the writing of a software programme, intended to support the manual task. In the examples I have endeavoured to illustrate albeit briefly, some of the complexities associated with the flow of flight data and also to demonstrate the versatility of the computer to react to rapid changes in the data flow. Whilst the details of the operating procedures described will doubtless differ at other world locations, the principles of the flow of this information between operational ATS units will however be basically similar.

Example 1 – flight plan Liverpool to Gatwick – Gatwick to Manchester

Details of a flight from Liverpool to Gatwick will either be stored on the bulk store file or, since Liverpool is within the Manchester sub-centre area of responsibility, will be input on a teleprinter at the sub-centre. At the appropriate time (as programmed into the computer) warning strips will be printed on flight strip printers at the Manchester sub-centre and at any location at the London air traffic control centre where advance information of the flight is required.

When the Manchester sub-centre receive an airborne time for the flight from Liverpool they input an activation message to the computer using their alpha-numeric keyboard which is linked to the central computer. This will generate an update message for the sectors at the sub-centre and those sectors at the London centre that had warning strips. Additionally, live strips will be printed at any sector or location concerned with the flight that did not have a warning strip; for example, approach control and aerodrome control at Gatwick will receive 'live' strips. In all cases the computer will have calculated and printed times for 'reporting points' based upon the airborne time input by Manchester. The 'reporting points' are usually associated with the ground-based navigation aids which delineate the route structures, and over which aircraft are required to report to the controller. The controller usually requires a flight progress strip for each of these reporting points which he then sequences in time order under the particular geographical position on his flight progress display. The computer is therefore programmed to produce the number of strips which are required for each specific operational position, concerned with that particular flight. As mentioned earlier, the computer then calculates, from the input airborne time of the aircraft, or from any input amendment of that time, which may have occurred during the course of the aircraft's flight, the estimated time at which the pilot should report over the subsequent reporting points, and then includes these times on the printed strips. In the case of a flight from Gatwick to Manchester that is not, for example, carried in the bulk store file, Gatwick flight clearance will, on receipt of the flight plan, extract the essential details and input them to the computer by teleprinter. At the appropriate time warning strips will be produced at Gatwick and the concerned sectors at the London centre. When the flight is airborne Gatwick, using their alpha-numeric keyboard, will input the airborne time causing 'update' messages and 'live' strips to be printed at the London centre. Following a process of the production of printed strips for all the concerned operational positions, similar to that as described for the Liverpool – Gatwick flight. 'Live' strips will also be printed at the Manchester sub-centre and Manchester tower; the receipt of the 'live strip' by Manchester being the first intimation to them of the pending flight.

Example 2 – flight plan Rome to London (Heathrow)

The first information on such a flight, unless programmed through the stored flight plan system, would be the receipt at the flight plan reception section of the London centre of a flight plan by teleprinter on the AFTN. On receipt of the flight plan the essential details required by the computer are extracted and passed in written form to a specialist teleprinter operator for 'input' using the input/output typewriter. The details will include a provisional time for Abbeville on the French coast and for the first reporting point within U.K. jurisdiction, for which a 'live' time will be received from the Paris centre. The message is checked by the computer which will print out an accept on the back-roll, if there are no errors on the input. At a specified time before the flight is due at Abbeville (the time being governed by the pre-programmed routine) warning strips are printed at the strip printer associated with the Dover/Lydd sector at the London centre.

When a firm time and flight level are received by telephone at this sector from the Paris centre an activation message is entered into the computer by the Dover/Lydd sector staff using the touchwire display. This action produces live strips at this sector, the TMA South sector and Heathrow aerodrome and approach controls.

Variations on Example 2

(1) Let us assume the aircraft decides to divert to Gatwick

The sector handling the flight at the London centre inputs to the computer an 'amendment' message which produces flight progress strips at aerodrome and approach control at Gatwick and also an 'update' message for Heathrow which tells them to discard their flight progress strips as the aircraft is no longer coming to them. Additionally, a plain language message will be sent to Heathrow saying to which airfield the flight is now going, and why. At the same time the sectors at the London centre which are concerned with the flight will receive new strips showing the amended flight plan details.

(2) Let us assume that, because of bad weather, the approach to Gatwick proves unsuccessful and the pilot decides to go to Manchester

A further amendment message is input to the computer by the concerned sector (London terminal area (south)). This input will produce flight progress strips at the concerned sectors and because the flight is 'live' will also produce strips for the Manchester sub-centre and Manchester aerodrome control. A 'discard strip' message will be activated to Gatwick.

(3) Let us assume the aircraft is held en-route before setting course for Manchester

If the aircraft is held en-route whilst re-clearance is organised for its flight to Manchester a 'hold' message is input to the computer by the concerned sector. As a result of this input an update message is sent to the Manchester sub-centre and concerned sectors within the London centre giving notification to them of the 'hold' – when the flight is cleared to continue the sector in which the aircraft is being held inputs a further update message into the computer which will result in time updates being sent for all reporting points within the concerned sectors at the London centre and Manchester sub-centre and Manchester aerodrome control. Finally, when the aircraft arrives at its destination the computer will drop the flight plan details from the core store in accordance with a pre-programmed interval. If the flight was a bulk store flight plan it would be 'dropped' from the core store but the original flight plan details (Rome to Heathrow) would be retained on the disc store for future use.

The foregoing explanation and examples will, I hope, give a general impression of the actions which are required to compile and amend the flight data which the controller requires to assist him in the performance of his task. As explained earlier it is this data which, when transposed onto flight progress strips and displayed in front of the controller, enables him not only to recognise the history of a particular aircraft's flight but also when relating it to other flight progress strip data, enables him to plan the future movements of that aircraft in relation to other traffic movements within his sector of responsibility. In other words the flight progress strip display is a planning tool, essential to supplement the radar viewing unit which is displaying 'now' time to the controller, and not, at the present time, predicting ahead. Clearance prediction and resolution through computer techniques can be displayed to the controller on his radar viewing unit in certain sophisticated air traffic control units, but the existence of this valuable aid still requires the controller to have available a separate display of air traffic for planning purposes. As also mentioned earlier in this chapter, a future development, planned by some air traffic control authorities, envisages the replacement of the printed flight progress strip displays by an electronic data display linked to the computer data base. It is a challenging development, for not only have the flight data to be displayed in time sequence, but also in a geographical context. Additionally, this information will be required to be continually updated in both of these dimensions.

This then is a particular area of the air traffic control task where the benefits which can be derived from the use of computers have to be very carefully tailored to ensure that the controller does indeed gain the advantage over the present manual application of the computer-derived flight data base.

To assist readers in following the processing of data beween one ATC unit and another, Figure 20 shows, in diagrammatic form, how this information would pass between the four

ATC units concerned with the flight of an aircraft from one airport to another.

This paragraph and its examples have dealt with but one aspect of the application of computer technology to air traffic control, but it will, I hope, have given an indication of the manner in which this technology can assist the controller in carrying out his tasks. Whilst, however, flight plan processing (FPP) as described, can be considered a relatively simple illustration of the application of computers and their processors, I hope a reference to their use at this stage in the book, will have indicated the very wide horizons which lie ahead. It is for this reason I have included Chapter 8 ('Automation'), in which readers will, I trust, obtain further knowledge of how computers associated with advances in avionics are at present being applied to the control of air traffic. I hope also that possibly those readers who are directly or indirectly concerned with ATC systems, can gain some appreciation of how their future use should be sensibly developed.

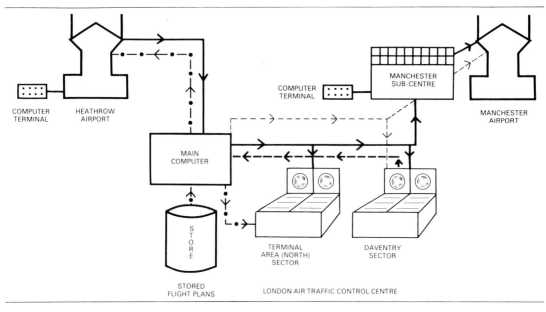

— •— •—   'Warning' F/P strip activated 40 minutes in advance of the flight.
          'Airborne time', activates computer to produce F/P strips for each sector and Manchester Sub-Centre.
━━━━━   'Sector amendment' derived from 'active' flight information.
– – – – –   'Amended' F/P strips based on the 'sector' amendments.

FIGURE 20. Flow chart of computer-assisted flight plan processing functions

7

The Provision
of Air Traffic Services

Introduction

Having explained the procedures, and the facilities which are available to air traffic control, to put these procedures into operation I wish now to explain the 'services' which are provided by this organisation. However, before doing so, it might be of assistance to spare a moment to clarify the terminology which is used. The term 'air traffic service' is a generic term, meaning variously

(1) Flight information service;
(2) alerting service;
(3) air traffic advisory service;
(4) air traffic control service;
(5) area control service;
(6) approach control service; and
(7) aerodrome control service

The term 'air traffic control service' is defined as a service provided for the purpose of:

(1) preventing collisions
    (a) between aircraft, and
    (b) on the manoeuvring area between aircraft and obstructions; and
(2) expediting and maintaining an orderly flow of air traffic.

Thus, whilst the air traffic 'control' services are contained within the general description of the air traffic services, which are available to aircraft, the definition of 'control' is categoric, and in effect means that to provide a 'control service', persons so doing require to be properly qualified and licensed. For example, an air traffic control officer's licence normally carries ratings for aerodrome control, approach control, area control and radar control. If the officer concerned wishes to practice his profession then these ratings, or those of them he possesses, require to be validated. That is, he must be assessed by the appropriate authority as being capable of carrying out the conditions attaching to the particular ratings, and furthermore should he cease to practise, for more than a period of 90 days, in regard to any of the ratings he possesses, he is then required to undergo a further re-validation. It will be appreciated that these rules, which are attached to the exercise of the privileges of a controller's licence, are intended to ensure the highest possible standards of safety in the exercise of his duties.

Whilst in this book we are concerned primarily in explaining those air traffic services related to which 'control' is exercised, it is also intended to describe the flight information service, the alerting service and the air traffic advisory service, for not only can they be discharged by a licensed controller but also because they are essential elements of the totality of the service provided. Similarly, whilst each of these services will be described separately, there are many locations throughout the world where the separate functions associated with these services can be, and are, combined.

For example, at a small aerodrome with relatively few aircraft movements it is quite practical and convenient to perform the duties of the approach control service and the aerodrome control service from the visual control room of the control tower building. Alternatively, it is not uncommon at some locations for a single approach control unit to carry out combined approach control services for a number of neighbouring aerodromes. There is also an increasing tendency for the air traffic control centres to provide the initial phase of the approach control service for aerodromes and airports, within their operational complex. The reason for this particular telescoping of functions is that air traffic control centres are normally responsible for the control of terminal areas, which as you will recall from the chapter on 'The management of the airspace', surround a number of busy airports/aerodromes. As a result they are equipped with facilities and staffs to handle large concentrations of aircraft and are able to retain control of aircraft destined to land in the terminal area, thus relieving the work-load on the individual approach control units. The functions therefore, which are performed by the air traffic control staff, in the provision of these services, are flexible and can expand or contract, dependent upon the demands of air traffic at particular geographical locations.

Before proceeding to explain in general detail the responsibilities of the various elements of these services I should like to summarise the objectives, and the control services which are provided to carry these out.

Objectives

The objectives of the air traffic services are to:

(1) prevent collisions between aircraft in the air;
(2) assist in preventing collisions between aircraft moving on the apron or the manoeuvring area, and between aircraft and obstructions on the manoeuvring area;
(3) expedite and maintain an orderly flow of air traffic;
(4) provide information useful for the safe and efficient conduct of flights;
(5) notify appropriate organisations regarding aircraft in need of search and rescue aid, and assist such organisations as required.

Air traffic control service

An air traffic control service with or without the use of radar is provided to achieve objectives (1), (2) and (3) and takes the form of either:

(a) area control service for IFR flights within control areas and special rules areas;
(b) zone control service for IFR flights within control zones and special rules zones;
(c) approach control service for flights under the jurisdiction of an approach control unit; or
(d) aerodrome control service for aircraft in the vicinity of the aerodrome traffic zone flying with visual reference to the surface and aircraft operating on certain parts of the aerodrome.

Air traffic advisory service

An air traffic advisory service is provided to assist in achieving objectives (1) and (3) in airspace within which a control service has not been established.

Having introduced these services, it is now my intention to detail the responsibilities of the various units which are involved in their provision, and then in Chapter 9, 'The air traffic control environment' explain how these varying functions come together to achieve the overall objectives of a safe and orderly flow of air traffic. For reference purposes the international definitions of the air traffic services are contained in ICAO Document 4444 ('Rules of the Air and Air Traffic Services') and Annex 11 (Air Traffic Services) but it is usual for each state to reproduce its own documentation, based upon ICAO and normally in the form of a *Manual of Air Traffic Services*. These manuals which are produced by States are usually in two separate parts:

Part 1, which contains instructions that apply to all air traffic service units; and

Part 2 which contains instructions that apply to a particular air traffic service unit. They are intended to amplify and interpret, at local level, the instructions contained in Part 1.

Generally speaking, however, there are three broad divisions of the air traffic services described in these manuals they are:

> aerodrome control,
> approach control, and
> area control (air traffic control centres)

and it is these headings I will now use for explanatory purposes.

Aerodrome control

An aerodrome control unit provides services principally to aircraft flying with visual reference to the surface within the vicinity of the aerodrome traffic zone and to those aircraft which are operating on the manoeuvring area. It is normally a separate unit, but as was mentioned earlier its functions may be combined either temporarily or permanently with an approach control unit. There is, however, an important proviso which applies to those occasions where a combined aerodrome/approach service is being provided, and that is: an aerodrome controller is not permitted to provide an approach *radar* control service, whilst engaged on aerodrome control duties. The reason for this proviso will, of course, be fairly obvious, for it will be clear that a controller who is viewing a radar display for the purpose of providing a radar control service cannot at the same time be physically observing the aerodrome circuit and ground manoeuvring traffic; therefore a separate controller must be provided for this service.

The responsibilities of aerodrome control associated with this definition are, therefore, the issuing of information and instructions to aircraft under its control to achieve a safe, orderly and expeditious flow of air traffic and to assist pilots in preventing collisions between:

(1) aircraft flying in the aerodrome traffic zone;
(2) aircraft taking off and landing;
(3) aircraft moving on the apron;
(4) aircraft and vehicles, obstructions and other aircraft on the manoeuvring area.

To achieve these objectives it is necessary for the aerodrome controller to have authority not only over aircraft flying within the aerodrome traffic zone but also over aircraft, vehicles and personnel on the manoeuvring area and aircraft which are moving on the apron.

Additionally, there are a number of specific responsibilities which are a necessary part of the functions of aerodrome control. They are:

(1) the alerting of the safety services;
(2) informing aircraft under its control of any depletion of the aerodrome's emergency services;
(3) supplying information as required by approach control in regard to:
   (a) IFR and VFR traffic, including departures, missed approaches and overdue aircraft,

71

(b) supplying details to aircraft, approach control and other designated authorities in regard to essential aerodrome information;

(4) Informing the authority responsible for the operation of the aerodrome (e.g. the aerodrome owner) when it becomes apparent that there is a deterioration in the state of the aerodrome (e.g. ice and snow on the runways or any associated facilities (e.g. the instrument landing system, ILS);

(5) the initiation of overdue action at those aerodromes where no approach control unit is established; and

(6) as mentioned previously – provision of an approach control service when this function has been so delegated.

One of the items mentioned above was 'essential aerodrome information' and as, apart from the actual controlling of the aircraft, this information is vital to the safety of an aircraft, irrespective of aerodrome size, it would be as well to explain this item a little further. Essential aerodrome information is that which concerns the state of the manoeuvring area and its associated facilities, which may constitute a hazard to a particular aircraft. It is required to be issued to pilots in sufficient time to ensure the safe operation of the aircraft. In many instances some of this information is automatically broadcast on a repetitive basis, known as the automatic terminal information service (ATIS), and is included amongst such other general information as the runway in use, the aerodrome QNH, weather conditions, etc. But even where an ATIS is in operation a check is required to be made to ensure that the pilot has received the latest available information.

In detail, essential aerodrome information includes:

(1) construction work or maintenance on the manoeuvring area;

(2) rough portions of the manoeuvring area, whether marked or not;

(3) failure or any irregular function of the aerodrome lighting system;

(4) failure or any irregular function of the approach aids;

(5) details of any aircraft which is parked close to the runways or taxiways;

(6) the depth of the snow layer on runways and taxiways, snow piled or drifted on the manoeuvring area and details of melting snow, slush and rutted ice and snow – associated with this information any details regarding the sweeping and sanding of taxiways and runways and also where possible an estimate of the braking action;

(7) information on bird formations reported or observed on or above the manoeuvring area or within the immediate vicinity of the aerodrome;

(8) any reports which may have been received of 'standing water' on the runways;

(9) mainly in regard to military aerodromes, information on the location and operational status of any arrester gear installation.

I trust it will be clear to readers, from the foregoing, that the aerodrome control service is not simply a question of issuing instructions to aircraft to land and take off or to taxi on the surface of the aerodrome, but is an amalgam of instructions and information, all of which are intended to ensure the safety of the aircraft within the vicinity of the aerodrome and on its surface. There is, however, one further function to mention, and it is one which will appear throughout this chapter; that is 'co-ordination'. Co-ordination is the vital link between the various elements of the air traffic control services and between the various functions which can exist within a particular control service. In this explanation the adjacent service with which aerodrome control is concerned is approach control. Therefore:

(1) aerodrome control are required to co-ordinate with approach control:

(a) departing IFR flights, and

(b) arriving aircraft which make their first call on the tower frequency, unless they are transferred to approach control;

(2) approach control are required to co-ordinate with aerodrome control:

(a) aircraft approaching to land,

(b) arriving aircraft which are to be cleared to a visual holding point, and

(c) aircraft which are being routed through the traffic circuit.

Before leaving this chapter mention should be made of the fact that at busy aerodromes provision is made for dividing the responsibilities of the aerodrome control service into an air control position and a ground movement control position. Where this is done the division of responsibility is usually as follows:

Air control – provides services for:

(1) aircraft flying in the aerodrome traffic zone; and

(2) aircraft taking off and landing.

Ground movement control – provides services for:

(1) aircraft moving on the apron; and

(2) aircraft and vehicles, obstructions and other aircraft on the manoeuvring area, *except* on active runways and their access points.

In regard to ground movement control, readers will recall that when explaining the instrument landing system in the chapter on air navigation I made mention of completely automatic landing. This capability of an aircraft to land in exceptionally poor forward visibility does, of course, promote difficult problems for both controller and pilot in regard to taxi-ing on the surface of an aerodrome, where the unaided human eyes can no longer provide the necessary intelligence for forward movement. There is, of course, taxiway lighting, direction arrows and stop bars, but in conditions of 'all-weather

operations' there are occasions where these aids are insufficient to provide the necessary guidance. Radar is then once again one of the facilities which can and does provide a partial solution to this problem. One such facility which is in use to assist the ground movement controller in these conditions is known as an aerodrome surface movement indicator (ASMI). It is a ground-based radar, the aerial head of which rotates at a very high rate and which, when allied to the short frequency of the transmitter, enables the controller to see, on a viewing unit in the tower, all objects which are moving on the surface of the aerodrome. There are a number of similar detection devices but at present the development of their techniques and operational application only permit guidance to be used, and not control. However, the pressures for all-weather operations will doubtless provide the impetus for considerable advances in this particular stage of an aircraft's movement. Further details on the use of ASMI is given at Chapter 9 ('The ATC Environment') in the section dealing with the ground movements controller.

Approach control

At busy aerodromes, it is usual for the approach control service to be conducted from a separate room and, as approach control do not physically require to see the aircraft under their control, their operations are normally conducted from an operations room immediately below the visual control room. However, as mentioned earlier, the demands of air traffic, and the environment within which specific air traffic control units are operating, requires a flexible approach to the services which are provided, and therefore an approach control unit may be combined with an approach radar unit, an aerodrome control unit, or may even share their responsibilities with an area control unit. Whilst the method of operation may vary, the services which are required to be provided, remain the same and they are:

(1) an approach control service;
(2) a flight information service; and
(3) an alerting service.

The application of the separation standards which were described in the previous relevant chapter do, however, vary, dependent upon the geographical situation of the aerodrome for which an approach control service is being provided. On a world-wide basis this can generally be accepted as being in two broad divisions; those aerodromes which are situated within controlled airspace and special rules airspace, and those which are situated outside these airspaces. In qualification of this statement therefore:

At aerodromes which are within controlled airspace and special rules airspace approach control is required to provide standard separation between IFR flights and between IFR and special VFR flights, from the time and place at which:

(1) arriving aircraft are released by area control until control is released to aerodrome control;
(2) aircraft approaching from outside controlled or special rules airspace cross the airspace boundary until control is transferred to aerodrome control;
(3) departing aircraft are taken over from aerodrome control until:
   (a) they are transferred to area control, or
   (b) they are clear of controlled or special rules airspace;
(4) overflying aircraft are within the relevant controlled or special rules airspace.

At aerodromes outside controlled and special rules airspace approach control is required to provide standard separation between IFR flights from the time and place at which:

(1) arriving aircraft are released by area con-

trol until control is transferred to aerodrome control;
(2) arriving aircraft place themselves under the control of approach control until control is transferred to aerodrome control;
(3) departing aircraft are taken over from aerodrome control until:
   (a) they are transferred to area control, or
   (b) they no longer wish to receive a service or are 10 minutes flying time away from the aerodrome, whichever is the sooner;
(4) overflying aircraft place themselves under the control of approach control, until they are clear of the approach pattern, and either no longer wish to receive a service or are 10 minutes flying time away from the aerodrome, whichever is the sooner.

The reason for the differing responsibilities of approach control at aerodromes outside controlled and special rules airspace, is that there is no legal requirement for flights which are conducted in the airspace which is outside aerodrome traffic zones and special rules or controlled airspace, to comply with instructions, because these instructions are 'advisory' only. However pilots are assumed to be complying with air traffic control instructions unless they state otherwise.

Additionally, approach control, wherever situated, have the following specific responsibilities:

(1) the issuing of pertinent traffic information on known VFR flights to IFR flights;
(2) the provision of standard separation between special VFR flights (unless a reduction is permitted by the concerned authority of a specific state);
(3) the initiation of overdue action;
(4) the passing of information to aircraft under their control in regard to any failure or irregular functioning of the aerodrome lighting system or approach aids.

At the commencement of this chapter I explained the 'objectives' of the air traffic control service and the three broad divisions of the services into aerodrome, approach and area control. Having explained the responsibilities of aerodrome control and approach control it is now essential to indicate how these two services and subsequently, the area control service, link together to provide a continuity of responsibility throughout the phases of an aircraft's flight. This is conducted through the supply of information from one to the other and of specific co-ordinations relating to individual flights. At a later stage I will explain, by example, how this occurs; but I wish to reiterate that the flow of information and co-ordination, whether conducted by manual methods or computer techniques, is fundamental to the achievement of these objectives. Therefore the operation of the procedures related to them are designed to ensure the dovetailing of one service into another, thus providing the continuity which is essential for the safe conduct of a flight. To illustrate how this is achieved the following details of the supply of information, co-ordination and delegation cover the main principles of application.

Information

Approach control is required to supply the following information to *aerodrome control:*

(1) pertinent flight data on all relevant aircraft including the type of flight, i.e. whether IFR or VFR, the height of the arriving aircraft and its ETA;

(2) the anticipated order in which control of the aircraft is to be transferred;

(3) any anticipated delay to departing IFR flights, and the reason for this delay;

(4) Where approach radar is operating, approach control shall supply to approach radar control the current weather report and any other significant aerodrome information, i.e. runway in use, state of the airfield lighting.

Approach control is required to supply the following information to *area control* in regard to IFR flights:

(1) the lowest level at the aerodrome 'holding' facility which is available for use by area control;

(2) the average time interval which is being achieved between successive approaches to the runway/s in use;

(3) the revision of the expected approach times, which have been issued by area control to arriving traffic, when approach control calculations show a significant variation (usually 5 minutes or more);

(4) the arrival times of aircraft over the holding point/s serving the aerodrome if these vary by 3 minutes or more from the estimates previously passed by area control;

(5) details of any missed approach if a re-routing of the concerned aircraft is necessary;

(6) the departure times of aircraft;

(7) all available information in respect of any aircraft which is deemed to be overdue.

Co-ordination

Approach control is required to co-ordinate with *aerodrome control:*

(1) aircraft which are approaching to land at the aerodrome;

(2) any arriving aircraft which has been cleared to a visual holding point;

(3) any aircraft which has been routed through the aerodrome traffic circuit.

Aerodrome control is required to co-ordinate with *approach control:*

(a) departing IFR flights

(b) arriving aircraft which make their initial contact on the aerodrome control R/T frequency.

Delegation to approach radar

At many aerodromes throughout the world, both civil and military, radar is used extensively to assist approach control in achieving its objectives. This does not necessarily imply that every aircraft is required to receive a radar service, but where circumstances of traffic density or the requirement for a radar-assisted approach, (surveillance radar approach (SRA) or precision approach radar (PAR) make such a course desirable, approach control may delegate its functions to approach radar. Where this is done, however, the following information must be supplied to approach radar:

(1) the callsign, type, level, route ETA or position, and the R/T frequency to be used;
(2) the expected approach time (EAT) (these are only normally used where heavy traffic may be causing delays in the landing sequence);
(3) the type of radar service required;
(4) the release and contact instructions which had been issued by area control;
(5) information on any conflicting traffic;
(6) the actual time of departure (ATD) of any outbound aircraft.

Delegation to aerodrome control

As mentioned earlier, the functions of approach control can in some circumstances be carried out by aerodrome control, in which event the objectives and responsibilities as detailed for approach control are assumed by this delegation. Where this is done, however, the aerodrome controller, carrying out this task, must possess an approach control rating which is valid for that aerodrome.

Approach radar

Whilst in the earlier chapter on radar, I outlined its role in the approach environment, I consider it could be advisable to risk a certain degree of repetition in this chapter on air traffic services, if only to point out the difference between radar used for approach purposes and radar used for area/en-route purposes. As a general rule the area for which radar services are provided by an approach radar unit is determined by the coverage of the equipment and does not normally exceed an overall limit of 40 nautical miles from the aerodrome traffic zone. In detailing the services provided, kindly bear in mind, as previously stated, that as some aerodromes are situated outside controlled airspace the radar service differs, dependent upon the category of the airspace: namely:

(1) for aircraft which are flying within controlled airspace and special rules airspace a radar *control* service is provided;
(2) for aircraft which are flying outside these areas, a radar *advisory* service is provided.

The services which are provided by an approach radar unit are:

(1) Surveillance radar approaches (SRA)

A surveillance radar approach is a method of providing the pilot of an aircraft with assistance to enable him to execute a landing. Such an approach would normally only be provided where an instrument landing system (ILS) was not installed or was inoperative. The assistance consists of providing the pilot with information regarding his position in azimuth in regard to the extended centre line of the landing runway and of the distance he is away from the threshold. The approach radar does not have a height element, but pre-computed advisory heights, through which the aircraft should be passing are relayed to the pilot.

(2) Radar vectoring and sequencing onto the ILS

Radar is used extensively for vectoring aircraft from the holding stacks which serve an aerodrome, onto the extended centre line of the runway in use. The interception of the ILS is usually made at between 10 and 8 nautical miles from the runway threshold and at a height which is compatible with a 3° glide path. The sequencing by the approach radar controllers is intended to use a minimum spacing between arriving aircraft. This is usually 3/4 nautical miles but can vary, dependent upon the type of aircraft. For example, if a light aircraft is following a heavy aircraft the distance is increased to take account of the turbulent wake generated by the heavy aircraft.

At some aerodromes, particularly military, approach radar is used to vector aircraft into the azimuth and elevation elements of precision approach radars (PAR) at a height and distance which permits the PAR controller to carry out his task of guiding the aircraft down to the runway threshold for the final 'flare' manoeuvre.

(3) Radar monitoring of ILS approaches

Whilst the interpretation of the ILS signals is entirely a pilot responsibility, radar can be used to monitor ILS approaches and information can be passed to the pilot if any undue deviation from the centre course is observed.

(4) Radar control of departing aircraft

Whilst the radar control of departing aircraft is normally a responsibility of area radar, the approach radar can be used, within its area of coverage, to provide radar separation standards to departing aircraft, once they are clear of their minimum noise routes (MNR).

(5) The control of transit aircraft

Where aircraft are transiting the area for which approach control are responsible, radar can be used to provide separation from other transiting or arriving and departing aircraft.

Area control (air traffic control centres)

As explained in the chapter on 'Airspace Management', the world's airspace is divided into flight information regions (FIR) usually below 20,000 feet, and upper flight information regions (UIR), superimposed on this level. The geographical boundaries of these regions are agreed through the machinery of ICAO and are contiguous between states. Located within these FIRs and UIRs are the controlled and special rules airspaces. The task of area control is to provide air traffic services within these regions, that is the area which is outside the confines of the airspaces designated for the provision of air traffic services by approach control and aerodrome control. In summary they are responsible for the control of the airways route networks and of the larger terminal areas, located in the FIRs and also the upper air routes which are located in the UIRs. Additionally, they are responsible for the alerting and distress and diversion services, and for the provision of flight information services to aircraft which are flying within the totality of this airspace.

The unit which is established to discharge these services is known as an air traffic control centre and dependent upon the size of the airspace there can be one or more units in a particular state, FIR/UIR. The air traffic control centre itself does not necessarily require to be physically associated with an aerodrome, its location being primarily determined by access to facilities such as power supply, telephone/teleprinter networks and radar data. In this regard it is of interest to note that at the larger centres more than 100 separate R/T frequencies can be in operation at any one time, radar data can be received from a multiple number of separate sites, and the centre can be responsible for controlling several thousands of aircraft movements in a 24-hour period. They are possibly the least understood of the operational facilities provided by the air traffic control service, for even when sited on an aerodrome the building itself is usually tucked away, at a remote location, out of sight of the public gaze and even when seen, the modern air traffic control centre has the appearance of a contemporary building which could be used for a variety of purposes. They are in fact a pulsing nerve centre, controlling and co-ordinating the world's aerial highways. Aircraft, as such, are never seen by the controllers and technical staffs that work in the environment of these centres, to them they are represented in the form of radar responses or pieces of paper, but the safe separation of aircraft, flying hundreds of nautical miles away from the air traffic control centre's geographical position, depends upon the skill and judgement of the controller's interpretation of a continuing stream of electronic, computer and verbal data, backed by the technical efficiency of the support organisations.

I propose now to explain the air traffic services which are discharged by these air traffic control centres and then, as I mentioned earlier, I intend, in narrative form, to endeavour to convey something of the atmosphere surrounding the manner in which these tasks are carried out.

Responsibilities

The responsibilities of area control are defined as:

(1) The responsibility for providing separation between aircraft operating in controlled or special rules airspace. (The air traffic control clearances which are issued to aircraft are based upon the standards of separation which are explained in the chapter on 'separation standards'.)

(2) The responsibility for the provision of radar services which are limited to the area of cover of the equipment/s in use and the separation applied must be in accordance with agreed standards (see chapter on 'separation standards').

(3) By agreement, the responsibility for the provision of air traffic services in airspace which would normally be the province of zone control or approach control.

Earlier in the book I explained, separation standards, the management of the airspace, navigation and communication aids, radar and flight planning and flight data. The reason I am making reference to these earlier chapters at this stage is that it is of particular importance to an appreciation of the responsibilities of area control that their role should be understood. To summarise therefore, there has to be an air traffic control system, which is achieved by the management of the airspace and the application of rules (rules of the air) relating to the use of that airspace. Navigational aids must exist not only to delineate this airspace but to enable pilots of aircraft to navigate within its confines. Flight data arising from the flight plan, in its various forms, must be available to the controller. Further, to enable the separation standards to be applied which ensure the safety of aircraft, communication facilities such as the telephone and radio telephony must be available to enable the essential co-ordinations and executive instructions to be issued. Additionally, where radar and computer technology is available these facilities should be used to assist the controllers in the discharge of their responsibilities. In regard to these latter facilities, radar and computers, it has to be borne in mind that, in many areas of the world, radar is either not available or does not provide coverage for the entire airspace; similarly, computers/automation are still in the formulative stage. Therefore, at the time of writing (and, I suggest, for the foreseeable future) a basic air traffic control system must exist which is capable of safe operation, either without these two facilities, or within their partial operation.

To return however to the 'responsibilities', I am certain readers will appreciate that the amount of work involved requires a division of these responsibilities in respect of the large volume of airspace which is being provided with air traffic services, and I wish now therefore to explain how this is done.

Area control sector organisation

For ease of operation the work of an area control unit is divided into sectors of responsibility. These sectors are usually longitudinal in dimension, having specific boundaries which are normally delineated by en-route reporting points. However, in some states, sectors are also divided vertically, permitting a separate sector responsibility for the air routes within the upper airspace. The sectors are required to work in close liaison one with another, their manning and method of operation being primarily determined by the nature of the technical equipment which is provided to carry out the tasks. In practice there are three types of sector organisation.

(1) Procedural control sectors

In many instances radar is still not available either throughout the area for which the unit is responsible or for certain sectors of the airspace. In these instances the non-radar separation standards are applied and control is exercised from a display called a flight progress board upon which the flight data are represented by flight progress strips, which are amended and moved manually, by the controller, to represent a moving picture in time, geographical position and height.

(2) Procedural control sector (assisted by radar)

In many area control units, when radar first becomes available, it is used to assist the procedural controller in resolving his traffic problems by the application of radar separation

standards in respect of certain delegated aircraft. However, where this type of operation occurs it is the non-radar controller (procedural) who is in the executive position, i.e. the officer in charge of sector operations.

(3) Radar control sector (supported by procedural control)

Many modern area control units now employ a radar-based system, supported by a procedural system which acts not only as the provider of information but also as a fall-back capability in the event of radar failure. Where this situation pertains the radar controller assumes executive control with usually an assistant controller positioned alongside him to assist in the maintenance of a traffic display, which is either in the form of a flight progress board or possibly in future systems an electronic data display (EDD). In a radar-based system it is also not unusual to have more than one radar controller working at a sector, in which case a chief sector controller is nominated as the executive responsible for the overall management of the sector team. Whichever type of sectorisation is employed by an area unit, it is, however, essential for each sector to have the following information and equipment available.

(1) a traffic display on which current or intended aircraft movements can be displayed, capable of being used by the controllers as a basis to achieve separation and co-ordination;
(2) radio telephony facilities;
(3) telephone circuits;
(4) radar data (where applicable);
(5) associated displays of essential information such as weather, pressure settings, serviceability of navigational aids, airfields' states, etc.

In order to convey an impression of what the sector suites look like, Figure 32 shows a typical layout, from which can be observed the radar consoles and the flight progress board displays. The space immediately surrounding the radar consoles will be occupied by telephone panels, radio telephony circuits, secondary radar code select panels and where appropriate computer interface devices. Figure 33 is an overall view of the operations room of a modern air traffic control centre, within which there could be approximately 100 operating positions.

Co-ordination

As with aerodrome control and approach control, so with area control, co-ordination is the vital function which links all of these services. Aircraft which are receiving an air traffic control service or an advisory service from an air traffic control centre (ATCC) or from a sector within that ATCC, must not be permitted to penetrate the airspace of another ATCC or sector unless prior co-ordination has taken place. In all co-ordinations it is important to recognise that they must take place ahead of the concerned aircraft's movement, and that the responsibility for initiating this action rests with the controller of the unit or sector which is transferring control. It is further a requirement of this co-ordination that the transferring controller must comply with any conditions specified by the accepting controller. For example, the accepting controller may require the aircraft to go to a higher or lower level or require the aircraft to be delayed, due to traffic in his sector. The reason, quite simply, is to ensure that no aircraft is transferred from one controlling authority to another until the airspace is clear to receive it, in accordance with the standards of separation previously described. The steps in co-ordination, which take place progressively, can be described as 'notification', 'negotiation' and 'agreement'. How this process is achieved is the subject of local agreement between the units concerned, often including neighbouring foreign states. There are,

of course, occasions where it is not necessary to co-ordinate each individual movement, but these instances are subject to detailed operating procedures, agreed to and implemented by both parties.

In regard to co-ordination with aerodrome control and approach control, the role of area control is that of a parent body, whose task is to ensure the overall efficiency and safe operation of the air traffic services. Approach control and aerodrome control units are required to comply with instructions which area control issue to achieve the objectives of the air traffic control service, throughout the specific airspace for which they are responsible. For example, when it is necessary to co-ordinate the departures from one or more aerodromes, the time at which individual aircraft can take off is specified by area control. Similarly, with traffic which is inbound to aerodromes, it is area control who issue the ATC clearance to the aircraft, either to proceed to a holding facility serving the aerodome or, if the arrival flow into a particular aerodrome permits, clear the aircraft to make R/T contact direct with approach control.

You will recall it was mentioned earlier that area control were responsible for providing air traffic services in the controlled and special rules airspaces outside the immediate vicinity of aerodromes, that is, the airways, upper air routes and the larger terminal areas. The reason that area control are responsible for issuing aircraft departure clearances, and if necessary specifying times of departure, is that they are aware of the air traffic which is operating on the airways or routes along which the departure aircraft wishes to fly and also of the demands of aircraft waiting to depart from other aerodromes, within terminal areas or overflying the terminal from distant departure aerodromes. Therefore, only area control are in a position to know if a particular aircraft can fly along a certain route at a certain time, in accordance with the information contained in the original flight plan or if the aircraft has to be delayed, or offered a different height to fly, or a different route to follow. Similarly, arriving air traffic bound for an aerodrome not only arrives from a variety of directions, dependent upon their aerodrome of departure, but also can be in such numbers that they require to be regulated; that is, held in reservoirs known as holding stacks, until they can be released in an orderly manner to approach control, at the aerodrome of destination. I will illustrate in the narrative example how this all happens but in describing area control I considered it would be of advantage, at this stage, to give some idea why it is that an aerodrome cannot operate independently but is required to co-ordinate its activities in relation to the surrounding airspace through the medium of area control. It might be as well to recall also, a point made earlier, that a busy aerodrome situated in a terminal area can be dealing with aircraft arriving and departing in excess of one a minute; additionally a busy terminal area usually has a number of aerodromes, of varying activity within its confines. Also many terminal areas of the major states are positioned at the crossroads of aerial activity, which means that a great deal of air traffic bound for other destinations crosses the area as they follow the airways and upper air routes, and of course occupy flight levels quite often desired by aircraft awaiting departure from the terminal aerodromes. It is therefore into this surrounding aerial activity that area control has to inject departing aircraft, and from which it has to descend terminal arrival aircraft.

To assist in achieving this objective, and as was stated earlier, the aerodrome traffic service units are required to keep area control promptly advised of the following data on IFR traffic:

(1) the lowest level at the holding point/s available for use by area control;
(2) the average time interval between successive approaches;
(3) the revision of expected approach times

(EAT) which have been issued by area control (this is normally done when the approach control calculations show a variation of 5 minutes, or more);
(4) the arrival time over the holding point/s if these vary from the estimates by 3 minutes or more;
(5) missed approaches, if a re-routeing is entailed (this is essential to co-ordinate the flight in respect of any other aircraft which may be in the vicinity);
(6) the departure times of aircraft;
(7) all information on any aircraft which may be overdue.

Similarly area control are required to keep the aerodrome units promptly advised of the following information on aircraft on IFR flight plans. This information must be passed ahead of the release of the aircraft from the jurisdiction of area control to approach control with, if possible, at least 15 minutes warning.

(1) A 'release' on each inbound aircraft, giving the following details:
　(a) aircraft identification and type;
　(b) point of departure;
　(c) release point;
　(d) estimated time and level at the holding facility or the arrival time and level at the holding facility if the release is given after the actual arrival of the aircraft in the hold (this situation can occur in heavy traffic where aircraft are stacked in the hold awaiting a turn to approach for landing);
　(e) the expected approach time;
　(f) the contact point.
(2) the anticipated delay for departing aircraft due to traffic congestion and the reason for the delay (this information is necessary for it may prevent an aircraft starting its engines too soon or even embarking passengers).

There are three expressions which I have used in this explanation in respect of arriving and departing traffic which, although explained in the glossary of terms, would, I consider, be worthy of a rather more detailed explanation in respect of the ATC activities which I have been explaining in this paragraph, they are: 'ATC clearances', 'releases' and 'contact point'.

Air traffic control clearances

The ICAO definition of an air traffic control clearance is: 'authorisation for an aircraft to proceed under conditions specified by an air traffic control unit' – in practice the word 'clearance' is used on its own, prefixed by the particular portion of the aircraft's flight to which it relates, e.g. taxi clearance, take-off, departure, en-route, approach, landing.

The request for a clearance is initiated by the pilot, by the submission of a flight plan, and you will recall from the chapter on the subject that this can be done either on the ground, or in the air, in certain circumstances. It is this information passed by the pilot or other person/organisation acting on his behalf which gives ATC the essential data on which to base an ATC clearance.

The clearance when issued, relates solely to 'known traffic'; that is, traffic, the current flight details and intentions of which are known to the controller concerned, through either direct communication or co-ordination, and is required to be issued for any flight, or portion of a flight, which is provided with an air traffic control or an advisory service.

The contents of an ATC clearance includes the following items:

(1) aircraft identification;
(2) clearance limit;
(3) route to be followed;
(4) levels of flight and any changes of levels;
(5) any further additions pertinent to the particular clearance, such as time restriction – communication instructions – departure/approach manoeuvres.

One of the items in the above list, 'clearance limit', requires explanation, for it has a very important bearing on the conduct of a flight particularly in the event of radio failure. A clearance limit is in fact the point to which an aircraft is granted an ATC clearance, and is specified by naming this point which is usually:

(1) an aerodrome;
(2) a reporting point; or
(3) a controlled, advisory or special rules airspace boundary.

Also where an aircraft has flight planned to remain within controlled, advisory or special rules airspace throughout its flight, and where there is reasonable assurance that prior co-ordination will be effected ahead of the passage of the aircraft, the 'clearance' relates to the entire route of the flight to the aerodrome of first intended landing. If, therefore, we refer to the example flight plan given in Chapter 6 ('Flight planning and flight data') depicting a flight from Rotterdam to Lisbon, the clearance issued to that aircraft, because its entire flight is being conducted throughout the controlled airways network of Western Europe where ATC co-ordinations will take place, will be to its destination Lisbon. Even in event of radio failure, the ATC clearance limit would still be valid and the aircraft would continue its flight to its destination in accordance with this clearance. There are complex procedures to ensure the safety of the aircraft under these circumstances but the point is made to underline the nature of a clearance limit.

To ensure international uniformity of understanding, as you know from reading the section on radio telephony, (Chapter 4 'Navigation and communication aids') standard phraseologies are used by air traffic control when communicating with aircraft and you will find examples of the phraseology which must be used when issuing an ATC clearance, in the Appendix at the end of the book.

The release point

The 'release point' is the position, time, or level at which an arriving aircraft comes under the jurisdiction of approach control or approach/radar control. The release point must be within controlled or advisory airspace and all other landing aircraft at lower levels must also have been released by area control. For reasons which will be clear, approach control may not climb the aircraft released to them unless co-ordinated with the area controller.

Where radar is in operation, aircraft may be released in order to expedite traffic by the application of radar separation standards, but where this is done the prefix 'radar release' must be used and details passed by area control to approach/approach radar control, of any specified traffic which may conflict with the aircraft's progress.

The contact point

The 'contact point', is the 'position', 'time' or 'level' at which an arriving aircraft is to establish R/T communication with approach control. It is a point normally ahead of the 're-lease' and its purpose is to enable approach control to pass to the aircraft any essential information which may be pertinent to the aerodrome of landing. The clearance limit, however, remains the same and no executive instructions can be issued until the aircraft reaches its 'release point'.

Flight information service

Flight information is defined as a service provided for the purpose of giving advice and information useful for the safe and efficient conduct of a flight; that is to say, such information as the state of an aerodrome, the service-ability of navigational aids, the weather at aerodromes or en-route, the altimeter pressure settings and any special information in regard to danger areas, air displays or special flight re-strictions. From the reading of the previous sections I hope it will be clear that where an aircraft is flying within an ATC system, such as within controlled airspace or when leaving or departing controlled aerodromes, flight information is an integral part of the air traffic services provided by the ATC units. However, where an aircraft is flying in the open flight information region (FIR) – that is, the airspace outside controlled and special rules air-space – the responsibility for the provision of flight information and for the alerting service rests with the air traffic control centre responsible for that specific region of the FIR.

At ATCCs special positions are established for the purpose of passing flight information to those aircraft with whom they are in R/T contact. The positions are manned by qualified controllers and although they are unable to provide a 'controlled' service, they do provide every assistance possible to this type of flying, including the initiation of the alerting service, if they have reason to believe this action to be necessary. The alerting service is so called, because it is the commencement of the procedure for 'overdue action' which is then followed by 'search and rescue' should this be required. The FIR controller is, then, the link between the pilot and the safety facilities, and the organisation which exists to assist aircraft which may be in need. However, R/T contact between the FIR controllers and aircraft flying in the FIR is not mandatory, and, as you will recall from the chapter on 'Airspace management', the only safeguard is that all aircraft which are flying above 3000 feet in the FIR, are required to comply with a simple quadrantal height rule, related to the aircraft's heading. To assist these aircraft, however, the FIR controller can issue 'proximity warnings' to pilots who are in communication with him.

Proximity warnings

A proximity warning is information offered to

a pilot by the FIR controller, when he, the controller, considers from the information presented to him that aircraft are in dangerous proximity to each other. This may sound a rather vague statement to make, but it has to be considered against the limited information and organisation available in the FIR. For example, civil and military aircraft may fly on random tracks, and the absence of navigational aids makes position fixing unreliable. Also the large size of the FIR makes it almost impossible to readily identify a variety of geographic locations, and finally there is no requirement for aircraft to be in communication with the FIR controller or to file a flight plan.

At this stage in the development of world aviation the services which are available to aircraft which are flying outside the organised route structures may seem rather casual, but I am certain that a glance at the totality of global airspace will doubtless indicate the immensity of the problem of even contemplating the provision of a 'controlled' service, to every vehicle flying in that airspace. Additionally there is a strong body of opinion that would object to the application of too many restrictions upon the freedom of movement, which obtains at present. However, the rapidity of technical advance changes both man's attitudes and capabilities, and we may well see in the not-too-distant future a further extension of the safety services, beyond the present restrictions of designated airspaces. An example of this additional assistance to aircraft flying in the FIR, is where, in a number of countries, military aerodromes with a radar capability offer a radar advisory service to civil aircraft who are within the coverage of their equipment. There are, however, additionally certain areas of the world where, due to the large distances involved and the sparse nature of navigational assistance, the application of an air traffic control service is required. These are the large oceans, such as the North/South Atlantic and the South Pacific, and desert areas like the Sahara. In these areas the methods which are employed to achieve separation between aircraft differ somewhat from those previously described. One such area is the North Atlantic oceanic area and whilst it has more air traffic than other similar areas, the procedures which are employed for the application of air traffic services are similar to those employed elsewhere in the world.

Oceanic area control

Approximately 500 aircraft cross the North Atlantic daily to and from destinations in Europe and North America; an interesting statistic, when it is recalled that in 1937 the total air traffic was a bi-weekly trans-atlantic flying boat service.

Because the aircraft operating on the North Atlantic are of similar types, desiring to operate at similar speeds and similar heights, and the performance of which is still affected by the pattern of weather (particularly the wind direction), procedures have to be adopted to provide a lateral track structure as a basis upon which to provide a separation service.

The track structure to be used is agreed once every 12 hours, by consultation between the authorities responsible for the control of the area. In the case of the North Atlantic the oceanic control centres involved are the Scottish, Gander, New York, Reykjavik and Santa Maria oceanic centres. The number of parties in the discussions depends upon where the weather pattern dictates the optimum positioning of the tracks. In practice the normal pattern of weather on the North Atlantic usually results in these tracks lying within the airspace controlled by the Scottish and Gander centres. The lateral spacing of the tracks is based upon an agreed separation standard of 60 nautical miles (1°), although this figure may be varied subject to a number of procedural safeguards agreed between the states concerned which can require certain categories of aircraft to be separated by 120 nautical miles (2°). Once the track structure for a 12-hour period has been agreed, the geographical co-ordinates of the tracks are promulgated through the AFTN to the North American and European states. This information then enables the operators who fly the North Atlantic routes to include on their flight plans details of the particular track they wish to fly. Figure 21 reproduces with the kind permission of the U.K. Civil Aviation Authority, a copy of the track structure which was in operation on the North Atlantic for the period 12.00 hours to 20.00 hours on the 11 February 1982.

As I stated earlier the separation standards which are used over these long distances vary somewhat from those described in the chapter on separation standards. Aircraft flying between flight level 275 and flight level 400 in the airspace covered by the track structure shown on Figure 21 (latitude 27N to latitude 67N) are required to have a specified navigation performance capability (MNPS) but even so the spacing of the tracks, with a lateral separation of 60 nm, allows for a considerable margin of error in navigation, when compared with the frequency of positional information which is possible with the multiplicity of navigational aids which are normally available to aircraft using overland airways and air routes. Similarly longitudinal separation is increased from 10 minutes to 20 minutes on the same track, except that this can be reduced where Mach number techniques are in use in respect of the concerned aircraft. The Mach number tech-

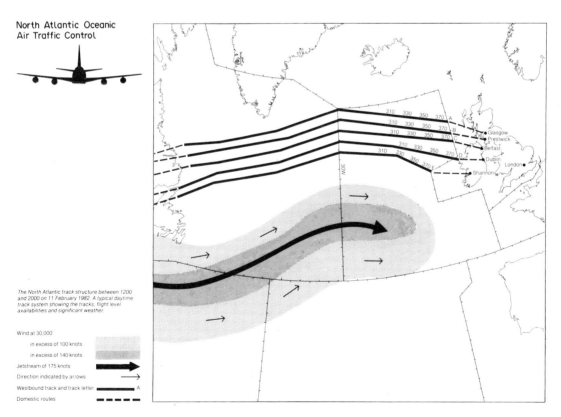

FIGURE 21. The North Atlantic track structure

nique is a method of maintaining longitudinal separation between turbo-jet aircraft where the pilots are required to adhere to a Mach number issued by air traffic control as part of the ATC clearance. Vertical separation remains unaltered, that is 1000 feet up to flight level 290 (29,000 feet, approx.) and 2000 feet above that level, except that above flight level 450 (45,000 feet approx.) the vertical separation is increased to 4000 feet. It is, however, possible, as I stated earlier in Chapter 2 ('Separation standards'), that the increase in vertical separation above flight level 290 may be reduced, and certainly at the time of writing I am aware that certain member states of ICAO are submitting proposals for such a revision.

Supersonic aircraft also operate in this area but because of their fundamentally different characteristics and the height at which they operate (50,000 – 60,000 feet) it is possible to organise fixed tracks, which do not conflict with the subsonic track structure, and which take into account the acceleration and deceleration phases of flight. Also the longitudinal separation between SST aircraft on the same track can be reduced to 10 minutes under certain specified conditions.

The application of an air traffic control service on the North Atlantic is exercised in a manner similar to that of any other ATC unit, except that whilst radar is used in the initial phase of a transatlantic flight to shepherd the aircraft onto the allocated tracks and to sequence them onto the relevant domestic route networks, thereafter, the controller has to use a flight progress board display to provide him with a pictorial presentation of traffic under his control. Aircraft pass position reports at designated intervals along the tracks and co-ordination takes place ahead of the transfer of control at the boundaries of the oceanic areas, usually 30° West. Communication between the aircraft and the ground is through high frequency radio communications (HF/RT) and specialist wireless operators are normally used for this

purpose. Ionospherical conditions can still, however, make communications difficult on H/F, and therefore when these conditions are known to exist, provision is made to provide greater separations between aircraft than those described.

It is also of interest to note that the use of computers to assist controllers in the deployment of aircraft onto the track structures has been in use on the North Atlantic for many years. Therefore, with the possible exception of their use within the domestic airspace of the U.S.A., it is fair to say that oceanic control on the North Atlantic has pioneered many of the techniques of the application of computers/automation, which are now being applied to other ATS units.

Whilst I have only been able to deal briefly in this section with control over large distances, I am certain readers will appreciate that it is an aspect of air traffic control which demands a high degree of specialisation and is also one area in which it is hoped that satellites will in the future make a contribution towards rapid and clear communications and improved accuracy in navigation.

General

In this chapter on the provision of air traffic services I have endeavoured to cover the main objectives and responsibilities. In doing so there are inevitably a number of 'services' which I have not mentioned, but their omission does not detract from the main principles which I trust I have been able to convey. In fact it is my opinion that were I to try to include all of the minutiae it could divert the reader's attention from my purpose of primary explanation. I do, however, appreciate that there may be readers who would wish to be aware of this detail, and in this regard I have presented the ATC services in such a manner that they can if necessary be supplemented by this additional information. The reference books which would be required to do so are:

Internationally
Procedures for Air Navigation Services.
Rules of the Air and Air Traffic Services
Doc. 4444 – RAC/501/11, published by the International Civil Aviation Organisation.

Nationally
The Manual of Air Traffic Services and
Air Information Publications
(published by concerned states).

To assist in an understanding of the air traffic services which an aircraft uses from a depar-

ture aerodrome via an airways network, to its destination aerodrome, I have included a Figure 22, which shows the ATC functions associated with each phase of its flight. I should also like to make the point that I have tried not to make any distinction between civil and military aircraft, for whilst the requirements of military aircraft will differ from their civil counterparts a military aircraft which participates in the services described operates in exactly the same way as a civil aircraft. There is in fact a major participation by military authorities in the provision of air traffic services, and these I will describe in detail at a later stage.

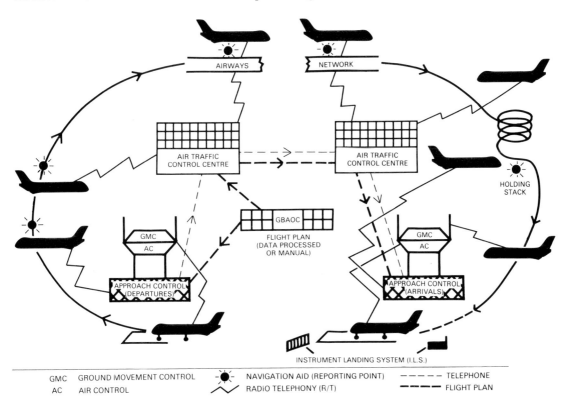

FIGURE 22.   Air traffic control functions

8

Automation
and Air Traffic Control

Introduction

Before I proceed to explain how the facilities and procedures which I have previously described come together to provide an air traffic control service it would, I consider, be of value to examine the role of the computer in its application to modern air traffic control systems.

Our first problem is to rationalise the words 'automation' and 'computer'. The dictionary describes 'automation' as, 'a piece of mechanism with concealed motive power' and 'computer' as 'a calculating device'. Personally I think both these descriptions are in need of revision and therefore, whilst risking the wrath of linguistic experts, I propose for our purpose to regard automation in this context as the result of the application of computer techniques to specific ATC processes. The second problem is how to approach an explanation of the subject. There are so many computer devices available today, even for application to domestic appliances and leisure games, that I suggest the only reasonable way is to approach it from the point of view of the user. In other words, what is the computer and its resultant automation doing for the controller.

In Chapter 5, I explained the principles of

primary and secondary radar and how secondary radar can be used to provide the controller with information on the identity and height regarding those aircraft responses which are of concern to him. Collectively this information is known as 'radar data'. In Chapter 6, I explained about 'flight data' and how computers are used to assist in the preparation of flight progress strips, and in the flow of information between those air traffic control units which are concerned with the conduct of the flight of a particular aircraft. It is then these two elements, radar data and flight data, which form the basic ingredients for the application of computer technology, and I now propose to explain how these elements, when computer-assisted, form the basic foundations of an automated ATC system. For ease of understanding and to eliminate continuous back-referencing, there will of necessity be some reiteration of parts of the information contained in previous chapters in the explanation that follows.

The computer

The electronic computer, although a versatile machine with an immense capability, is inher-

88

ently an unintelligent device, which cannot perform even a single function without being told, in almost infinite detail, precisely what to do in a logical step-by-step manner. Telling the computer what to do in the form of a 'program', translated into computer language, requires that the 'functions' to be programmed are understood and examined in detail. These programs, when translated into computer language, are known as *'software'* and the computers themselves are, not surprisingly known as *'hardware'*.

In considering the application of the techniques of automation to the processes of air traffic control it is essential to have an understanding of the basic ATC system of operation and of those functions to which it is intended to apply these techniques. It is also desirable to appreciate why the need for automation exists and what the advantages are, to both controllers and pilots, of its introduction into an air traffic control system. From an air traffic control point of view these advantages can be briefly summarised as the handling of repetitive tasks, to ensure that the right data, in the right form, are in the right place at the right time, with the objective of reducing the workload on the controller by relieving him of these repetitive manual tasks.

As a generalisation there are three recognisable elements in the application of automation to this particular discipline: they are:

(1) flight data processing;
(2) radar data processing; and
(3) the correlation or marriage of flight data processing and radar data processing.

Within each of these stages there are variants and the stages can be, and often are, telescoped and, of course, the air traffic control systems to which they are applied will vary from state to state and often within states themselves. There are, however, within the ATC and flight radar data functions a sufficient number of common factors which, when evaluated, form the basis

of a standard foundation. It is advisable also that the associated 'hardware' and 'software' philosophy should, if possible, be based upon a 'stage-by-stage' build-up principle. The advantages of this approach benefit not only the operators and technicians who have to use and maintain the system but also those ATC authorities who do not require fully advanced sophisticated systems, either for air traffic or economic reasons, at a specific point in time, but who would be able to build-up their system further should occasion so demand.

In this regard it is of interest to note that the International Civil Aviation Organisation in the 'Guidance Material on the application of automation to ATC' (Doc. 4444 Attachment D) states:

> It should not be necessary to install the complete system before any advantage can be obtained from it. Every attempt should be made to design the first stage so that by development and addition, rather than replacement, the system can be made capable of performing more functions, or of performing them in a different manner.

This sounds a very simple and logical statement to make, particularly as computers are relatively expensive pieces of hardware in economic terms, and the preparation of their related software routines, equally demanding in hours of dedicated manpower. Regrettably, however, it is a statement which is often overlooked, possibly for good reason, by both the customer, the concerned aviation authority, and the provider, the avionics industry. I appreciate that it is not always possible to follow good intentions, particularly when they are formed for international application. However, I hope that at least by discussing, in this chapter, the application of automation to air traffic control, concerned readers will gain an understanding of the major elements which are of concern in this development of automation and its associated avionics, for these developments are certainly the most important factor in the future of the world's ATC systems.

The ATC system

The basic principles of the control of air traffic have been explained in the previous chapters but it is suggested that it would be worthwhile considering what are the functions associated with air traffic control to which automation can be applied on a stage-by-stage basis.

Functionally, the flight of an aircraft can be divided into the following phases:

Phase I   Pre-flight planning
Phase II   Aerodrome departure
Phase III   Terminal area departure
Phase IV   En-route
Phase V   Terminal area arrival
Phase VI   Approach control
Phase VII   Aerodrome arrival

The air traffic control functions designed to separate aircraft one from another, associated with each of these phases of flight, have been described in detail at Chapter 7 ('The provision of air traffic services') but briefly they can be described as follows:

Aerodrome control (departure) phase

On initial departure from an aerodrome, ATC issue a departure clearance based upon the pilot's flight-planned request. This is normally obtained from the parent air traffic control centre, which usually has control of the terminal area as well as the en-route phase of the flight, and to whom details of the *flight plan* will have been transmitted (or computer-stored) ahead of the aircraft's request for a departure clearance.

Terminal area/departure control phase

As the aircraft leaves the vicinity of the aerodrome the pilot-in-command receives an onward clearance from the terminal area controller which is intended to position the aircraft into the en-route phase. The terminal area clearance is based upon prior knowledge of the aircraft's intentions (the flight plan) and the initial clearance which was issued as the result of the request from aerodrome control. Further updating of this clearance may occur, following the receipt of active information that the aircraft is airborne. As inbound routeings to aerodromes are designed not to conflict with outbound routeings, aircraft do not normally work approach control on departure.

En-route phase

As the aircraft progresses through the terminal area a further revision of the initial clearance will be issued to ensure the aircraft's climb to the most appropriate cruising level and on a routeing structure compatible with the aircraft's destination. The clearance is based upon a knowledge of the aircraft's intentions (the flight plan) updated by the departure clearance issued by the terminal controller and knowledge of the aircraft's progress through the terminal area.

In this phase of flight an aircraft may pass through more than one airways sector within the parent air traffic control centre; each sector being advised in advance of the aircraft's progress, based upon up-to-date flight data, which in turn amend the original flight plan.

Similarly an aircraft, during the course of its flight may progress from one air traffic control centre to another. In this case the receiving air traffic control centre will already be in possession of the *flight plan* which was originated at the point of departure. It is, however, the responsibility of the transferring centre to update this information from active flight data which have been received from the aircraft during the time it has been under their jurisdiction, and to transmit this information ahead of the transfer of control of the aircraft, to the air traffic control centre which will be accepting control of the aircraft.

Terminal area arrival phase

When the aircraft approaches the terminal area serving the destination aerodrome a further clearance will be issued to the pilot stating the point at which to enter the terminal area and the route which is to be followed, which can be either to proceed directly to the aerodrome of intended landing, or to the holding facility which serves that aerodrome.

This clearance depends upon the receipt of a *flight plan* and the updating of this information from flight data supplied by the en-route sectors, which have previously been in control of the aircraft's flight.

Approach control phase

As the aircraft proceeds through the terminal area, control of the aircraft will be transferred to the approach controller at its destination aerodrome; the point of transfer being dependent upon the current air traffic situation. It will then be the responsibility of approach control to issue a clearance to proceed, either direct from the aircraft's geographical position on its transfer from terminal area control, or to proceed on a heading from the holding facility, or to descend to a lower level overhead that facility.

This clearance depends upon the receipt of prior information (the flight plan) and of the updating of that information ahead of the transfer of control by the terminal area controller responsible for arriving traffic.

Aerodrome control (arrival) phase

After an instruction has been issued by ap-proach control for the aircraft to intercept the ILS or other landing aid, to enable an approach to land to be made, control of the aircraft is transferred to aerodrome control. The final clearance to land is issued by aerodrome control, during the course of the approach.

This clearance depends primarily upon the prior information passed by approach control (flight data) and of other aerodrome traffic not necessarily known to approach control. However, in many cases, a copy of the original flight plan is also passed to aerodrome control so that they may be kept informed of future air traffic requirements.

The flight plan and flight data

From the foregoing explanation of the ATC functions related to the flight of an aircraft, it will be clear that the flight plan, the data extracted from it for ATC purposes, and the subsequent updating of this information, is an integral part of the ATC system and its functions.

The flight plan, which is filed in advance of the flight, by the pilot of the aircraft or by his operating agency on his behalf, is a composite document containing a great deal of information, all of which is essential for the entirety of the operation for a particular flight, and part of which is essential for the ATC aspect of its operation. Therefore, the concerned ATC authorities, to whom the flight plan is addressed, extract from it the *data* essential for their particular part of the operation. Universally at the present time, this data, when extracted from the flight plan, are transferred to a *flight progress strip* and it is this flight progress strip, and the family it produces, which forms the basic pre-planning tool for air traffic control and which requires continuous updating with 'live' information, as a flight proceeds through the various ATC functions.

Attempts are being made, and will doubtless

be successful in the future, to replace this ubiquitous piece of paper by, for example, an electronic data display (EDD) but as the present flight progress strip represents to the controller a three-dimensional display in time, height and geographical position, continuously updated by 'live' information, it will be apparent that its replacement promotes a challenging problem both for the computer software routines and the controller/computer interface.

To assist in an understanding of these basic ATC functions readers may wish to refer back to the air traffic control functions diagram at Figure 22, and the computer-assisted *flight plan flow chart,* Figure 20.

Flight data processing

The foregoing sections have set out, in general terms, the functions of air traffic control and the relationship of the flight plan and flight data to these functions. The reason for so doing, is to try to illustrate that they are functions which are general to any location, and therefore should be capable of forming the basic foundation of any approach to system automation; from this software routines can then be developed to suit the requirements of specific locations.

Flight data processing, then, is that function which is concerned with the input into the computer of the flight data which have originally been extracted from the flight plan, and thereafter the updating of this computer information by reference to the 'live' or 'active' situation, and readers will recall that a detailed explanation of the computer's role in flight data processing was given in Chapter 6. The activation of the computer can be carried out manually, by a controller or other member of the control team, either by the use of an 'input' keyboard, known as an ANK (alpha-numeric keyboard) or alternative devices, such as, for example, a TWD (touchwire device). Whatever the system used, however, the person operating the 'input' device must in the first instance identify to the computer the particular aircraft's flight data, which are stored in its memory, and to which the update message is to be addressed.

It is also possible to activate and update the flight data carried in the computer automatically, by correlating it with the radar data which are being received by the radar sensors. How this is achieved, and the consequences of this marriage of flight data and radar data, will be subsequently explained.

Radar data processing

The term 'radar', as explained at Chapter 5, is an acronym of the phrase radio detection and ranging, and the range and bearing signals which are received by the antenna are in 'analogue' form. Whilst all signals so received require to be processed before being transmitted to a radar display, the term 'radar processing' used in this chapter is in respect of the processing of the received radar signals and their relationship in regard to computers. Technically, computers are concerned only with those radar signals which relate to responses from aircraft, and it is therefore unnecessary and uneconomic to feed them with all of the unwanted echoes which occur as a radar antenna sweeps through 360°, out to the range of its transmitted power. To be able to achieve this situation the radar signals of the concerned targets require to be converted into a digitised format. In this form the radar signals, or radar data, can be fed into a computer, to be either displayed directly onto a radar display or, if the computer has the capacity or is linked to an additional computer containing the relevant flight data, then both types of data can be correlated before being further processed onto the controller's display. In this regard there are many occasions where the radar transmitters and receivers are located at a considerable distance from the control positions. In these cases it is possible to process the radar signals at the radar sites and then by using either telephone lines or micro-wave links, transmit the data to the air traffic control unit concerned. A further key factor in this correlation, as explained at Chapter 5, is the allocation of identity codes to individual aircraft, through the use of a secondary surveillance radar (SSR) facility, and the ability to carry out multi-radar tracking, which enables those aircraft which do not carry a transponder (SSR) to also appear on the controller's display with a computer-related indication of their identity.

Correlation of flight data and radar data

We now, therefore, have the situation where the computer contains not only the *flight data* concerned with the movement of aircraft, but additionally, for those aircraft which are airborne, *radar data* relating to the aircraft's actual position in space and time.

By allocating to the concerned aircraft a discrete SSR code, and also by informing the computer that the code so allocated refers to the specific flight data relevant to that aircraft, the computer is able to recognise the radar data which it receives, and to correlate this data with the flight data already in its possession.

This act of relating flight data and radar data then begins to open up wide horizons for the application of automation to the tasks of controlling air traffic. The extent to which this automation is applied then forms the basis of the term 'air traffic control systems', and the formulation of computer programmes to bring these 'systems' about.

However, before, explaining some of the facilities which the application of computer technology can offer, it is worthwhile making the point that whilst the 'programming' of a computer, in this context, is the process of analysing the various air traffic control functions which are to be automated, and then breaking them down into simple step-by-step operations for translation into computer language – the controller himself acts as a communicator, a navigator and a calculator and predictor of future events. As was stated at the commencement of this chapter, it is essential to recognise that the advantages in automation are in the handling of repetitive tasks, to ensure that the right data, in the right form, are in the right place at the right time, thus reducing the workload in the performance of repetitive tasks. Therefore, to be effective, automation should be applied primarily to those of the controller's functions which limit his capability to discharge his primary responsibility, which is that of *a decision-maker*.

The application of automation

Chapter 6 gave an example of the standard form of the flight plan from which air traffic control extracts the data which are essential for the control of an aircraft's flight, and whilst there may be some variation between ATC authorities who use computer assistance, the following sub-headings can be accepted as a standard format of the type of data in general use:

> Aircraft type
> Aircraft callsign
> SSR code
> Point of departure
> Destination
> Route
> Height/desired cruising level
> Airspeed
> ETD and/or time over navigational facility

I propose now to explain how automation can be applied to these listed items. Before doing so however, I wish to describe briefly the practical objective of the application of this technology. For ease of explanation, this can be simplified into two main objectives:

(1) the display of radar-derived data, and
(2) the display of flight data.

The display of radar-derived data

When radar was first introduced to assist in the control of air traffic, the standard controller's viewing unit was a cathode ray tube (see Chapter 5, 'Radar') upon which the echoes of aircraft appeared as 'blobs' of light, known as radar 'responses'. Identification of these responses, to ensure that they were indeed the aircraft of concern to the controller, was a laborious business of turning the aircraft through 90° and then turning it back again. Direct observation of the viewing unit and notation of *both* turns was essential to confirm that the response was indeed that of the concerned aircraft.

The prime objective of the use of automation in this regard is to assist in this process of identity, by placing alongside the particular response a *'label'* which carries, in written characteristics, the identity of the response and other pertinent data, which will be explained later.

To be fully effective the concerned aircraft needs to carry an airborne SSR transponder and in many areas of the world's airspace the carriage of this equipment is increasingly becoming a mandatory requirement.

Methods do exist, however, for alerting computers to the requirement to display responses from aircraft not so equipped, or alternatively for overlaying responses from transponder equipped aircraft on viewing units which are displaying radar responses, of both primary and secondary targets.

The radar viewing units have also changed dramatically from the original cathode ray tube. It is usual, in ATC units to which this type of automation is being applied, to use a 'synthetic' type of radar display. Synthetic displays, whilst being a processed representation of the signals which are being received by the radar sensors, have the advantage that all responses, irrespective of the weakness of the returned signal, can be displayed at a constant level of brilliance and clarity.

In fact, the displays which are available today, for use by radar controllers, are truly remarkable pieces of equipment and although I shall be explaining their operational setting in Chapter 9, 'The ATC environment', I consider it would be of assistance, in this present chapter on automation, to spend a short time on a brief explanation of the main characteristics of a modern radar controller's display console, for without the facilities which these display systems provide it would not be possible to apply the automated techniques described in this chapter.

In describing these facilities, it is essential to include not only the display upon which is portrayed the air traffic, and which is the controller's 'viewing' unit, but also the furniture in which the display is housed, known as a console. The console of the type of equipment I am describing contains a high proportion of the avionics which are essential to provide the controller with the interface between his operating position and the radar data and flight data contained within the ATC system, and also with the capability to interpret, alter or add to the information on his display, and to co-ordinate automatically with other operational positions contained within the system. Therefore the display and the console are an integral unit and, not surprisingly and quite simply, are referred to as the 'display console'. With the kind permission of the Displays Division of Plessey Electronics Systems Ltd I have included the photograph in Figure 23 which clearly demonstrates the integrated nature of the display and the console, Figure 24 shows a close-up view of the control function keys and the input keyboard, associated with the display console.

This particular equipment contains within the console its own computer, which is capable of performing all of the processing required by the ATC operation within which it is required to operate. However, whilst it is capable of operating completely independently, it would be normal practice to have several of these units connected together to form a system, and in this configuration each display is able to communicate with the others. This intercommunication is carried out through the processors which are contained within the individual consoles, and their capacity is such that a separate processor is not required.

From the explanations I gave at Chapter 5 ('Radar') you will be aware that the displays must be able to accept inputs from primary radar and secondary radar and from radar sites where the primary radar and secondary radar are co-located and/or where the secondary radar is remotely sited. Whichever situation obtains, however, the position symbols to be displayed to the controller must be the positions at which the primary radar would show them, if he were viewing them on the conventional cathode ray tube display as described in Chapter 5.

The facilities which this type of display console adds to the conventional primary radar presentation can be summarised as follows:

(1) secondary radar position symbols;
(2) labels adjacent to the position symbols of selected aircraft displaying the following data:
    (a) aircraft callsign or SSR code,
    (b) flight level or height if the aircraft is below the transition level (see chapter 2, 'Introduction' for explanation of flight level),
    (c) supplementary flight plan data, such as route information, aircraft's destination, etc.;
(3) a 'leader' line, from each aircraft position symbol to its label;
(4) visual alarms for an aircraft emergency, special hi-jack code, or radio failure –

these are in the form of flashing symbols and labels;
(5) trail dots, which appear behind the aircraft's symbol to indicate the track which it has been following;
(6) a range and bearing line with reflective range and bearing, displayed at each end of the line;
(7) tabular areas – these are areas of the display which are not being used to control air traffic, and upon which can be displayed data of interest to the controller, such as, for example, advance details on aircraft which are due to enter his sector of responsibility;
(8) synthetic map displays, such as the outline of the airways, and air-routes, the coastline, danger areas etc – these maps are usually programmed within the console's computer memory but facilities also exist for the controller to draw-in on his display a synthetic map for any special purpose, such as, for example, a military exercise area or a temporary prohibited area for an air display;
(9) a direction-finder vector with bearing displayed at one end (this would normally be used in conjunction with a direction-finding facility operated in conjunction with the aircraft's R/T transmissions);
(10) a rotatable 'cursor', comprising seven parallel lines with bearings displayed at each end of the central line.

Additionally the controller can select the amount of data he wishes to see on his display, related to his sector and area of responsibility. He does this by setting up messages known as data selection parameters, which he notifies to the processor within the console, by using a keyboard input which is associated with the display. An example of such a selection programme could be as follows:

(1) *Azimuth filter* – the selection on the display of the sector for which he is responsible –

FIGURE 23. A radar display console This photograph shows a modern radar display console which houses its own computer with the capacity to carry out the functions described in the relevant chapter. Several of these display consoles linked together can provide the basis for an ATC system without the requirement of a central computer.

(Photograph Courtesy Plessey Displays Ltd)

FIGURE 24. Close-up view of an input keyboard associated with a display console. This photograph shows the input keyboard and function keys associated with the radar display. The yellow object to the left of the panel is the 'rolling ball' which the radar controller uses to position a symbol over any target on the radar display for which he may require information additional to that being displayed to him. Alternatively it may be used to initiate a 'software' routine.

(Photograph Courtesy Plessey Displays Ltd)

say from 000° to 160°. Therefore only this sector of the 360° sweep of the radar's antenna would be shown on his display out to an agreed range in nautical miles.

(2) *Height filter* - quite a number of ATC systems operate on a vertical split of responsibilities where one controller will look after traffic up to a certain level and another the traffic above that level, even though the aircraft are operating in the same geographical area, albeit vertically separated. In these circumstances a height band would be selected say from flight level 050 to flight level 240.

(3) *Mode and code filter* - aircraft operating within an ATC system, where the carriage of an SSR transponder is a requirement, are advised in advance of the SSR mode and code upon which they are required to operate. Therefore as it is only these aircraft for which the controller wishes to have labels related to the aircraft's symbols, the processor is notified of the concerned modes and codes required to be displayed.

This filtering facility therefore allows each controller to have an uncluttered display which shows full information only on those aircraft which are of interest to him. However, in order that a controller can check the information on aircraft which are not displaying full labels there is an 'all data' switch on the display console, which, when activated, overrides the filters and gives full labels on all of the aircraft on the display. The deactivation of the switch automatically restores the display to 'filtered' targets only.

From time to time, however, a controller may wish to query the information on a single radar target on his display. To do this he has a facility on his console known as a 'rolling ball'. The rolling ball produces an electronic symbol which can be moved to any position on the display, and the action by the controller in using this device is to position the symbol over

the target on the display. This action automatically alerts the computer processors to the fact that information is required on this specific radar target which has been selected by the controller. The processors, having been alerted, will then display to the controller the radar data and flight data on the selected target, which is stored within their memory. An alternative method of initiating this action is to use a 'light pen' as the interface between the controller and the computer data base and reference to Figure 35 shows a controller using such a facility. These devices can also be used for a variety of other 'functions', such as the movement of a tabular area from one part of the display to another, or the movement of the origin of the radar data source, known as 'off-centring', or the initiation of a 'hand-off' routine, that is the transfer of control from himself to another operating position. The rolling ball/light-pen therefore provides a link between the radar controller, the radar display and the software functions with which the computer has been programmed.

I have described in some detail the facilities which are available on modern display consoles, so that readers will appreciate, when reading the following chapter on the display of flight data, the equipment which is available at the controller's operating positions. It is these facilities which enable him not only to view the results of an automated or semi-automated ATC system, but also emphasise the essential role of the controller as the interface between the automated information which is displayed to him and the demands and requirements of the minute-to-minute operational changes and alterations which are necessary to ensure the safety of the aircraft under his control, and of which he alone must be the arbiter.

An additional point I wish to make before proceeding further is that for the purpose of providing as full a description as possible of the application of automation, I have of necessity described, at today's standards, a fairly high level of the application of these techniques. However, readers will, I am certain, appreciate that the elements I have described at present apply primarily to a limited number of busy ATC units, and that at the majority automation is relatively simple, albeit with the capability to advance towards the type of system I have outlined, as the future growth in air traffic and/or its associated problems may demand.

The display of flight data

The requirement for a display of flight data to the controller, additional to the radar data presented to him on his viewing unit, has been explained in detail in Chapter 6, and is also the presently accepted method of displaying this information on flight progress strips. This chapter also gave an example of the role of the flight progress strip and how computers are used to assist in their production, their updating and the flow of information between the various ATC units concerned with the conduct of a particular flight.

A further development, which is receiving the attention of many of the world's leading aviation authorities responsible for air traffic control, is to take additional advantage of computer technology by replacing the printed piece of paper (flight progress strip) with an electronic data display (EDD).

The electronic data display is a device similar to the synthetic radar viewing unit, although smaller in dimensions, upon which is displayed, in written electronic characters, the flight data contained in the computer, and which are required to be viewed by the controller. The data on the displays can be amended by the controller through an interface between his operating position and the computer and/or automatically by the computer itself, through its 'software' routines, which compare the 'static' (flight data) with the 'live' (radar data) data.

It is emphasised, however, that this use of EDDs to replace the computer-printed information is, at the time of writing, still in the evaluation stage.

Having specified the two main objectives of the application of automation, it is now intended to explain how this technique, when applied to the items specified earlier, begins to form the basis of an automated air traffic control system:

Aircraft type

The performances of modern aircraft, both civil and military, vary considerably in rate of climb/descent and cruising speeds. The types of aircraft under control can cover a range from, say, a light Cessna 172 to a supersonic Concorde, or from a Hercules air transport to a Tornado or Mirage-type fighter aircraft. In technical terms these various types of aircraft have what is known as differing 'flight profiles'. These flight profiles can be fed into the computer's data base and as a result the computer is able to recognise and associate the correct profile to the aircraft type specified on the aircraft's flight plan. Further the forecast wind direction and speeds which will occur throughout an aircraft's route of flight can also be added to the data base. This combination of information then enables the computer to work out the estimated times that it will take the concerned aircraft to fly on the various segments of its route, and relay this information to the controller and/or other ATC units concerned with the conduct of the flight.

When an aircraft is live – that is, airborne within the system – the weather data may be different from that forecast, or the profile being followed in practice by the aircraft may differ from the computed program. In this event the controller himself will, if required, update the computer with the 'live' situation and cause amendments to the displayed information to be made. In a system where flight data and radar data are being correlated this latter action may not be necessary, as the computer will recognise the difference between its static or flight data and automatically amend that data in accordance with the received 'live' radar data.

Aircraft callsign/SSR code

Each aircraft operating within an automated system is allocated its own discrete secondary surveillance radar (SSR) code. When a code is allocated to an individual aircraft the computer is also programmed with that same code, which it then relates to the other flight data relevant to the concerned aircraft. As, amongst, this data, is the callsign which has been allocated to it by the aircraft's operator, the computer can then convert the SSR code to the aircraft's actual callsign and then relay this information for display alongside the aircraft's response on the controller's viewing unit. In many parts of the world aircraft proceed from one sector to another, and also from one country to another. Therefore to avoid continuous updates of the computers within ATC units, which may be separated by many hundreds of miles, the SSR code allocated to an aircraft can, by arrangement, be used through the aircraft's entire flight. The various computers will recognise this code and relate it to the correct flight data, either as the aircraft enters the airspace of an adjacent sector/ATC centre, or when control of the aircraft is handed over from one authority to another. For example, if we take a flight from Vienna to London, where the flight can progress through Austrian, German, French and British airspace and/or the upper airspace centres of Maastricht and Karlsrhue, the same SSR code is used throughout the aircraft's entire flight and the computers at all of the air traffic control centres which control the flight as it progresses on its journey, will be alerted, either by manual input or upon radar data correlation recognition. This method is known

as the originating region code assignment method (ORCAM) and results from agreements within the regional organisations of the international Civil Aviation Organisation (ICAO). The objective of this method is to ease the load on the pilot of continuous changes of code, as he proceeds from the control of one authority to another, and to assist in the radar identity and transfer of control of the aircraft as it is handed over from one ATC authority to another.

Point of departure

It is probably an obvious statement to say that the point of departure is an important item of information, but in computer programming it means rather more than the fact that an aircraft is departing from a named airport. The computer will need to know the route structure the aircraft will follow immediately after departure, and this can vary with what direction of runway is used for take-off, and what airways sectors will be concerned, following the initial departure of the flight, from the terminal area. It will also need to be programmed with any special operating procedures which may apply in the departure phase of flight, and what flight data have to be passed on the aircraft's departure. It also needs information on when updates on this data need to be made, and to whom they should be addressed. From this information the computer is then able, in conjunction with the aircraft's profile and weather data already in its store, to compute the time at which the aircraft will be expected to arrive (ETA) over the various reporting points on its flight planned route.

Destination/route

The destination of an aircraft generally determines the route which it will follow, out of the terminal area within which its aerodrome of departure is situated, and also the airways and/or upper air routes it is intended should be followed during the course of its flight. These routes are complex, and whilst standard routeings are published between internal domestic and international destinations the access to these routes, and the use of alternatives, depends upon the live traffic situation which exists as the aircraft proceeds towards its destination. It is necessary therefore for the computer to be programmed with these standard routeings and their alternatives.

As stated at Chapter 6 ('Flight planning and flight data') a great majority of flights and their associated routeings are permanently stored within the computer memory, awaiting programmed activation, usually 20/30 minutes prior to an aircraft's estimated time of departure (ETD). Flight plans for aircraft which are not 'stored' require to be input to the computer and also be associated with the standard routeing relevant to the concerned flight.

Alterations which may be required to be made to these routeings by the controller for reasons of safety and/or expedition of air traffic will also be required to be known by the computer. Thus it is essential for the ATC organisation to have access to the computer for this and other control functions. A simple illustration would be, for example, where an aircraft is being diverted from its original point of intended landing. The computer will know of the intended alternative destinations but it will not know that the decision has been made by the captain/company/controller, to divert the aircraft. Therefore it must be informed of the new route to be followed and of the time this route is to be taken up by the pilot. It can then produce this revised information and relay it to all of those authorities which will now be concerned with the control of the aircraft's flight.

The structure of these air routes, allied to the internal air traffic control sectors within a state, and the adjacent ATC units of foreign states, vary considerably from one centre of aviation activity to another. Vienna differs from London; London differs from Manchester; Chicago differs from New York, etc. Therefore, in programming a computer it is not a simple matter of having a standard package; each location requires its own dedicated programme; the only constant factor is the basic information previously described.

Height, cruising level, ground speed

Information on the cruising height or flight level which the pilot of an aircraft considers optimum for his route of flight, and also the speed at which he wishes to operate the aircraft is made available to the controller from the computer's data base, and this enables him to endeavour to meet the requirements of the pilot, in regard to the optimum flight conditions for a particular type of aircraft. From the computed estimates for a given route, presented to him either in written form on a flight progress strip, or electronically on a data display, the controller is then able to assess the best method of achieving the desired intentions of a particular flight. Achieving this desirable objective does, of course, depend upon the amount of air traffic which is following the same route, and on the feasibility of applying separation standards described in Chapter 2 to enable this to be done in a safe manner. Inevitably there are a number of occasions where the flight planned requirements cannot be met; in this case once again the controller must instruct the computer of the changes to be made to the information which is in its memory.

To assist controllers in the task of assessing the feasibility of a 'clearance' to achieve an optimum solution, facilities do exist, at present in the experimental stage, for computers to predict the future intended flight path of an aircraft. For example, because the computer has been programmed with the profiles of aircraft and where additionally the flight data and radar data have been correlated, the computer can, on demand from the controller, cause a 'line' probe to appear on the display viewing unit, which extends forward from the response of the particular aircraft for, say, 20 nautical miles, thus enabling the controller to theoretically move his air traffic 'picture' forward in space and time.

Comment

In this chapter I have tried to describe the main elements which are concerned with the application of automation to air traffic control. Readers with a knowledge of these techniques will realise that there are a number of aspects of this operation which I have left out; for example, computers can be programmed not only to 'alert' the controller to probable conflict between aircraft but also offer to him solutions to 'resolve' such a possible conflict – also the knowledge of the air traffic contained within a computer's memory can be used to predict at what stage it would be prudent to 'regulate' the flow of traffic into a given airspace to avoid congestion and delay. The automatic 'hand-off' of aircraft, sector to sector, the interrogation of aircraft and the passing of messages air/ground without using radio telephony (Mode S), and the correlation with airborne collision-avoidance systems – these, and many more examples, lie in the realms of computers and automation either for present or future application.

It will, of course, be clear to readers, particularly from the paragraphs in this chapter on 'The display of radar-derived data', that the facilities available to the controller in an automated ATC system and the associated avionics equipment in the concerned aircraft, are already at a relatively high level of sophistication, and further that many of these facilities are already in use at ATC units throughout the world.

However, I wish to reiterate that the control of air traffic is a relatively complex art, and the application of computer technology equally so. The success of this application depends upon a detailed operational knowledge of the tasks a controller is required to perform in a specific location, and an understanding of the principle, that the computer is there to *assist* him in his task of the safe and orderly flow of air traffic, and must in no way go beyond the capability of the human being to retain control of decision-making.

Before concluding this chapter I should like to make the point that the application of computer techniques to radar data and flight data apply equally to the control of military aircraft. The content and programming may vary somewhat from those contained in this description, but the basic principles of assistance to the military controller in his task of the safe separation of aircraft remain the same.

9

The Air Traffic Control Environment

Introduction

Before proceeding to give an explanation of the control of the flight of a civil aircraft operating within an air traffic control system, I should like to try to convey something of the environment within which air traffic control operates. In the previous chapters I have explained the rules, the procedures and the technical equipment, which must all come together to form a foundation for the application of the art of the control of air traffic. Not all of the facilities described are of course necessary at all of the ATS units providing air traffic control services. These facilities can range from radio telephony and the telephone, at a small aerodrome operating within its aerodrome traffic zone, to the availability of instrument landing facilities, radar, computers and sophisticated communications and air traffic displays at the busier aerodromes and at air traffic control centres situated in a complex of airways and terminal areas/control zones. However, for the purpose of conveying an atmosphere, it is necessary for me to use as a background the latter situation. To do so I will proceed from aerodrome control to approach control and then to area control. It should also

be appreciated that the operating positions I describe will doubtless vary from one location to another. A further factor which I should mention at this stage is that in some states, and the United Kingdom is one, all aircraft which are operating within controlled airspace must do so in accordance with instrument flight rules. What this means is that, irrespective of the weather conditions which are being encountered by aircraft, they must receive and adhere to an air traffic control clearance, and the separations standards explained in Chapter 2 are applied even though there may be unlimited visibility and not a cloud in the sky. Before the knowledgeable take me up on this point, there is one exception, and that is 'special VFR' flights, where, under certain specified weather conditions, visual flight is permitted in controlled airspace. These flights are described by ICAO as 'a controlled VFR flight authorised by ATC to operate within a control zone under meteorological conditions below the visual meteorological conditions'. The authorisation of such a flight by ATC is dependent upon the traffic conditions which exist at that particular time, and a controller having issued a special VFR clearance is required to provide separation between that aircraft and all other special VFR flights in accordance with the minima prescribed by the appropriate ATS authority. Additionally he is required to provide separation between these flights and all other IFR flights in accordance with the separation minima as described in Chapter 2 ('Separation standards'). Other states do permit a mixture of VFR flights and IFR flights within certain of their controlled airspaces. Pilots flying in accordance with visual flight rules, however, are only permitted to do so in weather conditions which accord with laid-down standards of forward visibility and of distance/height from cloud. These weather conditions must, of course, be maintained to continue VFR flight. But what it does also mean is that under these conditions the responsibility for avoidance of collision rests with the pilot of the VFR aircraft. Where an air traffic unit does have a radar capability they can, and do, assist the pilots of IFR aircraft by passing information, known as 'radar advisories' on this VFR air traffic. A radar advisory is the passing of information usually in accordance with the 'clock code' in regard to the plan position of the target aircraft and details of its probable intended flight path, as observed from the radar display.

This subject of visual flying is one I shall return to in Chapter 11 on 'Airborne threat alert and collision-avoidance systems', but I have made reference to it at this stage, to add to the scenario that does exist in many parts of the world, and which affects the general atmosphere of operation particularly at a busy aerodrome/approach control facility.

That having been said, my following explanation, and the narrative on the control of the flight of a civil aircraft that follows, is set against the background of busy ATC units, located within a close-controlled ATC system: that is, where all aircraft in the system operate on an air traffic clearance irrespective of the weather conditions.

Aerodrome control

The modern aerodrome control room sits on the top of a concrete stalk, or on the top of a brick building, placed at as high an elevation as is permissible within the clearance angles of the aerodrome's runways. It is usually built entirely of non-reflective glass and the discerning airline passenger can often see disembodied heads constantly moving to and fro. Visitors are not normally welcome, for the very good reason that the room is surprisingly much smaller in area than one would imagine, and any unwanted physical presence not only adds to the congestion, but more importantly can obstruct the line of sight of the controller. Seeing, by eye, what is actually happening within the immediate environment of the aerodrome and on its surface is what this part of the ATC service is all about.

Usually at a busy aerodrome there would be two controllers: the air controller and the ground controller. From the division of duties between these two controllers which I described in Chapter 7 you will be aware that the *air controller* is responsible for aircraft which are flying in the vicinity of the aerodrome traffic zone and for aircraft taking off and landing. As he is the officer responsible for issuing the clearances to aircraft to take off and land, he must ensure visually that his runway is unobstructed before issuing such a clearance. In many locations this can involve a single runway for the use of both departures and arrivals, and therefore it is a fine judgement whether or not to permit a departure in between a sequence of arriving aircraft which are due to land on the same runway. He has to bear in mind not only that he has the correct spacing between the arriving and departing traffic but must also be aware of the route which the departing aircraft will be following immediately after take-off, and whether or not it is subject to wake turbulence in regard to its weight category, relative to the previous departing aircraft. To assist in this decision the human eye can be aided by the distance from touchdown indicator (DFTI). This is a cathode ray tube type of display which is clearly viewable in daylight conditions and upon which the distance from the end of the runway is indicated by the response of the arriving aircraft, being displayed as a symbol on the tube, relative to the extended centre-line of the runway in use. The centre-line is marked on the tube in distances from the runway threshold, and therefore the position of the aircraft's response will clearly indicate whether or not the controller has sufficient time in which to clear a departing aircraft from the runway, before the next arriving aircraft. To help him in this task the air controller will normally have the services of an air traffic control assistant, who will be receiving all details of the sequence of arriving aircraft from approach control, amending where necessary the flight plan information previously received, and in regard to departing aircraft, advising the parent air traffic control centre of the departure time, either by telephone or via a computer terminal.

As technology progresses in regard to the ability to view radar displays in daylight conditions, more and more visual control rooms will become equipped with surveillance radar displays, to assist the air controller in his observation of what the air situation is like in his immediate vicinity. Figure 25 shows such a display in use in the aerodrome control room of Austria's Vienna airport, and demonstrates the advance which has been made in this type of display in recent years. The display shown however in the photograph is a 'digitised' display, which is more easily adaptable to these conditions. Digitising means that the radar responses from aircraft, have been electronically processed, usually at the radar transmitter and receiver, and as a result of this processing the aircrafts targets are reproduced as symbols on the radar controller's display. There are certain problems in regard to their use in the close-in environment of an aerodrome, foremost amongst which is probably track 'jitter'. Track jitter is where the trail dots which appear behind an aircraft's position symbol to indicate its previous flight path history, move from side to side. This phenomenon can be disconcerting to controllers when they are radar-directing aircraft in the approach sequencing phase of flight. However, the advent of Monopulse SSR, which is described in Chapter 11, and the resultant improvement in tracking accuracy, which is clearly demonstrated in Figure 39, could materially affect the use of digitised displays in the aerodrome environment. It has to be remembered, however, as stated earlier, that this display cannot be used for radar control purposes by the air controller, unless a separate controller is provided to carry out this task or alternatively the air controller's other duties. Additionally, the air controller must ensure that all arriving traffic is aware of any pertinent essential aerodrome information and also initiate any emergency action should this be necessary.

The *ground movements controller* is, as his designation implies, responsible for all movements on the surface of the aerodrome. He has to liaise with the aerodrome management in regard to the position at the passenger terminal, which is vacant to receive an arriving aircraft; pass this information to the aircraft and similarly give permission for engine start-up and clearance to manoeuvre to the runway in use, in respect of departing aircraft. Like the air controller, it is essential for him to see as much as possible of the surface of the aerodrome, including its taxiways and exit points from the runway/s in use. To assist him he has usually the services of an air traffic control assistant, who will be receiving information on the flight plans of departing aircraft and liaising with area control, for the essential en-route air traffic clearance, which has to be issued to the aircraft once it has started its engines and is

FIGURE 25. A radar display in an aerodrome control room at Vienna airport This photograph shows a digitised radar display in use in Aerodrome Control at Vienna airport. It demonstrates the clarity of the display even in a relatively high level of illumination.
(Photograph Courtesy Plessey Displays Ltd)

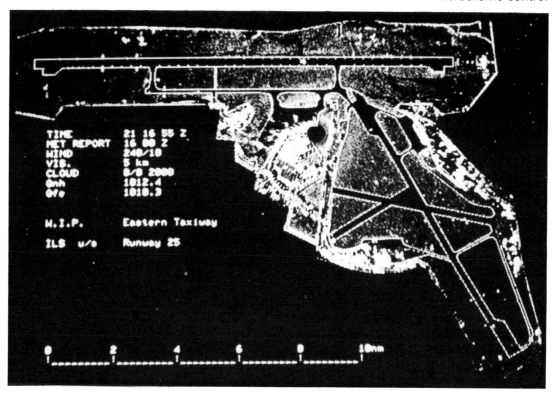

TIME   21 16 55 Z
MET REPORT   16 00 Z
WIND   240/10
VIS.   5 km
CLOUD   8/8 2000
Qnh   1012.4
Qfe   1010.3

W.I.P.   Eastern Taxiway

ILS u/s   Runway 25

FIGURE 26. The airport surface movements guidance indicator (ASMI) at Edinburgh airport. This is an actual photograph of an ASMI display which is installed at Scotland's Edinburgh airport. The runways and taxiways are clearly visible and demonstrate the value of the use of this equipment in conditions of poor forward visibility on the surface of aerodromes.

in the process of taxiing out. At night-time and in poor visibility the controller is responsible for setting up taxiway routeings for both departing and arriving aircraft. The taxiway routeings are usually in the form of green or white centre-line lights which are 'flush set' into the taxiways with, at intervals, a line of red stop-bar lights, which can be used in much the same way as road traffic lights. The pilot, after clearing the runways, then follows these lights which provide him with an obstruction-free route to or from the passenger terminal/s. At the busier airports, that have complex taxi routes and multiple terminals, it is usual to have in the aerodrome control room a lighting panel operator, whose task is to select from a miniaturised display of the aerodrome's surface lighting, the surface routeings designated by the ground controller. Figure 27 shows the lighting panel operator at London's Heathrow airport. In these days of automatic landings, where aircraft can and do land in conditions where forward visibility is insufficient to permit the pilot to taxi by human vision alone, it is also desirable to provide the ground controller with facilities which enable him not only to see for himself the position of the aircraft on the surface of the aerodrome but also be able to assist the pilot in clearing the runway and thereafter further assist him in taxiing to his appointed parking position. This facility is known as 'airport surface movement indicator' (ASMI). Internationally there are various other acronyms, and ICAO has yet to pronounce definitively upon their use, particularly in regard to the relationship between the controller and the pilot, in these circumstances where the responsibility for the safe navigation of the aircraft on the aerodrome's surface could pass from the pilot to the controller. Therefore it is politic at the present time to refer to this equipment in general terms, as 'surface movement guidance equipment', the emphasis being on the word 'guidance' which still leaves the pilot with the responsibility for the safe navigaton of his aircraft. The most popular of these items of equipment is radar-based with an antenna which rotates at very high revolutions and transmits energy on a very high frequency, with the result that vehicles and aircraft which are moving on the surface of the aerodrome are clearly visible to the ground movements controller on his radar display. So efficient are these devices that at London's Heathrow Airport, which has an underground tunnel to the central area, it is even possible to detect motor vehicles passing to and fro in this tunnel. Figure 26, which has been reproduced with the kind permission of Racal Avionics Ltd, shows the latest in this generation of surface movement guidance systems. It is located at Scotland's Edinburgh airport, and clearly displays the runway layout and the associated taxiways. So sensitive is this equipment that it is capable of detecting all moving and stationary vehicles on the airport surface ranging from B747 aircraft to a small car head-on, in all weather conditions, including fog, mist, heavy rain, wet snow and blowing sand; and can even detect a person at 2 kilometres, walking, kneeling or crawling on the runways or taxiways.

In regard to the environment within aerodrome control the popular image of a control tower, with loudspeakers squawking out messages in staccato language, is rare. In most units the controllers wear headsets with boom microphones for use both on the R/T and on the telephone. When their 'walkabout' for visual purposes permit, they are provided with desks into which are mounted the R/T and telephone select panels, electronic data displays (EDD) showing essential aerodrome information and other pertinent details and, at a growing number of locations, computer terminals. Finally, because aircraft are still subject to the vagaries of the wind speed and its direction, no tower would be complete without an indicator displaying both of these parameters. Figure 28 is a view of the aerodrome control room at London's Heathrow airport, which clearly indicates the visual nature of the room and shows the air and ground movements controllers and their support staffs wearing headsets.

Approach control

We now move to approach control which, whilst it does not of necessity need to be physically associated with aerodrome control, can usually be found situated in the control tower building on the floor immediately below the aerodrome control room. There is indeed a growing philosophy for the approach control services to be provided by the parent area control unit, and a strong case can be made for this, but for the purpose of this explanation I will deal with the classic situation of approach control co-located in the same building as aerodrome control.

From the explanation of the duties and responsibilities of approach control which I gave in Chapter 7, you will be aware of the fact that, in providing these services, they do not require to have visual reference to either the aircraft or the aerodrome. Therefore, because approach control employs radar extensively in its operations the approach room is usually, to the casual observer, poorly lit. However, a more intimate scrutiny of the surroundings will reveal that those areas which require illumination have individual lighting of adequate candle-power, which is carefully directed to ensure

FIGURE 27.   Aerodrome control—lighting panel operator (London Heathrow) This picture shows the lighting panel operator at London's Heathrow airport, setting up a taxiway route structure for an aircraft to follow at night-time. The route is based upon the instructions which the operator has overheard, which had been issued by the ground movements controller to the concerned aircraft.

(Photo Courtesy UK/CAA)

that the source of the light is not reflected in the controller's radar displays. In recent years considerable advance has been made in the capability of radar displays to enable them to be viewable, in relatively high ambient lighting levels, so that the modern approach room is indeed well lit, compared with the Stygian gloom of its predecessors.

I shall be mentioning in greater detail in the next chapter that an approach control of a busy airport can be handling as many as five stacks of arriving aircraft, which have been transferred to it by the parent area control centre. Where such a busy situation exists it would be standard practice to have at least four radar director positions, two of these positions being responsible for sequencing the aircraft from the stacks and the other two positions being responsible for the 'fine tuning', which ensures that the flight-paths are neatly sequenced, with the objective of spacing the aircraft onto the final approach path to the runway, with the minimum radar separation spacing of 3–4 nautical miles between succeeding aircraft. In this equation the radar directors have to take into consideration the weight cat-

FIGURE 28.   A view of aerodrome control (London Heathrow) A view of the visual control room at London's Heathrow airport showing the air controller at the left of the picture.

(Photo courtesy UK/CAA)

egories of the aircraft in the sequence and the effects of turbulent wake created by the heavy (Jumbo) type aircraft. Therefore, if you look up into the night sky and see a more than usual gap between the 'string of pearls' formed by the landing lights of aircraft which are approaching to land, it is highly probable that the gap has been deliberately created to 'delay' the turbulent wake of the heavy aircraft, with due regard to the following smaller type of air transport.

The radar directors who carry out this task are seated in front of their radar displays, upon which is shown the geographical positions of the aerodrome's holding stacks and etched onto the displays is the extended centre-line of the runways in use, which, of course, is their target point. The economic use of runways plays a vital role in the management of aerodromes and the radar director's skill in maintaining a steady flow of arriving traffic onto the runway/s is paramount in this regard. I intend therefore to explain this sequencing operation in more detail in the next chapter. Each group of radar directors is also supported by an approach controller, who has a flight progress board display of the flight data on arriving aircraft and who is in contact with area control in regard to the actual order of arrival of the aircraft in each of the holding stacks. Supporting each of these approach controllers is an air traffic control assistant, who will be dealing with incoming and outgoing telephone calls, preparing flight progress strip information, informing aerodrome control of the actual sequence of arriving aircraft and, where applicable, operating the computer terminal which is linked to the parent area control centre. Each position is equipped with telephone and radio telephony select panels and at these operating positions engaged in exchanges with aircraft over the R/T, the controllers will be wearing headsets similar to those of their colleagues in aerodrome control. Figure 29 is an overall view of the approach control room at London's Heathrow Airport, showing in the foreground the four radar director positions which are supported on either side by the approach controller and air traffic control assistant positions.

Because of the varied duties which are the responsibility of an aerodrome/approach control ATS unit, it is usual also to have a senior controller or supervisor in charge of both units. He is normally positioned at a special desk in the approach control room, at which there will be a monitor radar display from which he can observe the general air traffic pattern con-

FIGURE 29. A view of approach control (London Heathrow). A view of the Approach Control Room at London's Heathrow airport, showing the four Radar Directors sitting in front of their Radar Display. Seated either end of the Radar Displays are the two Approach Controllers, who are using a flight progress strip display to indicate the position of arriving aircraft in the holding stacks. Immediately above these positions can be seen the television cameras which are relaying information to the Air Traffic Control Centre.

(Photo Courtesy of UK/CAA)

FIGURE 30. A terminal area sector suite. This picture shows a Terminal Area Sector Suite, where the airspace has been divided into an East/West split and where each subdivision has an Arrivals Controller and a Departure Controller

cerned with his area of responsibility. From this display, and from an appraisal of the landing and departure rates being achieved, he is able to assess whether or not the flow of arriving and/or departure traffic requires to be restricted, to avoid either an overload on the radar directors or unnecessary wastage of fuel by aircraft waiting on the taxiways for departure clearances. This regulation of traffic to try to avoid unnecessary congestion, particularly in the peak hours, is a continuing process and is carried out in co-operation with the supervisor at the present area control centres. There are detailed 'flow control' procedures which are designed to try to prevent an overload on the ATC system but the vagaries of weather and

delayed schedules of aircraft, often caused in other parts of the world, can conspire to defeat these well-laid procedures. Therefore the supervisor must at all times be alert to the air situation as it develops at any moment in time. The foregoing is, of course, but one illustration of the duties of the supervisor; he is in summary the officer who is responsible to the senior air traffic control officer in charge of the unit, for the efficient operational discharge of the responsibilities and objectives of aerodrome control and approach control which are detailed at Chapter 7.

However, within the context of the description I am endeavouring to convey, approach control is not alone. It has an umbilical cord attached to the area control centre. It is from area control that it receives its arriving aircraft, it is to area control that it hands over its departing aircraft, and it is area control who can assist by absorbing the delays to arriving aircraft and by regulating the flow of departing aircraft.

Area control

As you will recall from the reading of Chapter 7, the home of area control is called an air traffic control centre and, as I said in that chapter, its location is not necessarily that of an aerodrome. In many instances, presumably because aerodrome land is invariably expensive, the locations can be many nautical miles away. In many ways this physical divorce from the scene of aviation means that their activities are often little understood by those directly engaged in the profession of aviation, and I venture to suggest that many airline pilots know them only by their R/T callsigns. This observation is in no way intended as a criticism of those engaged in the aviation profession, but is made simply to underline the fact that it is more difficult to visualise the operational concept of area control than is the case with aerodrome control and approach control, where the control tower building, situated on an aerodrome, clearly proclaims the reason for its existence.

Most ATC systems, of which area control is an integral part, rely heavily upon the use of radar to achieve the objective of the safe, orderly and expeditious flow of air traffic. Therefore, when entering the operations room of one of these air traffic control centres, the ambient lighting level will appear lower than is customary in buildings used for general commerce or in business premises. However, as with approach control, those areas which need a higher level of illumination have individual lighting to an approved standard. It is a strange phenomenon that whilst present radar displays can accept a reasonably high level of background illumination without detracting from their clarity, and whilst most modern air traffic control centres are above ground and have windows to the outside world, the majority of control staffs prefer not to have the background illumination too high, and invariably draw the blinds over the window areas.

The second impression of the operations room is that whilst there can be up to at least 100 R/T frequencies in operational use, and countless telephone conversations in progress, and also the presence in the operations room of 100-plus personnel, the prevailing atmosphere is one of relative calm. This generation of a relatively relaxed atmosphere, in an environment of intense activity, is by no means accidental. It is the product of discipline in training, the attention to detail in the planning of operational responsibilities to ensure that physical movement about the operations room is restricted to the minimum, and the sensible positioning and provision of the technical facilities which are essential to the controllers in the discharge of their tasks.

From the reading of Chapter 7 you will be aware of the wide ranging responsibilities of area control, and of the large area of airspace to be covered. Therefore for ease of operation the network of airways, air routes and terminal areas, for which area control is responsible, is divided into a number of sectors. Each sector is responsible for the air traffic which is flying within its defined limits. Where a terminal area forms part of a sector, and at busy locations, the terminal can itself form a sector; this responsibility extends to the control of air traffic which is arriving at or departing from aerodromes sited within the terminal. Figure 30 shows a terminal area sector suite, where the airspace has been divided into an east/west split and where each sector of the airspace is provided with a terminal area arrivals controller and a terminal area departure controller. The controller in charge of the overall operations of the sector suite can be seen standing at the right of the picture, wearing a headset and overseeing the general air traffic situation. Complex procedures exist in regard to the transfer of responsibility for the handover of aircraft from sector to sector, or from sector to and from aerodromes. These procedures are in accordance with the responsibilities which are outlined in Chapter 7, and which I intend to illustrate in Chapter 10, when I describe the flight of a civil aircraft.

A busy area control centre would have in operation about 8 or 10 suites of sectors, each suite being composed of two or more airways sectors. The main feature of a sector is the radar console, which usually houses a radar display of approximately 16 inches or 22 inches in diameter, sited in either a vertical or horizontal position. Grouped around the display are the controls which enable the controller to select the particular radar he is required to use for his sector; also the range in nautical miles he is required to view; the off-centring of the origin of the radar site, to enable him to use the full diameter of his display; the selection of a variety of video map information, such as an outline map of the airways in his sector and symbols representing aerodromes and navigational aids (see Figure 16). Additionally, adjacent to the radar display is an SSR code select panel. This device will enable the controller to select those SSR codes which the aircraft within his sector are required to use. Also in this area is the radio telephony frequency select panel. Each sector has an R/T frequency specifically allocated for its use, but as sectors may from time to time be allocated differing functions, or even carry out the duties of an adjacent sector under light traffic conditions, it is essential for the controller to have available R/T frequencies additional to that normally in use. On the flat area in front of the console there are normally two additional panels; one is a digital telephone keyboard which gives the controller access to other operational positions within the operations room and to other area control centres and aerodromes. These telephones are, wherever possible, direct controller to controller, but when this is not the case the keyboard can be used to access the national and international exchanges. The other keyboard, in an increasing number of area control centres, is the interface with the computer and, dependent upon the level of sophistication of the ATC system in use, it will be used by the radar controller or the controller assisting him, to update the flight data in the computer or to carry out a variety of tasks such as automatic handover to another sector varying the type of information on the aircraft's 'label', or the selection of presentation of additional radar data, or even information on aircraft in an adjacent sector (see Chapter 8, 'Automation'). Figure 31 shows a radar console in the vertical position, showing the controls grouped around the console. The digital map display shows the Manchester terminal area and the airways and air routes leading up to the Scottish area and over the Irish sea.

To the side of the radar console, or immediately in front of, but not obscuring, the screen is a display of flight progress strips. The purpose of these strips is fundamental to the planning of the sector's operation, the detailed reasons for which I explained in Chapter 6 ('Flight planning and flight data').

Above the radar console, usually housed in a canopy, positioned so that it is easily viewable, are illuminated screens which display a variety of information. Some of these displays use closed-circuit television to display the weather and altimeter pressures, and additionally in the case of terminal area sectors, the latest state of the aircraft in the holding stacks; whilst others are used for the display of static information such as geographical maps of the sector's area of responsibility, the serviceability state of navigational aids and aerodromes relevant to the sector, and any special information such as air displays, military exercises, etc.

FIGURE 31. Close-up view of a vertical radar display (Manchester sub-centre). This close-up view of a Radar Controller's position conveys an impression of the environment within which he operates. In a vertical position is his radar display on which can be seen the aircraft's targets with their SSR identity and height alongside. The video map shows the Manchester Terminal Area and the airways linking the London area to the South, the Scottish area to the North and Northern Ireland to the West. The telephone, R/T and Display functions keyboards are grouped around the console and to the left of the picture can be seen the flight progress strip display.

(Photograph Courtesy Plessey Radar Ltd)

This then is the area radar controller's 'cock pit', in front of which he sits wearing a headset similar to his colleagues situated at the aerodromes. As the controller has to hear and speak on both R/T and telephone circuits, to assist him in his task the headset receives R/T speech in one ear and telephone speech in the other. Mounted on the headset is a light-weight microphone which incorporates a noise-cancelling device, and which is used for the R/T, by depressing a key on the desk-mounted R/T panel and for telephone speech, by selection of a circuit on the digital telephone keyboard. Intercommunication is also possible between controllers using the same microphone but without activating any of the other circuits.

I referred earlier to the atmosphere of relative calm which exists within the operations room and in this regard the headset I have just described plays a major role, for in a busy centre there can be up to 100 operational positions, all engaged in an unseen and unheard continuous vocal dialogue. Therefore in terms of modern technology, although it is a relatively simple device, its contribution towards efficient operation is nonetheless quite remarkable. Seated alongside the controller is an air traffic control assistant, whose task is to assist the controller in his administrative functions by receiving and initiating telephone calls, regarding estimates on aircraft entering or leaving the sector; accepting, from the computer print-out terminals, flight progress strips relevant to the sector, and sequencing them on the controller's flight progress board display. At some sectors the assistant is also provided with a computer terminal, either in the form of a keyboard or a touch-wire display, with which he/she can update the computer data base with information regarding revised estimating or re-routeing of aircraft.

The sector I have described normally forms part of a sector suite, which comprises two or more sectors, Figure 32 shows a typical sector suite layout at the United Kingdom's London air traffic control centre. From an appraisal of the photograph it will be observed that a third person is sitting in between the two controllers seated at their horizontal radar displays. This is the senior controller responsible for the operations of all of the activities which are taking place on the suite of sectors. He is required to oversee the entire operation and to take whatever action he deems necessary to assist in the flow of traffic on the sectors. This usually takes the form of liaising with the chief controllers on other adjacent sector suites in regard to any problems which may have arisen, or to forestall one arising, and additionally to watch carefully the traffic loading on his sectors so that he can take timely action with the supervisor of the watch to restrict the flow of traffic, if jointly they conclude that an overload situation could arise.

Whilst I shall be dealing with the co-ordination of civil and military air traffic in later chapters it will be noticed that to the left of Figure 32 is a military controller. He is also part of the sector team on this particular sector and is there specifically to deal with co-ordinating the activities of military aircraft. How he accomplishes this task will be explained in detail in Chapter 14.

Sitting with a view of the entire activities in the operations room is the watch supervisor. As his name implies, he is the officer responsible for the overall supervision of all of the air traffic services provided by the air traffic control centre. He is the man to whom all of the minute-to-minute problems which cannot be solved by sector chiefs are passed. He must decide what to do if any facilities upon which the centre is dependent fail, and what action to take to maintain a steady flow of air traffic through the centre's area of responsibility, and to initiate and co-ordinate action with the distress and diversion and safety services, should occasion so demand. To do so he must have a general appreciation of the operational situation which pertains throughout all sectors, and

FIGURE 32. A typical airways sector suite layout (London ATCC) This photograph shows an airways sector suite at the London Air Traffic Control Centre where the Radar Controllers are at present using horizontal radar displays. In a future re-organisation they will operate in a different layout where vertical displays will be employed. To the left of the picture can be seen a military controller who is part of the team and whose specific task is to facilitate the movement of military aircraft across this busy airways sector.

(Photograph Courtesy of Plessey Radar Ltd)

117

also be aware of the general air traffic picture which exists in surrounding territories, including adjacent foreign area control centres. His operating position is a nerve centre of communications and data displays, and to assist him in the discharge of these duties he would normally be supported at a busy centre by a deputy watch supervisor and two air traffic control assistants. Figure 33 is a view of the operations room of the United Kingdom's London air traffic control centre. It is taken from the supervisor's position, who you will see sitting in the foreground, and I trust this photograph will convey some of the atmosphere of bustling, yet ordered, activity which I have been endeavouring to convey in this chapter.

Before leaving this description there are two other positions in the operations room whose functions I should mention. The first of these is the 'flight plan reception position', which is discernible immediately in front of the watch supervisor. This is the position which receives information on all of the flight plans which are not stored in the computers memory (see Chapter 8, 'Automation') and is provided with keyboards to enable the information to be input to the computer in accordance with a standard format. Further down the operations room is the flow control and departure flow regulator position, at which intelligence is received from the computer regarding the amount of air traffic which is bound for the centre's area of operation and the forward estimated times and routeings of the concerned aircraft. Liaison with the chief sector controllers in respect of the current state of traffic flow on the sectors, including that of traffic departing from terminal aerodromes, enables the officer in charge of this position to assess whether or not it would be prudent to advise the watch supervisor that the control of the traffic flow on certain routes or sectors or from terminal area aerodromes may be desirable. It is from this position that 'departure flow regulation' will be exercised, a subject which I referred to briefly

in the earlier description of approach control. In Europe, as in the United States, it is planned that this position will link up with a 'central European flow control facility', whose task will be to assess the air traffic situation over a given geographical area, including adjacent states, and as a result try to regulate the overall traffic pattern with the objective of endeavouring to eliminate bottlenecks of traffic by, if necessary, the re-routeing of aircraft onto under-utilised routes. However, the subject of traffic regulation affects not only the scheduling of aircraft but also the future design of air traffic control systems on an international basis, and is a matter upon which there are on-going discussions through the machinery of ICAO. In fact the above very brief description results from one of the initial recommendations of this international body, and doubtless much debate lies ahead to try to resolve a problem which can cause airlines unnecessary expense and the air traveller frustrating delay.

In this regard it is possible for readers to visualise something of the problem facing these flow control positions. If we consider for example the air traffic which is daily bound from Europe for the North American continent. These aircraft depart from airports as far apart as Athens, Rome, Vienna, Frankfurt, Copenhagen, Amsterdam, Brussels, Paris and London. All of them from these varying departure points are bound for the track structure on the North Atlantic. All aircraft are of a similar type, and therefore wish to operate at similar flight levels at similar speeds and on the most optimum track. This is compounded by the fact that the airline operators all wish their aircraft to arrive at their destinations in North America at socially acceptable hours. Also all of these operators are commercially independent and wish to publish schedule services at times which are attractive to their customers, the airline passengers. Due to the geographical position of the United Kingdom these aircraft

FIGURE 33.   A view of the operations room at the London ATCC. This view of the Operations Room of the London Air Traffic Control Centre, taken from the Supervisor's position conveys something of the atmosphere of a busy Area Control Unit. The Airways Sectors are grouped down either side of the room and in the foreground is the flight plan reception position and immediately beyond that the Flow Control and Departure Flow Regulator position.

(Photograph Courtesy Plessey Radar Ltd)

must pass over the U.K. airspace, usually the crowded London terminal area, on their routes to the North Atlantic. From the nearer departure points, such as Paris, Brussels and Amsterdam, the concerned aircraft are often still climbing to their cruising levels as they transit this airspace and in doing so require to pass through the flight levels of the climbing and descending international air traffic which is proceeding to and from the European capitals. This is but one cause of the problem of the regulation of air traffic, but does, I think give some idea of the magnitude of the task. The subject is thought-provoking, and understandably because of the commercial interests which are involved, sometimes somewhat emotional. The International Civil Aviation Organisation, through its regional organisations, has done a great deal of groundwork but many hard tasks lie ahead if we are to provide a workable and equitable system of the regulation of air traffic acceptable to all air users.

It is, however, one of the functions of area control to try to expedite air traffic, if, as a pilot or air traveller, delay is unfortunately encountered, it might be as well to recall that the controllers concerned must always apply the first of their written rules: 'safety'. It may mean, in its application, delay, but 'tis better to arrive!

Before leaving this chapter I wish to reiterate a point I made earlier; that is that air traffic control systems, facilities and procedures are in a continuing process of development and therefore the atmosphere which I have endeavoured to convey, which many readers will recognise relates to the London air traffic control centre, is already undergoing change, both in its methods of operation and its technical facilities. To illustrate this point I have included at Figure 34 a photograph of a layout of an airways sector as it will appear in the new Vienna area control centre in Austria. As you will see the fully digitised radar display is in the vertical position, and whilst to the right of

the picture can be seen a display of flight progress strips, also partially visible to the immediate right of the radar controller is an electronic data display (EDD) which carries details of current flight data, and which is linked to the computer's flight data base. It is the intention that electronic data displays will gradually supersede the paper flight progress strips, which can then be held in an abbreviated support role in the event of any system failure. The role of the controller sitting to the right of the radar controller, also changes, in that he becomes a support or planning controller, carrying out all internal and external coordinations, amending the data display, interfacing with the computer and generally planning the operation of the sector. This method of operation then leaves the radar controller free to carry out executive or control instructions. For those interested in terminology it is referred to variously as the P and E concept (planning and executive) or the E and S concept (executive and support). What this change emphasises, however, is the progress from an ATC system which was originally a 'procedural system', that is, a system based exclusively upon the standards of separation as described in Chapter 2 (excluding radar separation) thence to a system where radar was used to assist a procedural system, and now to a system which is radar-based but where the procedural system is still retained as a fall-back capability. This statement does not mean that radar separation standards only are used; they are in fact only applied where to do so would expedite the movement of air traffic; but what it does mean is that increasingly the ATC systems require that aircraft using these systems must be co-operating; that is, they must be equipped with SSR transponders, thus enabling the computer to carry out its role of automation, as explained in Chapter 8. There are exceptions which cover the situation in respect of aircraft which are flying outside the area of primary and secondary radar cover of the concerned ATS unit,

FIGURE 34. A view of the operations room at the Vienna ATCC. This photograph shows the Operations Room of the new Austrian Air Traffic Control Centre, located in Vienna. It will employ the very latest automated technology and is scheduled to commence operation in the mid 1980s.

(Photo Courtesy Plessey Radar Ltd)

FIGURE 35. A view of a digitised radar display showing the use of a 'light-pen' (Vienna ATCC). This photograph shows one of the latest in the range of radar displays in use at the Vienna Air Traffic Control Centre. The Radar Controller is using a 'light-pen' as the interface between his display and the computer functions. The alternative to the 'light-pen' is the 'rolling-ball' and the use of either device is purely a matter of choice by the commissioning authorities.

(Photograph Courtesy Plessey Displays Ltd)

but in regard to busy airways/air routes the world is increasingly moving towards total radar cover for these areas.

Finally, there is an aspect of the environment of aerodrome control, approach control and area control which I have been unable to cover, and one which deserves a book of its own. What I have described in regard to these locations is the atmosphere and the physical sights which a visitor would experience. What I have not been able to describe is the vast technical organisation and highly qualified staffs who operate, unseen to public gaze, but who are responsible for the efficiency of the end-product upon which the controllers, and the aircraft which are their responsibility, de-

pend. Their world is as fascinating as the one I have tried to describe, and their skills an integral part of the successful operation of ATC systems. To demonstrate something of this world of high technology, Figure 36 shows the central computer complex of a modern flight data processing and radar data processing system.

I now intend to proceed to Chapter 10, in which I propose to describe the flight of a civil aircraft, and which will incorporate as many of the principles as possible, which I have described in the previous chapters. Later in the book, in Chapter 15, which follows the chapters dealing with civil/military co-ordination, I intend to provide a similar description of

FIGURE 36. A view of a central computer complex. This photograph is a view of a modern central computer complex and portrays the clinical efficiency of the technology which lies behind the controller and his operating displays.

(Photograph Courtesy Plessey Displays Ltd)

the air traffic control operations associated with the flight of a military aircraft. The two descriptions will, as far as is possible, be complementary, and I hope that when they are read in conjunction with the rest of the book, these two examples will convey, the practical application of the control of civil and military air traffic.

10

Detailed Description of the Control of the Flight of a Civil Aircraft

Introduction

In the earlier chapters I have explained the rules, the procedures and the technical facilities which are required to provide an air traffic service. In doing so I have emphasised that the level of facilities available to the controller depends to a large degree upon the amount and complexity of air traffic for which he is required to provide a service. However, for me to be able to describe as many as possible of the air traffic services and the technical support facilities, it is essential for me to use as a background a busy location. I have therefore chosen for this purpose the United Kingdom's London (Heathrow) International Airport, including its surrounding terminal area and airways route network. For international readers I apologise for the use of this particular geographical location, but it is an area with which I am familiar and therefore should enable me to provide a reasonably accurate account of a somewhat complex operation. However, whilst certain of the procedures which I shall describe

may vary at other geographical locations, the basic principles remain the same, and subject to minor procedural differences, the examples which follow reflect how air traffic is controlled on a world-wide basis, in a similar type of environment.

To enable me to provide a detailed description of the ATC operations I propose to take you through, in narrative form, the following phases of the aircraft's flight.

Departure – London to Manchester

(1) Pre-flight planning.
(2) Departure clearance – (aerodrome control – ground movements controller).
(3) Runway departure – (aerodrome control – air controller).
(4) Terminal area transit – (area control – terminal area controller).
(5) En-Route airway flight – (area control – airways sector controller).
(6) Manchester terminal area – (Manchester

sub-centre terminal area/approach controller).

(7) Manchester airport arrival – (Manchester air controller and Manchester ground movements controller).

Arrival – Paris to London (Heathrow)

(1) Pre-notification of aircraft's flight – (Area control – Paris and London airways sector controllers).

(2) En-Route airways flight – (Area control – the Paris/London inbound sector airways controller).

(3) Terminal area – (area control – terminal area controller).

(4) Approach phase – (approach control No. 1 and No. 2 radar directors).

(5) Aerodrome arrival – (aerodrome control – air controller) (aerodrome control – ground movements controller).

Note:– Reference to Figure 22 (Chapter 7) demonstrates the ATC functions associated with these phases of an aircraft's flight.

In the previous chapter, 'The air traffic control environment', I tried to convey something of the atmosphere which pertains in the locations which will be concerned with the phases of the aircraft's flight which I shall describe. Therefore it is my hope that this present chapter, when read in conjunction with its predecessor, will bring together in an understandable form, the various elements, previously described, which are essential to the art of the control of air traffic.

Also as this book is concerned with the control of military and civil air traffic, I propose, following the next chapters which deal specifically with the problems of civil/military co-ordination, to provide a detailed description of the air traffic control operations concerned with the flight of a military aircraft. The geographical location of this flight will also be the United Kingdom and I propose to link it to the description of the London – Manchester flight, described later, as one method of demonstrating the co-ordination of civil and military air traffic.

Finally I would ask readers to bear in mind that whilst the situation described, and the facilities and procedures employed, are correct at the time of writing, the application of new technologies and the requirements of increasing traffic may well alter the methodology of the events described. Also for the sake of the clarity of the narrative, only the main principles of the ATC operations are described. There are many detailed operating and co-ordination procedures specific to each ATS unit and to individual operating positions within that unit, but their inclusion would be confusing without adding to an understanding of the events described. I make the point, however, for my more learned readers, who will be aware of the multitude of unit supplementary instructions which, as their name implies, supplement the national instructions (*Manual of Air Traffic Control*) that exist to cater for the specific requirements of particular ATS units and/or for specific operating positions within those units.

The flight plan

All aircraft which are either required by law or who wish voluntarily to participate in the United Kingdom's national air traffic service are required to obtain, in advance, a clearance to do so. This prior notification normally takes the form of the filing of a 'flight plan'. The flight plan is a statement of the pilot's intentions and contains such information as the type of aircraft, its callsign, speed performance, destination and the height and route he wishes to follow. The flight plan is usually filed at the pilot's aerodrome of departure but provision is also made for filing 'in-flight' for aircraft who wish to enter the ATC system whilst airborne from destinations which may not be served directly by the system.

Many airline operators do, of course, fly regularly over the same route, and to prevent continuous paper repetition of this data, information on these flights are permanently stored in computer memories. Similarly, to assist in the extraction and presentation of this flight data to air traffic control, computer techniques as described in Chapter 6, are now used to carry out many of these tasks which were previously discharged on a manual basis. The use of flight plans and associated computer techniques is somewhat complex and subject to considerable variation from one locality to another. To try to illustrate the workings of the ATC system in a reasonably simplified manner it is therefore proposed, as stated in the Introduction, to describe a flight departing from Heathrow bound for Manchester and a flight arriving at Heathrow that originated in Paris. In both of these examples computer technology plays a vital role, and I hope to demonstrate how aviation authorities endeavour to provide their ATC services with the latest in modern methods to assist in the discharge of their functions.

Heathrow departure

For a departure of a scheduled airline operator from Heathrow to Manchester a copy of the flight plan will have been stored in the computer memory and that memory will have been programmed to activate the flight plan approximately 40 minutes before the estimated time of departure, which had previously been inserted on the flight plan, to concur with the operator's published timetable. The computer is housed at the London air traffic control centre, West Drayton, and the manner in which it reacts to this memory activation is to print out flight progress strips at each sector through which the aircraft will fly on its route to Manchester, including one for the ground movements controller in the tower at Heathrow Airport, where a 'tail-off' from the parent computer is positioned. These flight progress strips provide the controllers with the basic data they need to plan the movements of air traffic prior to the application of radar techniques. The information printed on them by the computer enables the controller to see at a glance the identity of the aircraft, its departure point and destination, the height at which the aircraft would like to cruise, and the speed at which it will be flown.

When the passengers are aboard the aircraft and it is ready to move out from the terminal buildings the pilot initiates a radio telephony call to the ground movement controller in the tower. The ground movement controller, who has already been alerted to the pending aircraft movement by the computer, issues to the pilot taxiing instructions in regard to the route to be followed to the runway in use and also the secondary radar code (SSR) which the pilot is required to select to establish his identity when airborne. Whilst the aircraft is in the process of taxiing the controller obtains from the terminal departure controller, who is situated at the London centre, a clearance for the aircraft to depart in accordance with the pilot's flight-planned request.

At an aerodrome such as Heathrow, which has a very high movement rate, there are detailed variables to this procedure which are arranged to prevent an aircraft starting its engines too early, or to regulate the traffic where delays in the system may require flow control to be imposed. Also the procedure for requesting an individual clearance from the terminal area departure controller can be dispensed with, which permits aircraft to free-flow on the appropriate standard instrument departure (SID). This procedure is based upon the premise that the terminal area radar controllers can accept all of the departures which the aerodromes can generate. Resort to individual requests for departure clearances, then only occur if there is any reason to anticipate any overload either upon the terminal area sectors or the airways sectors which they serve. The individual request for a departure clearance has, however, been described to demonstrate the link between the aerodrome and the area control centre. The clearance when issued will contain instructions to the pilot stating the route he has to take out of the terminal area, the navigational aids to follow and the height at which to cross them; also when he can commence climb to his cruising flight level and the airways to proceed along on his flight to Manchester. Within the London area these clearances are standardised and are known as standard instrument departure clearances (SIDs). They are published in documents available to pilots and alleviate the need for lengthy R/T messages. These SIDs also contain any noise-abatement procedures which may be conditional to the use of a particular runway. On arrival at the holding point for the particular runway which is in use for departing traffic, control of the aircraft will be transferred from the ground movement controller to the air controller. The air controller is in charge of the 'live' runway and it is his task to instruct the aircraft when to enter the runway for take-off. This instruction will depend upon a variety of factors such as, for example, the route which is being followed by the aircraft which immediately preceded the departure. The fundamental basis of the air traffic control system is that aircraft are separated one from another either by height, by time or by geographical position. The intervals between aircraft departing from the runway are therefore an essential element of the controller's plan to achieve separation between this particular departure and any other aircraft which may be flying on the same route or flying through the terminal area.

When the aircraft has been given instructions to take off control is transferred when the aircraft is airborne to the London air traffic control centre.

The London air traffic control centre is responsible for the control of the London terminal area and the airways and upper air route network that links London with internal centres of population such as Birmingham, Manchester, Glasgow, etc., and with its adjacent foreign neighbours Holland, Belgium, France, the Channel Islands, Eire, Denmark, and the North Atlantic, which serves the routes for aircraft bound for North America. The organisation of the London centre is extremely complex but in simple terms the airspace for which it is responsible is divided into a number of sectors with a team of controllers responsible for the control of aircraft within the sector, which is their direct concern. The terminal area is divided into two sectors, one north and one south, and it is to the departure controller of the northern terminal area that control of the aircraft will be transferred by the air controller at Heathrow.

Prior, however, to the transfer of control of the aircraft the Heathrow R/T frequency on which the instruction to take off was issued will have been monitored by an air traffic control assistant at the London centre and the information on the aircraft's movement is recorded on a screen placed in front of a television camera. A closed-circuit television display of this information is positioned adjacent to the terminal departure controller, who is thus alerted to the fact that the aircraft in respect of which he had previously received from the computer a warning flight progress strip, has departed Heathrow and is about to enter his sector. At the same time as the aircraft is airborne, the actual time of departure is entered into the computer from a keyboard adjacent to the Heathrow air controller's position. This input message activates the computer to produce new flight progress strips for the terminal area north sector and the Daventry sector through which the aircraft will fly on its route to Manchester. The computer having been previously programmed with the aircraft's profile, i.e. its climb/descent/cruise, speeds and the distances to be flown between the reporting points; also the wind direction and speed at varying levels, it can therefore quite readily calculate and print, at the two sectors, flight progress strips giving the estimated time at which the aircraft should arrive at these various points. Additionally as the Manchester sub-centre which is responsible for the Manchester terminal area is linked to the London computer, a flight progress strip is automatically printed at that unit giving the flight details and an estimated time of arrival for the aircraft at Manchester airport.

The control of traffic at the London centre is based upon the extensive use of radar, and once again by the use of computer technology, the secondary radar code which was earlier allocated to the aircraft by Heathrow is correlated with the flight plan information, with the result that when the aircraft's response appears on the terminal departure controller's display the call-sign of the aircraft appears alongside the radar response. Additionally, as the majority of aircraft also carry what is known as a Mode C transponder, the height at which the aircraft is flying is also shown in conjunction with the callsign.

The task of the departure radar controller – once he has identified the aircraft and the pilot has completed the 'minimum noise route' element of his standard instrument departure – is to start the aircraft on its climb to its cruising level, using, if necessary, radar separation standards to resolve any problems which he may have in regard to other arriving, transitting or departing traffic. To ease the task of the departure controller in regard to co-ordination with other sectors concerned with the airspace there is an internal procedure which permits him to climb the aircraft to an arbitrary level of 120 without reference to other sectors. Prior, however, to reaching this flight level, or alternatively when the aircraft is approaching the sector for which the Daventry sector controller is responsible, co-ordination is carried out, and when this

has been done the aircraft is instructed to change its R/T frequency to that of the Daventry sector and told to contact London centre on that frequency. There is a further sophistication of this procedure, termed 'silent handover', where prior co-ordination is only necessary if the aircraft is required to depart from the standard track and/or flight level.

On receipt of the R/T call the Daventry sector controller continues the climb of the aircraft to its cruising level, once again using radar separation standards if necessary to solve any conflicts which may occur in respct of any other traffic which he may have in his sector. It is also possible by this time to check the computer predictions on the lapsed time between reporting points, and if these deviate by 3 minutes or more the estimates for the rest of the flight are revised and a new expected time of arrival is passed to Manchester.

Because of the volume of military aircraft who wish to cross the main airway (Amber Airway One) for which this sector is responsible, a military controller is positioned at the same sector suite. This arrangement permits any essential co-ordination procedures to be carried out in the immediate operational environment.

Prior to the arrival of the flight at the boundary of the Manchester terminal area, co-ordination takes place on a direct telephone circuit between the Daventry sector controller and the Manchester terminal area controller, in regard to any descent instructions which may be dependent upon the traffic situation at Manchester. If the traffic is running normally and there are no delays due to poor weather conditions or other arriving traffic, the descent will be commenced and the aircraft instructed to call the Manchester controller on a specified R/T frequency.

Manchester arrival

The Manchester terminal area controller has a radar display similar to that used by the

Daventry sector, and the aircraft will be visible to him showing its callsign and height as it descends into his area. He will also have displayed in front of him the flight progress strips generated by the computer which have been updated by any revised estimates. It is the responsibility of the Manchester terminal area controller to continue the descent of the aircraft until it comes within the jurisdiction of the Manchester approach controller.

Approach control for Manchester airport are situated within the Manchester sub-centre and it is their task to sequence the arriving traffic which have been handed over to them by the terminal area, onto the extended centre-line of the runway in use at a distance and height which will enable pilots of aircraft to establish themselves on the instrument landing system. Therefore the control of the aircraft will pass during the course of its descent to the approach controller who will pass the necessary headings, descent and speed instructions which will enable the aircraft to close the centre-line at approximately 8–9 nautical miles at a height of 2000 feet and separated longitudinally from any preceding or succeeding aircraft. For ease of operation, approach control for not only Manchester but also for nearby Liverpool airport, is carried out by the Manchester sub-centre and is an example of a point I made earlier in the book (The provision of air traffic services – approach control, Chapter 7) that the approach function can be discharged by an area control TMA unit, and also that the approach controls for more than one aerodrome can be carried out as a combined function. When the aircraft has been given the final heading by the approach controller the pilot will be instructed to contact the Manchester airport air controller for final landing instructions.

The Manchester air controller is in charge of the runway and will already be aware of the expected arrival time, having previously received a copy of the flight progress strip information generated by the computer, and as a result of co-ordination between himself and the approach controller. When the aircraft has landed, control is then transferred to the Manchester ground movements controller who is responsible for issuing to the pilot instructions in regard to the terminal building arrival bay he is to use and how to taxi his aircraft to get there. Finally, the landing time of the aircraft is recorded and that particular flight plan is thus ended, but, of course, if it is a stored flight plan it will remain in the computer's bulk-store for use on the next scheduled flight.

Paris departure

An aircraft which is departing from Paris for London will have gone through the same flight planning process as described for a London departure. The French air traffic control centre which is at present located at Orly airport, Paris, employs computer techniques for its flight data in much the same manner as described in this chapter and in Chapter 6, and a tail-off from the French computer is located in the operations room at the London air traffic control centre. At the present time the Paris and London computers do not use the same language and therefore in computer terms they cannot 'talk' to each other. However, future developments in regard to a common language and formats will doubtless resolve this problem.

The air traffic control system, known generally as the 'airways system' and the procedures applied are compatible throughout Europe and therefore the movement of an aircraft from France to the United Kingdom differs little from the internal movement previously described. The departure of the aircraft from either Orly or Charles de Gaulle airport will follow a procedure similar to that for London, and when airborne the aircraft will be transferred to the control of the Paris centre. At the same time as the aircraft is airborne the Paris computer will originate a flight plan message which will be received in teleprinter form at the London centre. This message is then fed into the London computer which originates a warning flight progress strip for the Dover/ Lydd sector and for approach control at Heathrow airport. Thus both the London centre and the airport are made aware of the pending arrival, well in advance of its penetration into the United Kingdom airspace. The Dover/Lydd sector is the sector located at the London air traffic control centre which is responsible for the control of aircraft which are inbound to the United Kingdom from the Paris area. This responsibility includes air traffic which has over flown the Paris control zone in addition to those aircraft which have departed from aerodromes within that zone. For ease of understanding however, I shall hereon in this narrative refer to the sector as the 'London sector'.

The task of the Paris sector controller is similar to that previously described for the London departure, i.e. to climb the aircraft as expeditiously as possible to its desired cruising level within the constraints of other air traffic, and to apply the separations essential to provide for the safety of the flight.

As the aircraft progresses through the French airspace a positive check will be obtained on the aircraft's position in relation to its flight-planned estimates, and from this information the controller on the Paris – London sector is able to calculate a positive estimate for the aircraft's arrival within the area of responsibility of the sector controller at the London centre. This estimate, which is usually related to a navigational facility, is then passed verbally on a direct telephone circuit from Paris to London. On receipt, this information is fed into the computer which is programmed to produce flight progress strips for each of the reporting points which the aircraft is required to follow within the London airspace, including a strip for London airport giving an expected time of arrival. These strips then replace the 'warning' strips which had been issued on the initial Paris computer information.

Approximately 10 minutes before the expected time of arrival within the London sector, the Paris controller contacts the London sector controller on a direct speech circuit to co-ordinate the transfer of control of the aircraft. This co-ordination is necessary to ensure that the essential separation will exist in respect of any other traffic at the time of its arrival in the London sector controller's airspace. This co-ordination could require the Paris controller to alter the level of the aircraft or to delay its arrival for a specified time. It would be unusual for him to be required to do so but the one objective of co-ordination is to ensure that the control of an aircraft is not transferred unless and until it is safe for it to proceed. In practice this procedure is simplified by Letters of Agreement between the Paris and London centres but the cardinal principles still apply.

When transfer of control has been agreed the London sector controller identifies the aircraft on his radar display from the callsign which appears alongside the aircraft's response. This automatic identification is made possible due to the fact that the allocation of SSR codes throughout the major part of the European area has been co-ordinated to prevent the necessity of a change of code from one country to another. Thus the London computer is able to relate the code the aircraft is using to the flight plan data within its memory and thereby convert this code into the aircraft's callsign for display purposes.

It is the task of the London sector controller to instruct the aircraft on the route it is to follow into the London terminal area and to commence its descent from cruising level, initially to flight level 130, dependent of course upon the levels of any preceding traffic. You will recall that in the explanation of the London departure the departure terminal area controller could climb his aircraft to an arbitrary level of 120. Thus until co-ordination takes place, vertical separation exists between the arriving and the departing traffic.

Having started the aircraft on its descent, the London sector controller is then required to co-ordinate with the terminal area arrival controller the lowest level within the terminal area to which the aircraft can proceed. The arrival controller, who is already aware of the pending arrival having received in advance a copy of the flight progress strip, has to take into consideration a number of factors when determining the level to which the aircraft can be initially cleared.

The ideal objective is to continue the descent of the aircraft and so route it that on a radar handover to the airport approach controller it can be directed without interruption onto the extended centre-line of the runway in use. There are, however, a number of factors which prevent this situation occurring, such as conflicting traffic bound for other destinations, or more traffic arriving at Heathrow than can be accommodated without holding the aircraft clear of the arrival and departure paths awaiting a turn to land. To assist the arrival controller in his decision he has available to him at his operating position a closed-circuit television picture which provides him with a view of the traffic display board at Heathrow, and which shows the levels that are occupied at the holding facilities serving the airport.

Under these circumstances the standard practice would be to arrange with the airways sector to instruct the aircraft to descend to the lowest level then available in the holding stack and to specify this geographical position as the clearance limit, i.e. a point beyond which the aircraft must not proceed without permission.

When this instruction has been given by the London sector controller to the aircraft, and it is approaching the terminal area and is clear of any conflicting traffic, control is then transferred to the arrival controller. The arrival controller, who operates two 'stacks' for aircraft which are bound for Heathrow from the southern routes, will have previously agreed with Heathrow approach control a specific level at which control can be transferred from the centre to the airport. There are seven holding stacks operating in the London terminal area, five of which serve Heathrow airport, and this arrangement is arrived at to prevent an overload on the approach control facility. If the traffic demand is very heavy and delay in the holding pattern is likely to exceed 20 minutes, the arrival controller will issue to the aircraft an expected approach time – that is, a time based upon the sustained landing interval at which the pilot can expect to receive instructions to commence an approach to land.

When the aircraft has been descended in the stack to the agreed level at and below which approach control assume jurisdiction the aircraft is instructed to contact London approach control on a specified R/T frequency.

London (Heathrow) arrival

Heathrow approach control has a radar capability of sufficient coverage in range and height to provide a service throughout its area of responsibility and one of the major tasks of this radar is to enable the controllers to sequence the arriving aircraft into an orderly and expeditious landing stream. Before proceeding further with the Paris inbound flight it is proposed to explain the philosophy of 'holding stacks' and what is meant by the term 'radar sequencing'.

Radar sequencing of arriving traffic

When more traffic is in the ATC system and bound for an aerodrome where its interval of arrival is less than the separations essential to ensure the safe arrival of aircraft on the runway, i.e. the 'demand' exceeds the runway capacity -- it is essential to 'hold' this excess traffic at 'holding points' or 'stacks'.

These 'stacks' are usually positioned in such a manner that aircraft entering them at the lowest available level (in the London terminal area the minimum level in the stacks is the flight level equivalent of 7000 feet) could carry out a continuous descent approach to intercept a standard 3° glide path at approximately 8 or 9 nm out on the extended centre-line of the runway in use. When the first aircraft is held in the stack succeeding aircraft are separated vertically from each other at 1000 feet intervals. Where more than one holding stack is in use, as is the case with Heathrow, which has five, each stack is geographically separated to ensure that aircraft which are holding at the same level but in different stacks are separated laterally from one another.

Aircraft which are in the holding pattern normally carry out a 1 minute race-track pattern from/to the navigational facility. To this race-track pattern are applied criteria laid down by ICAO, which take into consideration the 'worst-case' flight path, and it is these criteria which enclose the pattern laterally and from which any adjacent pattern or any by-passing air traffic must have separation. For sequencing the traffic off the stacks and onto the runway centre-line the standard practice is for the radar director to instruct the aircraft at the lowest level in the stack to leave on a specified heading and to commence descent to an initial height which will later be lowered, so that on arrival at the glide path intercept the height attained will enable the aircraft to intercept the glide path from below and allow the automatic flight system to 'lock-on'. During the course of the descent further headings will be given by the director to enable the aircraft to close the runway extended centre-line at a distance usually between 8 and 9 nautical miles which will give the pilot time to settle his aircraft onto final approach.

The exact point at which the aircraft is given a heading to intercept the glide path will, however, depend upon the relative position of other aircraft in the sequence of traffic and also the exact height at which the aircraft carries out the interception may be dependent upon environmental considerations.

During the course of the descent the radar director will also be using 'speed control' to ensure the aircraft's profile is compatible with an approach to land.

At the time the first aircraft is instructed to leave the stack on a radar heading, the approach controller will instruct the second aircraft in the stack to descend to the vacant level and on the pilot's report that he has vacated his present level all other aircraft holding in the stack are similarly 'laddered' down. Figure 37 shows diagrammatically how aircraft are 'stacked' at 1000 feet intervals over a navigation facility and then laddered down in sequence, as the lower levels are vacated.

The radar director, having set the first aircraft on its course to the runway, then turns his attention to the second aircraft which is now descending to the lowest level in the stack. At an optimum position designed to prevent the aircraft from commencing an unnecessary orbit of the pattern the radar director will issue instructions to the pilot to leave the pattern and commence his descent.

The art of the issue of headings from the stacks and the control instructions thereafter, is to close the aircraft up to a 3 to 4 nautical mile spacing and thus ensure the maximum utilisation of the runway in use. As has been stated, Heathrow has five stacks serving the airport one of which is used for traffic bound for Stansted airport, and when each of them are containing holding traffic it is a complex art to arrange the aircraft in line astern with the correct spacing of 3 to 4 nautical miles, particularly as the positioning of the stacks is not equidistant. To do this radar-directing task, Heathrow has four directors – two looking after the three stacks to the north and two for the two stacks to the south. The number 'one' director carries out the task of issuing the initial heading upon which to leave the stack and the number 'two' director does the 'fine-tuning' to achieve the separation from other aircraft in the sequence, including the final turn on to intercept the glide-path. In

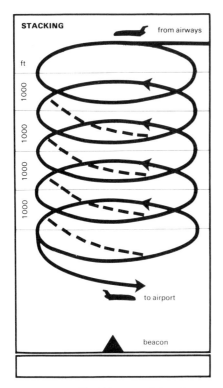

STACKING   from airways

ft

1000

1000

1000

1000

to airport

beacon

FIGURE 37.   Diagram of aircraft
in a stacking configuration

practice, it is of course, not always possible to achieve 3 to 4 nautical miles spacing because with a mix of heavy and light aircraft it is necessary to allow additional spacing due to the turbulent wake effect of the heavy aircraft. In the worst of these cases the spacing may have to be extended to as much as 8 nautical miles.

If we assume, therefore, that the aircraft from Paris has gone through this procedure and is now established on the ILS for an approach to land, transfer of control will take place at this point to the air controller. The air controller will have been notified in advance of details of the arriving traffic and their sequence in the arriving stream. The air controller is positioned in the tower or visual control room and has responsibility for the runway in use, and it is he who will issue to the aircraft its 'clearance to

land'. This final clearance is essential because a single runway can often be in use for departures as well as arrivals, and in any event the clearance cannot be issued until the air controller is confident the runway will be clear of all obstructions at the moment of touchdown.

During the course of the landing roll the aircraft will be instructed at what turn-off point to leave the runway and, having done so, control will be transferred to the ground movement controller who is positioned in the tower adjacent to the air controller's position. It is the task of the ground movement controller to issue to the aircraft the stand number he is to occupy outside the passenger terminal building and pass instructions on the route to be followed to that position. The stand allocation is the responsibility of apron control who have a continuous liaison with ground movements to ensure the most efficient utilisation of the very busy stand areas.

To assist the ground controller in poor visibility conditions, he has available to him a radar display called an airport surface movement indicator (ASMI) which is capable of detecting objects such as vehicles and aircraft which are moving on the surface of the airport. He also has a lighting operator who sets up the complex taxiway lighting which is needed for guidance during the hours of darkness. On arrival at the apron area, that is the area adjacent to the stand at which the aircraft will park, control of the aircraft ceases as far as air traffic control is concerned, and as the landing time has already been recorded the flight plan is finished as far as that particular aircraft movement is concerned.

Comment

In summary the foregoing examples of the air traffic control operations describe an 'air traffic control system'. To implement such a system requires controlled and/or special rules airspace to regulate the traffic and within which the rules of the air can be applied. The airspace requires to be delineated by navigational aids to enable pilots of aircraft to navigate within that airspace. To apply the standards of separation to ensure the safety of aircraft flying within this airspace requires the presence of licensed controllers qualified in the particular air traffic control service relevant to that airspace. To enable the controllers to discharge these tasks they require to be provided with advance information on a pilot's intentions, either in the form of a flight plan or a transfer-of-control message. Also they require technical facilities such as radio telephony and telephone circuits. Further, in the majority of systems, primary and secondary radar and the support of computer technology are essential to their efficient operation, and at aerodromes which are handling instrument flight rule traffic there should exist an instrument landing facility or a radar capable of carrying out a precision approach or a surveillance radar approach. Additionally, at those aerodromes where aircraft are permitted to operate in poor visibility it is advisable to provide the controller with a surface movement guidance system to assist the pilot in navigating on the surface of the aerodrome.

In conclusion I trust that this chapter, when read in conjunction with its predecessors, will have conveyed a mind picture of the art of controlling air traffic and of the organisation, technical facilities and personnel dedicated to the safety of all who fly for pleasure or reward in the air. The picture which I have tried to convey is related to the present aviation world, but as I have repeatedly remarked, technological advance, both in the air and on the ground, still progress at a remarkably rapid pace. Therefore before proceeding to deal with the problems associated with the co-ordination of civil and military air traffic, I am including a chapter (Chapter 11) on airborne threat alert and collision-avoidance systems. This chapter lifts the veil on the future, and as yet unresolved, developments on the aviation scene, and as some of these developments will doubtless impact upon air traffic control systems I considered they should be discussed in this book, even though at this stage I, and a great number of other people, are unable to be positive about their application or effect.

11

Airborne Threat Alert and Collision-avoidance Systems Including SSR Mode 'S' and Monopulse SSR

Introduction

Whilst the primary means of collision-avoidance within a controlled environment must continue to remain the responsibility of the ATC system, the carriage of threat alert and collision avoidance systems, and their use by aircraft, will undoubtedly have an effect upon ATC operating techniques, procedures and phraseologies. Therefore in looking towards the future it is desirable for me not only to acknowledge their existence but also to explain what the systems are and what they are supposed to do. The descriptions will of necessity be superficial for two main reasons:

(1) ICAO are still at present debating the procedures which are to be used in regard to these systems and also whether or not to approve the use of Mode 'S' on the same channel, since potential interference can

exist if a common SSR channel is used, and

(2) The systems themselves have only just reached the stage where an agreed technical specification can be issued for their manufacture.

Time, will, of course, invalidate both of the above statements, but such is the penalty of writing a semi-technical publication. However, I hope readers will agree with me that historical knowledge has its place, even in this world of rapid technological developments, and I therefore consider it desirable to devote a chapter to a subject which will doubtless affect world-wide ATC systems, rather than ignore it because it has yet to reach a final development stage. Because the equipment used in the systems is relatively technically complex and still subject to development, and also because concerned aviation authorities have still to agree to the transmissions which the system will generate, the descriptions I shall give will be in relatively simple terms. There are, in any event, many learned papers and publications which could be obtained by readers who desire more detailed explanations, but our concern in relation to the control of air traffic is not so much in regard to how they work but why they are necessary and what their impact will be in relation to ATC systems.

Before describing the systems themselves it would I think, be of advantage to provide a glossary of the terms which are generally in use, they are:

SSR Mode 'S'	This is a term adopted by ICAO, which in the interests of common international understanding is uniformly used when referring to SSR improvements, encompassing the characteristics of the discrete addressing of aircraft and data link functions between the air and the ground.
ADSEL	Selective address.
DABS	Discrete address beacon system.
BCAS	Beacon collision-avoidance system.
A-BCAS	Active beacon collision-avoidance system.
F-BCAS	Full beacon collision-avoidance system.
TCAS I ⎫ TCAS II ⎭	Threat alert and collision-avoidance systems.
AIRCAS	Air-derived SSR collision-avoidance system (included in RTCA Doc184 as TCAS I equivalent).

Not all of the above terms are at present in use, but for any reader who researches the subject more deeply they all occur, often just as acronyms, without explanation. A further point which I should make for non-U.S.A. readers, is that the term 'beacon' refers to an aircraft's SSR transponder (see Chapter 5, 'Radar'). It also might help in an understanding of the various terms for me to outline the situation as it is at this present time. The initial intention of airborne collision-avoidance systems was to link the airborne systems with the ground-based ATC systems. This has proved to be difficult to achieve both procedurally and technically, and therefore the proposal that has been adopted by the 'front-runner' the U.S.A. Federal Aviation Authority, is for a system which provides a 'threat alert' to the pilot of an aircraft, which is intended to assist him to discharge his existing responsibilities to avoid collision with other aircraft, and in some systems the ability to compute the best 'pilot' action to avoid an airborne detected collision. Hence the term *threat alert* and *collision-avoidance system*', (TCAS) instead of the term previously used, 'collision-avoidance system' (CAS). Therefore the present situation in the U.S.A. would appear to be that an airborne collision-avoidance system is intended to be as independent of the ground ATC organisation as is technically feasible so as to serve as an independent 'back-up' to the personnel and equipments of the ground system.

I shall be adding my 'comments' at the end of this chapter but wish at this stage to make the point that, whilst the foregoing is my interpretation of the U.S.A.'s objectives, it is an interpretation with which other contracting states of ICAO, who have automated ATC systems, may not necessarily be in agreement. In particular the 'back-up' role to the ground ATC system, its necessity, and how it could operate in practice, will doubtless be a subject of considerable debate.

The explanations that follow, therefore, refer to threat alert and collision-avoidance systems and whilst the general term 'TCAS' has been adopted as a self-explanatory acronym for these systems, I shall also give a brief description of a system with the acronym 'AIRCAS'.

Both TCAS and AIRCAS use the same SSR signals emitted by SSR airborne transponders and to avoid confusion at this stage AIRCAS although based upon ICAO SSR technology, does in fact comply with the principles of the systems which are now proposed for adoption. I therefore intend to explain the basic principles of:

(1) TCAS I
(2) TCAS II
(3) AIRCAS I
(4) AIRCAS II.

However, I ask readers to bear in mind that the technical specification for the international use of threat alert and collision-avoidance systems has, at the time of writing, still to be issued by ICAO. Only when this consultative process has been completed and pronouncement made, can this equipment be used for international pur poses outside the territory of a particular state. Also, following the promulgation of this internationally agreed specification, any of the world's avionics manufacturers can produce and offer for sale these items of equipment, provided they conform to the criteria as laid down in the specification. The U.S.A. quasi Government body RTCA has in fact issued a document approved by its Executive Committee (DO 184) for TCAS I.

The present concept, however, envisages two separate but compatible systems one for the smaller aircraft, such as light executive and privately owned aircraft (general aviation), and the other more complex system for airline users.

Later in this chapter I am also taking the opportunity to provide a brief description of SSR Mode 'S' and monopulse SSR. I am doing so because, if airborne collision systems are to be co-ordinated or even integrated with the ground ATC systems, a method of communi-

cation air/ground/air will be required other than the present method of radio telephony. Mode 'S' is one potential method of providing this facility and as it improves SSR, monopulse is also essential for efficient Mode 'S' operation. Appropriately these two developments in avionics will be described at the end of the chapter and I will now proceed to describe the airborne systems detailed above.

TCAS I

TCAS I is a basic system intended for use by small aircraft. The equipment in the aircraft consists of a Mode 'S' transponder with an encoding altimeter and an interrogation unit. It has a minimal display in the cockpit, possibly either a buzzer or a flashing light, to alert the pilot to the proximity of another aircraft. The alert is activated either by:

(1) Any aircraft only equipped with a conventional SSR transponder or
(2) Any number of TCAS I or TCAS II aircraft that exist in the vicinity of the aircraft.

To prevent unwanted alerts an altitude filter is incorporated into the TCAS I equipment, and thus only conflictions at or near the altitude of the concerned aircraft will activate the alert. Since TCAS I must decode the threats provided by the Mode 'C' altitude data, the pilot's display can contain an 'above'/'below' indication and also the number of hundreds of feet, which is a most useful aid to the pilot in his visual search. However, if the conflicting aircraft is equipped only with a conventional transponder, with no altitude encoder, the TCAS I equipped aircraft can still receive an alert, irrespective of the difference in altitude.

The objective of the alert is to enable the pilot to make a visual scan from the cockpit and thereafter determine whether or not evasive action is necessary. To assist the pilot in this process an option to the basic RTCA system is proposed incorporating a cockpit display which would show the approximate bearing and altitude separation of similarly equipped aircraft. However, since this bearing data could more than double the costs, RTCA does not require it in the basic use of TCAS I. Additionally, to ensure that TCAS can operate without dependence upon ground based ATC systems, and outside areas of radar cover, both TCAS I and the larger airline version TCAS II, are to be so designed that they can automatically transmit a brief interrogation message one to the other. Such active transmissions must be on the same channel as the ground SSR stations, and as a result can provide the identity of the aircraft and its range and altitude.

TCAS II

TCAS II is a more sophisticated and complex version of TCAS I and is intended for use primarily by airline operators. It incorporates a cockpit display and involves the use of a micro-processor to assist in the evaluation of a threat alert. For example, when there is a potential conflict between two or more similarly equipped aircraft each evaluates the threat and determines the optimum avoidance manoeuvres. The first of the equipped aircraft to reach a decision automatically transmits its intentions to the other similarly equipped aircraft, thus enabling the latter to be aware of the course of action which is proposed. Also if a TCAS I equipped aircraft is in the vicinity of a TCAS II equipped aircraft, the latter can determine the separation distance, the bearing and the altitude separation between the two aircraft, and can then transmit these data to the TCAS I equipped aircraft. This information passed to the TCAS I aircraft is 'advisory' giving details of the TCAS II aircraft's range, altitude and approximate angle but no command instruction is issued.

In this version of a proposed system for threat alert and collision-avoidance, the escape manoeuvre which is presented to a pilot on his cockpit display is limited to 'fly-up' or 'fly-down', i.e. climb or descend. However, at the time of writing, an 'Enhanced TCAS II' is proposed which involves the fitting to the aircraft of a directional aerial. I shall be describing the Litchford AIRCAS System in the next paragraph, but in regard to direction finding it is interesting to note that AIRCAS II accomplishes the same bearing angle data with possibly greater accuracy than the directional antennas at present being evaluated in the TCAS II system. Also, because AIRCAS does not require a hole to be cut into the hull of an airliner to enable an antenna to be installed, the overall cost should be considerably less than that of TCAS II with a directional aerial of comparable accuracy. Either solution should, however, provide for more accurate intruder bearing data, not only for providing a reduction in unnecessary alerts, but also for generating intelligence on horizontal man-oeuvres, i.e. turn left/turn right. It should also make possible a more easily assessable cockpit display of the surrounding air traffic for the pilot.

Figure 38, which has been reprinted with permission from the September 1981 *Air Line Pilot,* the magazine of the U.S. Air Line Pilots Association, depicts one of the possible interrogation procedures between TCAS I and TCAS II equipped aircraft.

AIRCAS

Introduction

I am including a description of 'AIRCAS' for it introduces a different technological approach to threat alert and collision-avoidance systems. As a system it appears to meet all of the criteria as presently understood by me, and underlines the point I made earlier in this chapter, that whilst states/ICAO lay down the technical specifications, it is then a matter for private industry to provide the equipment and for the customer to decide which manufacturer is to be its supplier.

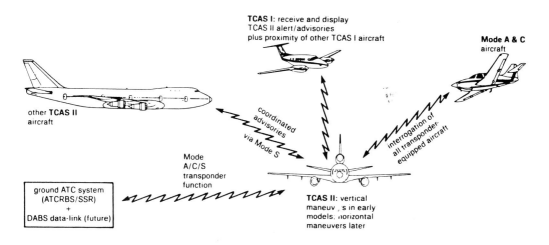

TCAS I: receive and display
TCAS II alert/advisories
plus proximity of other TCAS I aircraft

Mode A & C
aircraft

other **TCAS II**
aircraft

coordinated
advisories
via Mode S

interrogation of
all transponder-
equipped aircraft

Mode
A/C/S
transponder
function

ground ATC system
(ATCRBS/SSR)
+
DABS data-link (future)

TCAS II: vertical
maneuv , s in early
models; horizontal
maneuvers later

FIGURE 38.   Threat alert and collision-avoidance systems (TCAS) interrogation procedure
(Diagram Courtesy of 'Air Line Pilot')

AIRCAS is the invention of Mr. George B. Litchford of New York, U.S.A., and I am indebted to him for permitting me to include my version of this ingenious and flight proven system. I have, of necessity, had to abbreviate highly complex technical data and I trust that in doing so I have not departed too far from his principles of operation.

Although both can have 'Controlled/Active' modes, AIRCAS I and AIRCAS II are fundamentally passive 'threat alert' TCAS I and TCAS II systems relying on SSR interrogation signals generated by ground stations (such as TMA and en-route radars) and the consequent altitude and identity transmitted by other aircraft transponders. In fact, the universality of these aircraft transmissions has been determined by the U.S.A. as the only viable means to implement TCAS.

Although AIRCAS I and AIRCAS II units would be fitted in the aircraft in addition to the conventional airborne SSR transponders, it is very probable that because of the similarity in system techniques, later versions of AIRCAS systems could be combined with SSR transponders into a single composite unit.

AIRCAS I is a low-cost system intended for the general aviation (GA) market and provides the pilot with an indication (on a simple cockpit-mounted panel) of the range and differential altitude of the threatening aircraft together with that aircraft's identity.

AIRCAS II is a sophisticated system intended for the commercial aviation and military market, and provides the pilot with information on a cockpit-mounted colour CRT (in a similar presentation to a radar display) of the range, direction, altitude and identity of all aircraft in the vicinity, together with the predicted track and point of conflict of any threatening aircraft.

Outline System Description

AIRCAS I

The standard side lobe suppression receiver of an airborne SSR transponder is designed to detect only the signals transmitted in the main beam of the SSR ground station. This main beam would be 3° to 6° wide, which is equivalent to $1\frac{1}{2}$ to 3 nautical miles at 30 nautical miles from the radar head. A similar type of receiver is fitted to AIRCAS I, but being much more sensitive, will also detect the normally unwanted interrogation signals transmitted in the side lobes of the SSR ground antenna. The effect on the AIRCAS I aircraft is, that it is now able to 'listen in' to a ground radar's SSR interrogations of all aircraft, within approximately 20 beamwidths on either side of its 'own' beam from the SSR. This vastly increases the listening area surrounding the AIRCAS I, and means that all possible collision threats are detected. Assuming a sector of a normal interrogation beam to be 3° to 6° wide, then the sector that AIRCAS I can detect is about 30 times this single beam coverage, or about 90° to 120° wide. At a range from an SSR station of only 5 nautical miles, this represents a protected area 20 nautical miles across with the AIRCAS I always in the centre (no matter what path AIRCAS flies). Although side lobes get weaker and the angular sector gets narrower at a range of say, 30 nautical miles from the radar, the AIRCAS I listening area is still about 20 nautical miles wide.

It is the narrow interrogation pattern of an SSR that allows AIRCAS I to receive transmissions of altitude and identity from other aircraft outside of its own beam. Consequently, the AIRCAS I does not garble these transmissions when it replies only at the instant the beam is pointing towards it. If the 'threat' is in so close as to be in the same beam as AIRCAS I, 'sliding window' effect still allows AIRCAS I to detect the threat's presence, altitude, identity, and to establish its 'pseudo' range. At 60 nautical miles

the protected area is still 20 nautical miles even though the side lobes have diminished in strength. The side lobes near the main lobe and the scattering next to the main lobe (reflections from hangars, power lines, aircraft, towers, etc.) are also strongest next to the beam, so though the angle is less, the linear dimensions of the AIRCAS I protection area are the same. This is expected to be true, even at 100 nautical miles from a long range SSR and which is a more powerful SSR ground station with strong side lobes.

Aircraft fitted with AIRCAS I units will therefore monitor simultaneously, interrogation signals from the ground station and the resultant SSR responses from 'other' aircraft up to 15 nautical miles away. By relating the 'other' aircraft responses to particular ground interrogations and measuring the time delay known as time of arrival (TOA), simple mathematics will determine the approximate or 'pseudo' ranges (but not the azimuth positions) of other aircraft nearby. The differential altitude between the AIRCAS I aircraft and the 'other' aircraft may also be determined from the Mode C (altitude) responses contained in the SSR message. By setting appropriate gates and thresholds to specific ranges and altitudes, only those aircraft likely to pose a threat will be indicated on the pilot's AIRCAS I control panel. This is achieved by using extra sensitive receivers enabling the true threat to have an extremely high probability of detection without garble, thus eliminating what pilots dislike most, continuous false alarms. The result is that only the 'true' threat, and its identity and altitude, is displayed to the AIRCAS I pilot.

AIRCAS II

AIRCAS II receives the normal SSR interrogation signals when the narrow rotating beam centred on the radar ground station points at the aircraft's antenna. The several (20 to 40) interrogation pulses received during one pass of the ground radar antenna are routed to the AIR-CAS II processor. The processor determines the rotation speed of the ground radar normally between 6 and 15 rpm and also generates a continuous series of pulses exactly simulating the pulse repetition frequency (p.r.f.) of the ground-station. The simulated p.r.f. is synchronised, checked and updated at each pass of the ground radar signal, which is normally every 4 to 10 seconds depending on the turning rate of the radar installation, and the process is also repeated on up to 4 other ground stations.

AIRCAS II monitors the SSR responses from all other aircraft and is able, by referring to the simulated interrogation pulses generated in its processor, to determine exactly to which ground interrogation pulse and separate radar the SSR reply received from any 'other' aircraft is related. The processor measures the total time taken (a) for interrogation signals to leave the ground station and arrive at the 'other' aircraft, and (b) for the response from the 'other' aircraft to arrive at its 'own' aircraft. This total time is limited to values of less than 200 milliseconds to avoid 'non-threats' and is known as 'time of arrival' (TOA) and is the basis of the mathematics of the Litchford system. The TOA locates the 'other' aircraft anywhere on the locus of an ellipse (in fact an ellipsoid, as the situation is three-dimensional) with the two focus points of the ellipse being the ground radar station and the AIRCAS II equipped (i.e. 'own') aircraft.

Knowing that ground radar antennas rotate in a clockwise direction, and using the same simulated p.r.f. technique and rotation periods, the AIRCAS II processor is also able to measure the differential angle (DAZ) centred in the ground radar position between its 'own' aircraft and any 'other' aircraft. By other means it also knows its magnetic direction from any ground SSR.

With values of TOA and DAZ the AIRCAS II can determine the exact range of the 'other' aircraft from its 'own'. To establish the bearing

of the 'other' aircraft it is necessary for the AIRCAS II system to know the exact bearing of the interrogating ground radar. This bearing is derived by making a further calculation using the simulated p.r.f. and rotation periods mentioned above, and supplementary data received from the ground radar stations. All SSR ground radar stations have two antennas. One is the directional antenna which rotates at a steady speed, and the other is an omnidirectional antenna which is used to broadcast the side-lobe suppression pulse throughout 360, although in some cases an arc of about 100° is sufficient. In the Litchford AIRCAS II system it is proposed that the ground station transmits, as part of the SLS normal transmissions, discretely coded pulses through the omnidirectional antenna which will indicate every 45° point in the rotation of the directional antenna. These azimuth points are stored and related to the simulated p.r.f. and rotation periods, so that when carrying out any TOA calculation the AIRCAS II processor also has knowledge by accurate interpolation of the bearing of the ground radar station. It then calculates the bearing of the 'other' target from its 'own'. An alternative method of deriving AIRCAS II bearing from the ground station, has also been developed which requires no change or addition to any ground SSR station but which creates the same accurate bearing angle from the SSR as the TCAS II systems.

The AIRCAS II system can therefore, in a passive way, compute the range, bearing and decode identity and altitude of all aircraft within a selected range gate. As with AIRCAS I, differential altitudes are computed from the Mode 'C' responses from other aircraft. All this information will be presented on a colour display unit installed in the cockpit. The latest cockpit displays called 'EFIS' (electronic flight instrument systems) use cathode ray tubes which are ideally suited to AIRCAS II. The presentation will be similar to that of a ground radar operational display, but centred on the

AIRCAS II aircraft and oriented in the direction of its flight.

The Litchford AIRCAS II system will be able to store and process SSR data on p.r.f. rotation periods derived from up to 40 ground radar stations as would, for example, be desirable in airspace such as that in the U.S.A. Aircraft tracking data is derived from 5 of the best available radars with only one of these being essential for the AIRCAS calculation. However in the event that the aircraft is within radar sight of only one ground station (or even none), then the AIRCAS II integral interrogator will be brought into operation to interrogate any other aircraft in the vicinity.

The combined data on a single radar can provide range, bearing, altitude and identity on up to 50 aircraft targets and from these the 'threat logic' of AIRCAS II can identify any targets that threaten a collision.

Comment

The introduction into service of airborne threat alert and collision-avoidance systems does indeed raise problems, not only in regard to their use in an airborne situation but also how the results of any executive action by the pilot, to avoid what he considers to be a hazardous situation, is to be integrated with the ground ATC system. For example, the Litchford system, described in the previous paragraph, plans to use the available SSR messages, not yet assigned by ICAO, to simultaneously alert the ground ATC organisation and the pilot to a collision threat, and it could therefore be argued that this gives ATC data superior to that otherwise available.

The first question which arises, however, is why should such systems be necessary? For the answer to this question we must look initially at the continent of North America, particularly the U.S.A. You will recall that earlier in this book I have made mention of flight in accordance with visual flight rules (VFR) where the sole onus of responsibility for the avoidance of collision rests with the pilot of the aircraft which is operating in these conditions. For, whilst it is true that even when flying in accordance with instrument flight rule (IFR) and receiving an air traffic control separation service, the pilot is required to keep a look-out; in flight in accordance with VFR the pilot alone is responsible to ensure that he does not hazard the flight of other aircraft. With the increase in performance characteristics of both small and large aircraft, certain tragic accidents have underlined the fact that the unaided human eye, even when assisted by radar advisory information from the ground, is not always sufficient to prevent the development of a hazardous situation. Where, therefore, a mix of VFR and IFR traffic in a relatively busy airspace is permitted, the dilemma for the concerned authorities is either to re-classify the airspace as controlled airspace – and as a consequence eliminate operation in accordance with VFR, and require all air traffic to operate on an air traffic control clearance – or to provide for some alternative form of safeguard to assist in the avoidance of collision.

It is, not surprisingly, in North America where there are large fleets of intercontinental and transcontinental airlines and a much greater number of small (general aviation) aircraft (5000 vs 200,000) that the problem has caused the authorities there to take the lead in the development of airborne threat alert and collision-avoidance systems. Historically, in the U.S.A., freedom of flight in accordance with VFR is a feature of aviation development, which to a large degree does not apply to quite the same extent for example in north-west Europe, where the growth of aviation has been slower and where the ATC systems have evolved in step with this growth. However, attractive as it may be to argue the merits or demerits of restricting flight in accordance with VFR, our concern is with the effect of these systems upon the ground ATC organisation.

Before commenting upon the interaction with ATC systems there are two further occasions where it is considered that threat alert could have a role. Firstly, and regrettably, there are still at the time of writing many areas of the world where the ground ATC organisation is not always able to provide an adequate service. This can be due to a variety of factors, such as the lack of adequate communications facilities, particularly over long distances, or inadequate navigational aids for providing precise positional information. Secondly, as human error is still a factor, however long the odds, it could provide a final 'back-stop' to an error committed by the ground ATC organisation. In this regard it is interesting to observe that the U.S.A. Federal Aviation Administration plans to spend billions of dollars on the 'ATC automation' element of its National Air Space Plan (NAS). One of the objectives of this automation is understood to be to enable a reduction to be made in the present escalating growth of air traffic control staffs thus enabling controllers to handle a far greater load of air traffic than is possible with present systems. The exponents of airborne threat alert and collision avoidance systems could therefore well argue that under this proposed system of greater reliance on automation by the ground ATC system, TCAS could enable the controllers to be 'backed-up' by the pilots in the event of any unfortunate automation or human error.

In returning to the effect these systems may have on the ATC system I would ask you to bear in mind that we are very much looking into the future; therefore my observations can only be subjective. What is known, however, is that a decision has been made by the Federal Aviation Administration (FAA) of the U.S.A. and backed by the U.S. Congress, to introduce a threat alert and collision-avoidance system and that the carriage of this equipment may be a prerequisite of entry into certain nominated airspaces, just as indeed SSR transponders are today. Undoubtedly these airspaces will include the major intercontinental air terminals. As the majority of the world's states fly to and from the U.S.A. it means that their aircraft may also be required to fit the system. Therefore on the return journey, say from New York to London, is the pilot going to leave his TCAS active, or switch it off before entering the United Kingdom's IFR-only controlled airspace? I suspect that the pilot, having been provided with a device which enables him to see the air situation around his aircraft, will want to leave the equipment in an active state. If so, how is the pilot's interpretation of what he may consider to be a hazard, to be integrated into the ATC system on the ground? For example you will recall that at my 'Comment' in Chapter 8 ('Automation') I referred briefly to the fact that ATC computers can be used not only to alert the controller to a possible hazard but also to provide him with solutions to resolve the situation before it develops. Simply stated, conflict alert and resolution is a computer software package where the separation parameters are extended to, say, 1500 feet vertical separation, instead of 1000 feet; 8 nautical miles horizontal radar separation, instead of 5 nautical miles. If, therefore, any aircraft's responses came within these parameters, the controller would be alerted to the fact that the concerned aircraft were approaching the minimum separation standards and that action may be necessary to ensure that those minimums were not transgressed. The 'resolution' would result from the computer carrying out a check of the aircraft proposing threats, and thereafter providing solutions to the controller, such as climb/descend/turn left/right: solutions much the same as TCAS II is suggesting to the pilot. However, it would be quite remarkable if both the airborne and the ground based computers and the information carried in their respective data bases were in entire harmony. Therefore, other than in an emergency situation in these, at present theoretical circumstances, there is a need for co-ordination between the air and the ground. The arrival on the aviation scene of SSR Mode 'S', now provides a possible means whereby this co-ordination could be effected.

SSR Mode 'S' and monopulse SSR

You will recall that in Chapter 5 (Radar) I explained the basic principles of secondary radar, which permits an aircraft to be interrogated and information to be obtained without recourse to the use of a radio telephony speech circuit. Similarly, Mode 'S' is being proposed as part of this SSR family of avionic facilities. The 'S' stands for 'selective' and in the context in which we are considering its application, it acts as a data link between the aircraft and the ground. As its name implies aircraft carrying these Mode 'S' transponders can be contacted separately, without other aircraft being involved, which is the case when an R/T frequency is used. In other words, the aircraft has an automatic private line via the Mode 'S' transponder to the ground station's computer and therefore information can be exchanged by data transmissions rather than by voice. I should also mention that to be effective the selective addressing of aircraft requires the application of a different technique of interrogation of the aircraft's transponder, known as *'monopulse SSR'*. The present generation of SSR requires the aircraft to be interrogated several times as the beam sweeps the target radar response. It requires this number of interrogations to determine the azimuth position and identity of the concerned aircraft. However in this process, because so many transmissions are involved, there can be 'garbling', which is a technical term for interference with the SSR transponders of other aircraft which may be in the immediate vicinity. Monopulse SSR however relies on a very small number of interrogations to produce a single reply, and so considerably reduces any liability to interference and makes possible the selective addressing of a single aircraft.

For those readers who would like a rather more detailed technical explanation, monopulse SSR unlike conventional SSR measures the bearing of an aircraft from each received frame and code pulse of its transponder reply. An average of these measurements gives consistent, highly accurate azimuth data, even in areas where the 'sliding window' extractors used in conventional SSR would output track errors, caused by garbling and missed replies. This dramatic improvement in azimuth accuracy is achieved by determining the bearing of an aircraft with respect to the antenna boresight, by comparing the relative amplitudes of transponder replies received through the separate sum and difference patterns of the antenna. Because the bearing of an aircraft can be accurately measured it is possible to discriminate between the transponder replies of aircraft flying in close proximity, thus giving a higher probability of correctly decoding these transponder replies, which would appear garbled to a conventional SSR system. Therefore because only sufficient transponder replies to validate identity and altitude codes are required, the interrogation rates can be significantly reduced causing less interference and higher accuracy. Informed readers will, of course, be aware that there exists a variety of views on interrogation accuracy which is why in the foregoing sentence I have used the terms 'possible' and 'higher probability', for whilst I do not wish to be deliberately vague, the continuing advances in new technology do tend to invalidate positive statements.

Whilst at present we are discussing monopulse SSR in its relationship to its role as a data link between the aircraft and the ground (mode 'S') the characteristics of monopulse make an equally remarkable contribution, compared to the old SSR processors, towards the display of tracking accuracy of aircraft targets on digitised radar displays such as those described in Chapter 8 ('Automation') in the section on 'The display of radar-derived data'. To demonstrate this point I have reproduced, with the kind permission of Cossor Electronics, Figure 39 which shows the improvement in tracking accuracy obtained using a monopulse system as compared with the plots received from the same aircraft using a conventional SSR system.

To return however, to Mode 'S' the carriage of on-board computers by an increasing number of aircraft linked to this mode therefore opens up a wide range of use other than as an ATC data link, and to give an indication of what this statement means, and therefore what the future may hold, I have reproduced as Figure 40 (with the kind of permission of Cossor Electronics) a copy of a mode 'S' data link print-out which resulted from trials of this equipment which were carried out in the United Kingdom.

I hasten to add that the detail which is contained in the 'print-out' is not included to support any results which may have been obtained from these specific trials, but to indicate to readers the type of information which can be obtained from an aircraft, without recourse to the use of radio telephony.

I trust the foregoing 'comments' will illustrate the reason why I included in this book a chapter on airborne threat alert and collision-avoidance systems. These systems, when allied to or integrated with air traffic control, give an indicator to the future limitless horizon of technological development and the procedures to be used in their employment. How their application is to be developed will depend upon the opinions and sound judgement of aviation and air traffic control experts, particularly the International Civil Aviation Organisation, whose consultative and decision making machinery will be explained in Chapter 12. However, in this regard I wish to repeat a point which I made earlier in this chapter, that the primary means of collision-avoidance within a controlled ATC environment must remain with the ground based air traffic control system.

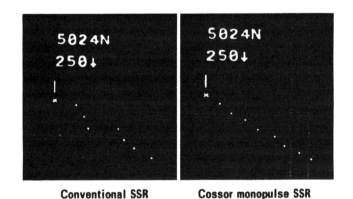

Conventional SSR **Cossor monopulse SSR**

SIMULTANEOUS PLOTS OF A REAL AIRCRAFT

FIGURE 39. Monopulse S.S.R. tracking of aircraft. This is an actual photograph of an aircraft which was being tracked simultaneously by 'standard' SSR and 'Monopulse' SSR. The accuracy of the tracking is depicted by the trail dots behind the aircraft's target and the superiority of monopulse is clearly demonstrated.
(Photograph Courtesy of Cossor Electronics Ltd)

				MODE 'S' DATA LINK PRINT-OUT FROM BRITISH AIRWAYS TRISTAR									
Time (GMT)	Range (nm)	Azimuth (deg)	Height (ft)	Air Temp (deg. C)	Wind angle	Wind speed	Ground speed	Track angle	Roll attitude	Pitch angle	Descent rate (FT/S)	Flap angle	Aircraft weight (Kg)
11:49:27	77·0	101·5	35,000	− 27·0	222	16	460	278	− 0·4	+ 3	0	+ 0	153,200
11:49:38	76·0	101·7	35,000	− 26·5	221	16	461	278	− 0·4	+ 3	− 5	+ 0	153,200
11:49:49	75·0	101·8	35,000	− 27·0	222	16	461	278	− 0·4	+ 2	0	+ 0	153,200
11:50:05	73·0	101·8	35,100	− 26·5	223	16	462	277	− 0·4	+ 3	0	+ 0	153,100
11:50:16	71·0	102·1	35,100	− 26·0	227	15	463	277	− 0·4	+ 3	0	+ 0	153,100
11:50:32	69·0	102·1	35,100	− 26·0	231	14	463	276	+ 0·0	+ 2	5	+ 0	153,100
11:50:43	68·0	102·4	35,000	− 26·0	231	14	461	276	+ 0·0	+ 2	10	+ 0	153,100
11:50:54	66·0	102·5	34,900	− 26·0	230	16	460	277	+ 0·4	+ 1	20	+ 0	153,100
11:50:59	66·0	102·6	34,900	− 26·0	229	17	458	277	+ 0·0	+ 1	20	+ 0	153,100
11:51:04	65·0	102·7	34,700	− 26·0	227	17	456	277	+ 0·0	+ 1	25	+ 0	153,100
11:51:10	64·0	102·7	34,500	− 25·5	225	18	456	277	+ 0·0	+ 1	30	+ 0	153,100
11:51:15	64·0	102·8	34,400	− 25·5	221	18	456	278	+ 0·0	+ 0	35	+ 0	153,000
11:51:21	63·0	102·9	34,200	− 25·0	219	18	455	278	− 0·4	+ 0	35	+ 0	153,000
11:51:26	62·0	102·7	34,000	− 24·5	216	18	456	278	− 0·4	+ 0	35	+ 0	153,000
11:51:31	62·0	102·9	33,800	− 23·5	215	18	456	278	− 0·4	+ 0	35	+ 0	153,000
11:51:37	61·0	102·9	33,600	− 23·5	215	18	455	278	− 0·4	+ 0	35	+ 0	153,000
11:51:42	60·0	103·0	33,600	− 23·5	216	18	454	278	− 0·4	+ 0	25	+ 0	153,000
11:51:48	60·0	103·2	33,200	− 23·5	217	18	453	278	− 0·4	+ 0	40	+ 0	153,000
11:51:53	59·0	103·2	33,200	− 23·0	218	17	452	278	− 0·4	+ 0	35	+ 0	153,000
11:51:58	58·0	103·1	33,200	− 22·5	219	17	451	278	− 0·4	+ 0	40	+ 0	153,000
11:52:04	58·0	103·2	33,200	− 22·0	218	16	451	278	+ 0·0	+ 0	40	+ 0	153,000
11:52:09	57·0	103·1	33,200	− 21·5	217	16	452	278	− 0·4	+ 0	50	+ 0	153,000
11:52:15	56·0	103·4	32,200	− 20·5	213	15	455	278	− 0·4	+ 0	50	+ 0	153,000
11:52:20	56·0	103·5	32,200	− 19·5	210	15	456	278	− 0·4	+ 0	55	+ 0	153,000
11:52:25	55·0	103·4	31,600	− 18·5	208	15	458	278	− 0·4	+ 0	55	+ 0	153,000
11:52:36	54·0	103·6	31,000	− 16·5	208	14	462	278	− 0·4	+ 0	55	+ 0	153,000

FIGURE 40.   Mode 'S' data-link print-out.

(Courtesy of Cossor Electronics Ltd)

We have now reached the stage in the book where I wish to deal with the specific problems associated with the co-ordination of civil and military air traffic, and therefore the following chapters are devoted to the outlining of the problems and the explanation of solutions to these problems. I would ask readers to bear in mind, however, that the principles of the control of air traffic, which I have previously explained, apply equally to military as well as civil air traffic, with the proviso that where military aircraft only are involved, occasions can arise, such as for example when aircraft are engaged in training or special exercises, where less than the standards of separation previously described may be applied. However, where military aircraft are participating in a civil ATC system, or where the flight of a military aircraft and aircraft operating in a civil ATC system might conflict, the standard separations, as quoted in Chapter 2, apply equally to both types of air traffic.

12

The International Civil Aviation Organisation (ICAO)

Introduction

I have left a description of what ICAO is, what it does, and how it works, to this stage in the book because in the following chapters I intend to deal with the co-ordination of civil and military air traffic, and it is this organisation, ICAO, which provides the international link between civil and military flying activities. Specifically the subjects which they have debated, and upon which they have issued written recommendations and guidance, cover the following:

(1) co-ordination between military authorities and air traffic services;
(2) co-ordination of activities potentially dangerous to civil aircraft;
(3) strayed or unidentified aircraft; and
(4) interception of civil aircraft.

As the foregoing subjects are of vital importance to the safe operation of both types of flying activity, I intend to examine them in detail in Chapter 13, and to refer to the relevant ICAO references. However, before doing so I consider it is desirable, for those readers who may not be conversant with the role

ICAO occupies in the affairs of world aviation, to provide an explanation of the workings of this international body. In this regard ICAO have themselves produced a booklet for international readership entitled *Facts about ICAO,* which is published by their Public Information Office located at their headquarters in Montreal, Canada. Having read this booklet, it seemed to me that as it is intended for an audience similar to that towards which this book is directed, and as its authors not only know their subject but also how to project it in understandable terms, it would make sense to reproduce its contents in this chapter. Therefore with the kind permission of ICAO, following is their account of the Facts about ICAO.

Less than eighty hours

In 1873 Jules Verne told the story of Philias Fogg's record-breaking trip around the world in eighty days. A century later, any tourist can go around the world in a scheduled time, including stops, of considerably less than eighty hours. The hero of the trip now, of course, isn't the passenger but the aeroplane, with its capability of flying at speeds rivalling that of sound and its ability to soar over the obstacles of terrain below, of mountains and oceans and rivers and deserts.

To achieve its potentialities however, the airlines must

have effective allies on the ground, thousands of trained men and women to guide the aircraft, to service it, to watch over its progress: air traffic controllers to protect it from collision with other aircraft, meteorologists to inform it of weather conditions and probabilities, technicians to operate communications and air navigation equipment, cartographers, personnel licensing and training experts, mechanics, flight dispatchers. In an afternoon's flight an airliner can cross the territories of several nations, nations in which different languages are spoken, in which different legal codes are used. In all these operations safety must be paramount, there must be no possibility of unfamiliarity or misunderstanding. In other words there must be international standardisation, agreement between nations in all the technical and economic and legal fields so that the air can be the high road to carry man and his goods anywhere and everywhere without fetter and without halt.

The nations of the world have therefore established the International Civil Aviation Organisation to serve as the medium through which this necessary international understanding and agreement can be reached. ICAO's membership comprises 151 sovereign states. With the signing of a treaty in December 1944, ICAO was created as an intergovernmental organisation and in 1947 it became a specialised agency in relationship with the United Nations. Its headquarters are in Montreal and it has regional offices in Bangkok, Cairo, Dakar, Lima, Mexico City, Paris, and Nairobi.

ICAO provides the machinery for the achievement of international co-operation in the air; successful results depend on the willingness of the nations of the world to make concessions, to work together to reach agreement. The success which international civil aviation has achieved in the past three decades is abundant proof that nations can work together effectively to achieve a public good.

Standardisation

One of ICAO's chief activities is standardisation, the establishment of international standards, recommended practices and procedures covering the technical fields of aviation: licensing of personnel, rules of the air, aeronautical meteorology, aeronautical charts, units of measurement, operation of aircraft, nationality and registration marks, airworthiness, aeronautical telecommunications, air traffic services, search and rescue, aircraft accident inquiry, aerodromes, aeronautical information services, aircraft noise and security. After a standard is adopted it is put into effect by each ICAO Member State in its own territories. As aviation technology continues to develop rapidly, the standards are kept under constant review and amended as necessary.

In keeping pace with the rapid development of international civil aviation, ICAO is conscious of the need to adopt in its specifications modern systems and techniques. In recent years, extensive work has been undertaken by ICAO in the areas of automatic reporting of data on aircraft accidents and incidents, all weather operations, automation of air traffic services, the application of com-

puters in meteorological services, aircraft noise, engine emissions and the carriage of dangerous goods by air. ICAO has dealt with the subject of unlawful interference with civil aviation and with questions regarding aviation and the human environment.

Regional planning

Not all aviation problems can be dealt with on a worldwide scale, and many subjects are considered on a regional basis. ICAO therefore, recognises nine geographical regions which must be treated individually for planning the provision of air navigation facilities and services required on the ground by aircraft flying in these regions.

In each of the regions, careful planning is necessary to produce the network of air navigation facilities and services upon which the aeroplanes depend – the aerodromes, the meteorological and communications stations, the navigation aids, the search and rescue bases – the thousands of facilities to be established and operated and the services to be rendered. This planning is done at ICAO regional air navigation meetings, held at regular intervals for each of the regions, where the need for each facility or service is carefully considered and decided upon. The plan which emerges from a regional meeting is so designed that, when the states concerned put it into action, it will lead to an integrated, efficient system for the entire region.

When states require assistance in this regard, help is available through ICAO's seven regional offices – each one accredited to a group of Contracting States. These offices have, as their main function, the duty of encouraging, assisting, expediting and following up the implementation of the Air Navigation Plans and maintaining them up-to-date.

As financial and technical resources vary widely between nations, and as air transport's demands involve some complex and costly equipment, and well-qualified personnel for manning and maintaining the facilities, there may be uneven implementation of parts of the Air Navigation Plans. ICAO can assist states through its Technical Assistance activities. It has succeeded also, in a few cases in arranging for "joint financing". Certain facilities in the North Atlantic are financed by the states whose airlines make use of them: a transatlantic cable for transmitting messages of interest to aviation, and air navigation aids and meteorological and air traffic control facilities in Greenland and Iceland.

Facilitation

The obstacles placed by customs, immigration, public health and other formalities on the free and unimpeded passage of passengers and cargo across international boundaries – have been a particularly serious impediment to air travel. This hindrance is inherent in the speed of air travel itself; if, for example, formalities at each end of a trans-oceanic flight of six hours take up one hour, this means that the passenger's trip time has been increased by one-third, while the same formalities only add about two per cent to a five-day sea voyage across the same ocean. For the past two decades ICAO has tried to persuade its member states to reduce red tape, and international standards on facilitation have been adopted to place an upper limit on what states may demand. In addition to reducing procedural formalities, ICAO's efforts are also aimed at providing adequate airport terminal buildings for passengers and their baggage as well as for air cargo, with all related facilities and services.

Economics

The Convention on International Civil Aviation requires that international air transport services be established on the basis of equality of opportunity and operated soundly and economically. In fact, ICAO's basic objective is the development of safe, regular, efficient and economical air transport. To assist states in planning their air transport services, ICAO collects and publishes comprehensive world aviation statistical data and undertakes extensive economic studies in line with resolutions of the ICAO Assembly and recommendations of world-wide Conferences. ICAO also produces manuals for the guidance of states in such areas as statistics, air traffic forecasting, airport and air navigation facility tariffs and the establishment of air fares and rates. Workshop meetings are conducted in various regions to provide states with information and advice on ICAO activities and to exchange pertinent information and views.

Technical assistance for development

From the beginning man has lived in communities connected to or separated from one another by surface conditions. Jungles and swamps, mountains and rivers and deserts have in the past presented almost insurmountable obstacles to his movement – a condition which is characteristic even today in so many developing countries where road and railway networks are insufficient or non-existent. The aeroplane's advantage here is obvious: it moves along a boundless highway in the sky and the only road building it needs is enough for take-off and landing. By the creation of an airstrip remote towns and villages can be linked quickly to the modern world, whereas surface connections could take years or even generations to build.

ICAO therefore pays special attention to promoting civil aviation in developing countries. A major instrument in this work is the United Nations Development Programme. So far most of the organisation's work in this area has been directed toward the development of the ground services required for civil aviation and in particular toward aerodromes, air traffic control, communications and meteorological services; in the past few years, and with the advent of larger and more complex aircraft, requests for assistance in the more sophisticated field of aviation are increasing in number.

Assistance in general has consisted in advising on the organisation of government civil aviation departments and on the location and operation of facilities and services, and particularly in the training of personnel. Many large civil aviation training centres have been created or assisted for example in the East African Community, Egypt, Lebanon, Mexico, Morocco, Nigeria, Thailand, Tunisia, Zambia; in most cases these are regional training centres which take students of many nationalities and for which the local governments pay a large share of the costs and take over complete operation of the projects after a set time. Smaller national training centres have also been established by ICAO technical assistance missions, and nationals of many countries have received ICAO fellowships for study abroad.

ICAO technical assistance missions consisting of one or more technical experts have gone to nearly one hundred states all over the world. Thousands of students have attended training schools operated by ICAO.

Unfortunately, the requirements for assistance in aviation have always exceeded the means available to satisfy them – and with the current development this pattern shows no indication of changing.

Law

Within the 151 Member States of ICAO there are many legal philosophies, many different systems of jurisprudence. There is need, therefore, for a unifying influence, for the development of a code of international air law. It is the duty of ICAO to draft international air law conventions and to try to arrange for their general acceptance. Until this date the organisation has been responsible for the preparation of international air law conventions, involving such varied subjects as the international recognition of property rights in aircraft, damage done by aircraft to parties on the surface, the liability of the air carrier to its passengers, crimes committed on board aircraft and unlawful interference with civil aviation.

How it works

The constitution of ICAO is the Convention on International Civil Aviation, drawn up by a conference in Chicago in November and December of 1944, and to which each ICAO member state is a party. According to the terms of the Convention, the organisation is made up of an Assembly, a Council of limited membership with various subordinate bodies and a Secretariat. The chief officers are the President of the Council and the Secretary General.

The Assembly, composed of representatives from all member states, is the sovereign body of ICAO. It meets every three years, reviewing in detail the work of the organisation and setting policy for the coming years. It also votes a triennial budget.

The Council, the governing body which is selected by the Assembly for a three-year term is composed of 33 states. The Assembly chooses the Council Member States under three headings: states of chief importance in air transport, states which make the largest contribution to the provision of facilities for air navigation and states whose designation will ensure that all major areas of the world are represented. As the governing body, the Council gives continuing direction to the work of ICAO. It is in the Council that standards and recommended practices are adopted and incorporated as Annexes to the Convention on International Civil Aviation. The Council is assisted by the Air Navigation Commission (technical matters), the Air Transport Committee (economic matters), the Committee on Joint Support of Air Navigation Services and the Finance Committee.

The Secretariat, headed by a Secretary General is divided into five main divisions the Air Navigation Bureau, the Air Transport Bureau, the Technical Assistance Bureau, the Legal Bureau and the Bureau of Administration and Services. In order that the work of the Secretariat shall reflect a truly international approach, professional personnel are recruited on a broad geographical basis.

ICAO works in close cooperation with other members of the United Nations family such as the World Meteorological Organisation, the International Telecommunications Union and the Universal Postal Union, the World Health Organisation and the Intergovernmental Maritime Consultative Organisation. Non-governmental organisations which also participate in ICAO's work include the International Air Transport Association, the International Federation of Airline Pilots Associations and the International Council of Aircraft Owner and Pilot Associations.

THE MEMBER STATES

Afghanistan
Algeria
Angola
Antigua and Barbuda
Argentina
Australia
Austria

Bahamas
Bahrain
Bangladesh
Barbados
Belgium
Benin
Bolivia
Botswana
Brazil
Bulgaria .
Burma
Burundi

Canada
Cape Verde
Central African Republic
Chad
Chile
China
Colombia
Congo

Costa Rica
Cuba
Cyprus
Czechoslovakia

Democratic Kampuchea
Democratic People's Republic of Korea
Democratic Yemen
Denmark
Djibouti
Dominican Republic

Ecuador
Egypt
El Salvador
Equatorial Guinea
Ethiopia

Fiji
Finland
France

Gabon
Gambia
Germany, Federal Republic of
Ghana
Greece
Grenada
Guatemala
Guinea
Guinea–Bissau
Guyana

Haiti
Honduras
Hungary

Iceland
India
Indonesia
Iran
Iraq
Ireland
Israel
Italy
Ivory Coast

Jamaica
Japan
Jordan

Kenya
Kiribati
Kuwait

Lao People's Democratic Republic
Lebanon
Lesotho
Liberia
Libyan Arab Jamahiriya
Luxembourg
Madagascar
Malawi
Malaysia
Maldives
Mali

Malta
Mauritania
Mauritius
Mexico
Monaco
Morocco
Mozambique

Nauru
Nepal
Netherlands
New Zealand
Nicaragua
Niger
Nigeria
Norway

Oman

Pakistan
Panama
Papua New Guinea
Paraguay
Peru
Philippines
Poland
Portugal

Qatar

Republic of Korea
Romania
Rwanda

Saint Lucia
Sao Tome and Principe
Saudi Arabia
Senegal
Seychelles
Sierra Leone
Singapore
Somalia
South Africa
Spain
Sri Lanka
Sudan
Surinam
Swaziland
Sweden
Switzerland
Syrian Arab Republic

Thailand
Togo
Trinidad and Tobago
Tunisia
Turkey

Uganda
Union of Soviet Socialist Republics
United Arab Emirates
United Kingdom
United Republic of Cameroon
United Republic of Tanzania
United States
Upper Volta

Uruguay

Vanuatu
Venezuela
Viet Nam

Yemen
Yugoslavia

Zaire
Zambia
Zimbabwe

I trust that from the foregoing facts, and the list of member states, readers will be aware of the far-reaching influence which ICAO has upon world aviation affairs, and will recognise that air traffic control which, although it is our immediate concern, is but one of the aspects of aviation dealt with by them.

It is therefore quite remarkable that this organisation, which has its origins back in 1944, has not only survived the continuing test of international debate but has also continued to consolidate its role as the arbiter of international standards of safety. However, as stated in the booklet, ICAO itself only provides the machinery for the achievement of international co-operation, and successful results depend upon the willingness of the nations of the world to make concessions, to work together, to reach agreement. It is this aspect of co-operation, not only between nations but also within nations, that I wish now to examine in the next chapter on the co-ordination of civil and military air traffic. The references which I shall make have resulted from debate within the machinery of ICAO and are intended for adoption by all of the contracting states with the objective of making prudent provision for the safety of flight of national and international air traffic. In this regard, and before proceeding to the next chapter, I consider it would be desirable for me to explain in rather more detail the differences between ICAO standards, recommended practices and procedures.

Standards, recommended practices and procedures for air navigation

International standardisation is essential in air operations supporting services such as aerodromes, telecommunications, navigational aids, air traffic services, search and rescue, aeronautical charts, and above all in the rules of the air. A minimum standard of safety is equally essential in the design and construction of aircraft, the training and testing of pilots, navigators, engineers and air traffic control officers, and in the operation of aircraft engaged on international flights.

To achieve this standardisation the ICAO Council adopts international standards, recommended practices, and procedures for the safety, regularity and efficiency of air navigation. Standards and recommended practices are contained in 17 Annexes to the Chicago Convention. They are shown in Table 2.

TABLE 2 *The Chicago Convention annexes*

Annex	Title	Abbreviation
1	Personnel Licensing	PEL
2	Rules of the Air	RAC
3	Meteorology	MET
4	Aeronautical Charts	MAP
5	Dimensional Units	DIM
6	Operation of Aircraft	OPS
7	Aircraft Nationality & Registration Marks	REG
8	Airworthiness of aircraft	AIR
9	Facilitation	FAL
10	Aeronautical Telecommunications	COM
11	Air Traffic Services	ATS
12	Search and Rescue	SAR
13	Aircraft Accident Inquiry	AIG
14	Aerodromes	AGA
15	Aeronautical Information Services	AIS
16	Aircraft Noise	
17	Security	SEC

(1) Standards

A standard is any specification for physical characteristics, configuration, material, performance, personnel or procedures, the uniform application of which is recognised as *necessary* for the safety or regularity of international air navigation and to which contracting states *will* conform in accordance with the convention; in the event of impossibility of compliance, notification to the Council is compulsory under Article 38 of the Convention. This notification of non-compliance with a standard is known as a 'difference'. These differences when notified to ICAO are then published in the relevant Annex under the name of the concerned state. This action is taken to ensure that other states are aware that a procedure which is different from the standard may apply in a particular location.

(2) Recommended practices

Recommended practices refer to any specifications for physical characteristics, configuration, material, performance, personnel or procedures, the uniform application of which is recognised as *desirable* in the interests of safety, regularity, or efficiency of international air navigation and to which contracting states *will endeavour* to conform in accordance with the Convention.

(3) Procedures for air navigation services

Procedures do not have the same status as standards or recommended practices. The latter are adopted by the Council in accordance with Article 37 of the Convention; Procedures contain detailed material which is approved by the Council and which amplifies the basic principles of the standards and recommended practices. Procedures for air navigation services are contained in the following documents:

Aircraft Operations	Doc. 8168
Rules of the Air and Air Traffic Control	Doc. 4444
Abbreviations and Codes	Doc. 8400

Regional planning

To assist in providing for specific geographical areas ICAO has set up nine geographical regions to cater for different types of flying operations and to facilitate detailed planning of facilities and services to support these operations. For example, long-range ocean flying predominates in the North Atlantic region while short/medium-range high-density flying predominates in the European – Mediterranean region.

Regional meetings result in the drawing up of regional plans. The purpose of a regional plan is to set forth in detail the facilities, services, and procedures required for international air navigation within the region. Each regional plan contains recommendations which governments can follow in programming the provision of their air navigation facilities and services, knowing that they are forming part of an integrated system which is adequate for the foreseeable future. The ICAO regions are:

European Mediterranean	EUM
Middle East	MID
Africa/Indian Ocean	AFI
South East Asia	SEA
Pacific	PAC
South American	SAM
Caribbean	CAR
North American	NAM
North Atlantic	NAT

To assist in administrative support and technical advice, seven regional offices provide secretariats for these regions; they are located at:

Bangkok	serve	SEA and PAC
Mexico City	serve	CAR and NAM
Cairo	serve	MID
Dakar	serve	AFI (WEST)
Lima	serve	SAM
Paris	serve	EUM
Nairobi	serve	AFI (EAST)

Additionally, as was stated in the transcript of the booklet, ICAO also provides assistance to developing countries by the provision of international experts, instructors, training equipment and fellowships for training abroad. This assistance covers ground services, flight safety, air law and regulations, and the organisation and administration of civil aviation.

Finally, I think it may assist if I were to amplify a little the structure of ICAO as it is explained in the booklet. It may reiterate a certain amount of the previous information but the purpose of this restatement is to emphasise the comprehensive consultative machinery and organisation which results in the prodution of the standards, recommended practices and procedures, and furthermore ensure their continuing review, in line with the development of the aircraft as a vehicle, and the facilities and personnel concerned with its operation.

The structure of ICAO

The Assembly

The Assembly is the sovereign body of ICAO; it meets every 3 years at a place and time convened by the Council. All contracting states may be represented, and decisions are taken by a majority of votes cast. The financial arrangements of ICAO are determined and a triennial budget voted. The work of the Council is reviewed and directions and recommendations given for future action.

The Council

The Council is the permanent governing body; it is composed of 33 members elected by the Assembly. The Council elects its own President.

The Council is responsible to the Assembly for taking whatever steps are necessary to maintain the safety and regularity of international air transport and to encourage and regulate the growth of air services throughout the world. One of its major duties is to adopt international standards and recommended practices and to incorporate them as Annexes to the Convention.

The Council controls and co-ordinates the work of six additional representative bodies; they are:

The Air Navigation Commission

The Air Navigation Commission is concerned with the development of international standards and recommended practices, and for the planning, co-ordination and examination of all ICAO work in the field of air navigation. It is composed of 15 Commissioners appointed by the Council after nomination by contracting states. It is assisted in its work by the technical secretariat of the Air Navigation Bureau.

The Air Transport Committee

The Air Transport Committee is composed of Council members. Its function is to advise the Council on problems associated with the economics of air transport. One of its main concerns is the removal of unnecessary customs, immigration, and other formalities which may increase a trans-ocean flight by one-third its time. Another concern is the provision of passenger facilities at international airports. Standards and recommended practices relating to facilitation are developed by the Air Transport Committee and, if adopted by the Council, find their way into Annex 9. The Committee is assisted in its work by the Air Transport Bureau of the Secretariat.

Committee for Joint Support of Air Navigation Services

The terms of the Convention require contracting states to provide navigation services and facilities in their own territory. In addition, services and facilities are needed in regions of undermined sovereignty and on the high seas. Furthermore, some states cannot afford to install and operate services. The Committee for Joint Support studies these problems and may recommend that air navigation services and facilities be provided through joint support. The nations whose airlines use the services make a pro-rata payment for such use. Examples of joint support are the North Atlantic oceans stations and the air navigation services established in Greenland, Iceland and the Faroes.

Legal Committee

The Legal Committee deals with the interpretation and amendment of the Chicago Convention and prepares drafts of international conventions such as:

The Rome Convention of 1952 dealing with damage caused by aircraft to third parties on the surface.

The Tokyo Convention of 1963 dealing with offences committed on board an aircraft.

Finance Committee

The Finance Committee is composed of nine members appointed by the Council from representatives of Council member states.

The ICAO Secretariat

Corresponding to each ICAO Committee and Division is a section of the ICAO Secretariat, made up of staff members selected for technical competence in their fields. Technical and administration aid and advice is given to the Council, the Air Navigation Commission and the Committees. The Secretariat is headed by a Secretary General – and is divided into five divisions:

The Air Navigation Bureau
The Air Transport Bureau
The Technical Assistance Bureau
The Legal Bureau
The Bureau of Administration and Services.

In addition to the regular staff, the services of experts are obtained from time to time by loan from member states.

13

The Civil/Military Air Traffic Problem

Introduction

In trying to rationalise the problems associated with civil and military air operations, it is essential to accept, from the outset, the differing roles of these two types of flying activity and to recognise that the majority of military operations are, by their very nature, not amenable to the strict rules and procedures which apply to civil passenger-carrying air traffic. Exempted from this statement are those occasions where military aircraft operate within controlled or special rules airspace, when they comply with the rules and procedures applicable to those airspaces. Also air traffic control at military aerodromes is exercised in much the same manner as explained in the foregoing chapters.

To look at the problem from a military viewpoint it is also essential to try to assess how the impact of the use of the air, for commercial purposes, impacts upon their operational role. In the early 1950s civil aviation commenced to expand very rapidly, on a world-wide basis, and continued to do so at an annual growth rate of approximately 10 per cent until the late 1970s; even in the period of economic recession of the early 1980s this expansion continued, albeit at a slower annual rate of approximately 3 per cent. The aircraft itself, both in performance and size, demonstrated an equally rapid evolution. In particular the introduction into passenger-carrying service of jet-powered air transport meant that for both operational and economic reasons these aircraft were required to operate in the higher levels of the airspace; an area which had previously been almost exclusively used by military jet aircraft.

Additionally, as you will be aware from the reading of previous chapters in this book, it was essential to create controlled airspace structures to protect the flight paths of these aircraft and within which mandatory rules and procedures could be applied. In this regard, if you refer again to Figure 3 (which shows the upper air routes over part of north-west Europe) I think you will appreciate this diagram illustrates very graphically the problem which faces both of these types of flying. To illustrate the problem further, let us consider for one moment one of the world's congested airspaces, the United Kingdom's London terminal area. As I have mentioned earlier at London Heathrow airport alone, aircraft take off and land in peak hours in excess of one a minute, and the terminal area itself handles approximately 3500 controlled flights in a period of 24 hours. Of this latter number a high proportion will be overflying the terminal area to other destinations and will be occupying the higher flight levels from approximately FL 250 (25,000 feet) to FL 370 (37,000 feet). Similarly, aircraft bound for and departing from aerodromes within the terminal area will be descending from or climbing to these flight levels. The airways en-route networks spread out from the terminal like three-dimensional motorways to link up not only with the major internal cities of the United Kingdom but also with the major capitals of continental Europe and beyond.

This abbreviated picture of civilian aerial activity is repeated to a larger or lesser degree throughout the aviation world, and it is therefore against this background that military aviation is required to conduct its operations in such a manner that they do not constitute a hazard to the safe conduct of flight. In this regard the tasks facing military aviation are many and varied, and most of them do not fall readily into the fairly rigid concept of control as practised in a civil capacity. Also the tactical role of military aviation is subject to changes dependent upon the 'threat analysis'. For example in recent years there has been a gradual shift of emphasis from the upper air space to low-level operations, and whilst in terms of airspace congestion this has introduced problems for the co-ordination of military aircraft with general aviation and aviation sports, such as hang-gliding and parachuting, it has reduced the conflict between military aircraft and civil commercial air traffic. Therefore the co-ordination procedures must be sufficiently flexible in application to be able to react to these changes and be subject to constant review by both organisations. It is appreciated that the successful planning and operational application of co-ordination procedures does create an extra work-load for both military and civil ATC authorities. However, the service pilot is as much concerned for the safety of himself and his aircraft, as is his civil counterpart, and therefore recognises that where a conflict may arise for the use of the airspace, co-ordination and co-operation must exist to provide for the protection of both types of flying.

To try to summarise, therefore, from a military viewpoint, the creation, by many states, of an air traffic control system of airways with their associated terminal areas and control zones, allied to the rapid expansion of the numbers of aircraft movements and their performance characteristics, has further complicated the question of civil/military co-existence, and the ability of each to carry out its differing tasks within the world's airspaces.

Further, it has to be accepted that on the one hand the civil operators demand the rigid application of separation standards between aircraft and protection by law of much of the airspace in which they fly, and therefore, by implication, acceptance of control of their flight paths by a ground organisation. From a military point of view, however, the adherence to predetermined flight paths and stringent separation rules, such as those required by passenger-carrying aircraft, negate the role for which they exist, which is one of freedom of movement and tactical flexibility.

It is then the co-existence of both of these types of air traffic within shared airspace to which solutions have to be found. To assist in the resolution of this dilemma it is suggested that it is desirable for states to have in existence civil and military traffic control organisations capable of co-ordinating these two types of flying, to ensure not only that their respective roles can be carried out safely and with the minimum of interference, but also that the world's airspace, which stubbornly refuses to get any bigger, can be used as flexibly and economically as possible.

The international aspect of the civil/military air traffic problem

In the previous chapter on the International Civil Aviation Organisation I referred to the fact that it was this organisation which provided the international link between civil and military air traffic, and in this regard I trust the foregoing introduction clearly indicates the need for states to take action on the deliberations of this body of world opinion.

To achieve this objective ICAO in its Annex II to the Convention deals both with co-ordination between military and civil air traffic services and with the co-ordination of activities which may be potentially hazardous to civil aircraft. Because the role of military aviation varies considerably from state to state, ICAO wisely does not try to advise states how this co-ordination should be carried out in detail, but leaves it to the concerned state to adopt procedures which are directed towards satisfying these objectives. However, to assist readers to appreciate not only the difficult task of international 'drafting', but also the manner in which ICAO has tried to place on record the difficult areas of civil/military co-ordination, I have reproduced, with their kind permission, a copy of the actual wording which is contained in Annex II.

2.13. Co-ordination between military authorities and air traffic services

2.13.1. Air traffic services authorities shall establish and maintain close co-operation with military authorities responsible for activities that may affect flights of civil aircraft.

2.13.2. Co-ordination of activities potentially hazardous to civil aircraft shall be effected in accordance with 2.14.

2.13.3. Arrangements shall be made to permit information relevant to the safe and expeditious conduct of flights of civil aircraft to be promptly exchanged between air traffic services units and appropriate military units.

2.13.3.1. Air traffic services units shall, either routinely or on request, in accordance with locally agreed procedures, provide appropriate military units with pertinent flight plan and other data concerning flights of civil aircraft.

2.13.3.2. Procedures shall be established to ensure that air traffic services units are advised if a military unit observes that an aircraft which is, or is believed to be, a civil aircraft is approaching, or has entered, an area in which interception might become necessary. Such advice shall include any necessary corrective action which might avoid the necessity for interception.

2.14. Co-ordination of activities potentially hazardous to civil aircraft

2.14.1. The arrangements for activities potentially hazardous to civil aircraft, whether over the territory of a state or over the high seas, shall be co-ordinated with the appropriate air traffic services authorities. The co-ordination shall be effected early enough to permit timely promulgation of information regarding the activities in accordance with the provisions of Annex 15.

2.14.1.1. *Recommendation* - In determining these arrangements the following should be applied:

(a) the locations or areas, times and durations for the activities should be selected to avoid closure or realignment of established ATS routes, blocking of the most economic flight levels, or delays of scheduled aircraft operations, unless no other options exist;

(b) the size of the airspace designated for the conduct of the activities should be kept as small as possible;

(c) direct communication between the appropriate ATS authority or air traffic services unit and the organisation or unit conducting the activities should be provided for use in the event that civil aircraft emergencies or other unforeseen circumstances require discontinuation of the activities.

2.14.3. The appropriate ATS authorities shall be responsible for initiating the promulgation of information regarding the activities.

2.14.4. *Recommendation* – If activities potentially hazardous to civil aircraft take place on a regular or continuing basis, special committees should be established as required to ensure that the requirements of all parties concerned are adequately co-ordinated.

In summary what this international statement provides for is the co-ordination of civil and military air traffic where both types of flying might be in conflict one with the other; the promulgation of any training areas, danger areas or special exercises with, where possible, the flexible use of the airspace, and the setting up of procedures where a civil aircraft may have inadvertently strayed into a sensitive military area. In the following chapter I intend to give examples of co-ordination methods and military airspace utilisation, but before proceeding to do so I consider it would be of interest to spend a short time in examining the problem of 'strayed' or unidentified aircraft.

Strayed or unidentified aircraft

Regrettably there still exist within the world's airspace a number of areas which are sensitive from a military viewpoint; equally regrettably, navigation errors can and still do occur, particularly on flights over long distances which have inadequate ground communication and navigation aids. To give an indication of ICAO's concern for aircraft in these circumstances they amplified the statement given in the extract from Annex II (para. 2.13) in Document 4444, 'Rules of the Air and Air Traffic Services'. This is a document which you will recall I have referred to before, and its purpose

is to specify, in greater detail than is possible in the relevant Annex, the actual procedures to be applied by air traffic services units, in providing the various services to air traffic. Once again I think it would be advisable for me to reproduce the actual wording, which in any event gives very clear and concise information on the procedures which should be adopted in these circumstances:

Note 1 The terms 'strayed aircraft' and 'unidentified aircraft' in this paragraph have the following meanings:

Strayed aircraft An aircraft which has deviated significantly from its intended track or which reports that it is lost.

Unidentified aircraft An aircraft which has been observed or reported to be operating in a given area but whose identity has not been established.

Note 2 An aircraft may be considered, at the same time, as a 'strayed aircraft' by one unit and as an 'unidentified aircraft' by another unit.

As soon as an air traffic services unit becomes aware of a strayed aircraft, it shall take all necessary steps to assist the aircraft and to safeguard its flight.

If the aircraft's position is not known, the air traffic services unit shall:

(a) attempt to establish two-way communication with the aircraft, unless such communication already exists;

(b) use all available means to determine its position;

(c) inform other ATS units that may be affected, taking into account all the factors which may have affected the navigation of the aircraft in the circumstances;

(d) inform, in accordance with locally agreed procedures, appropriate military units and provide them with pertinent flight plan and other data concerning the strayed aircraft;

(e) request from the units referred to in (c) and (d) every assistance in establishing communication with the aircraft and determining its position.

When the aircraft's position is established, the air traffic services unit shall,

(a) advise the aircraft of its position and corrective action to be taken; and
(b) provide, as necessary, other ATS units and appropriate military units with relevant information concerning the strayed aircraft and any advice given to it.

As soon as an air traffic services unit becomes aware of an unidentified aircraft in its area, it shall endeavour to establish the identity of the aircraft whenever this is necessary for the provision of air traffic services or required by the appropriate military authorities in accordance with locally agreed procedures. To this end, the air traffic services unit shall:

(a) attempt to establish two-way communication with the aircraft;
(b) if attempts in (a) fail, inquire of other air traffic services units within the flight information region about the flight and request them to attempt to establish two-way communication on the frequencies available;
(c) if attempts in (a) and (b) fail, inquire of air traffic services units serving the neighbouring flight information regions about the flight and request their assistance in establishing two-way communication with the aircraft.

The air traffic services unit shall, as necessary, inform the appropriate military unit as soon as the identity of the aircraft has been established.
Note: Requirements for co-ordination between military authorities and air traffic services are specified in Annex 11, 2.13.

Interception of civil aircraft

As soon as it is learned that an aircraft is being intercepted, an air traffic services unit serving the airspace within which the interception is taking place shall:

(a) attempt to establish two-way communication with the intercepted aircraft on any available frequency, including the emergency frequency 121.5 MHz, unless such communication already exists;
(b) establish contact with the intercept control unit maintaining two-way communication with the intercepting aircraft, with a view to relaying messages between the intercepting and intercepted aircraft; and
(c) in close co-ordination with the intercept control unit take all necessary steps to ensure the safety of the intercepted aircraft.

From the foregoing chapter, I hope it will be clear that the problems of the co-ordination of civil and military air traffic have long been recognised internationally. I accept that the quotations which I have reproduced may appear to be in somewhat stilted official language, but I would ask you to bear in mind that they result from lengthy debate between delegates of many nations and represent a sincere attempt to provide for the safe operation of both of these types of flying activity. Also the use of the words and phrases have of necessity to be carefully selected so that their intention can be clearly understood by nationals whose native tongue is not the English language. Turning these words into 'deeds' does, of course, depend to a large extent upon how the contracting states of ICAO decide to put into practice these standards and recommended practices. It is therefore my intention in the next chapter to describe some of the methods which can be used to achieve these objectives, and then to illustrate their practical application and to indicate the additional services which are provided by military air traffic control.

14

The Organisation for the Co-ordination of Civil and Military Air Traffic

Introduction

As stated in the previous chapter the International Civil Aviation Authority, when recommending that co-ordination between civil and military authorities should take place, did not, for the reasons stated, say how this should be accomplished.

In practical terms it is not possible, certainly at this time, to propound an overall world-wide organisational solution to this problem. It is, however, reasonable to suggest that there are three main definitions, and then to indicate by example how an organisation can be established to create the system to ensure the existence of co-ordination. These definitions are considered to be:

(1) *Total integration* That is where a single unified service provides air traffic services to all aircraft irrespective of the operating authority of the aircraft concerned.

(2) *Partial integration* That is where the organisation is composed of staffs belonging to both civil and military services and where the air traffic services are provided jointly by both authorities.

(3) *Procedural co-ordination* That is where air traffic services are provided separately by the civil and military authorities and where co-operation exists entirely through co-ordination procedures.

Probably the outstanding example of total integration is that practised in the United States of America, where a single authority, the civilian-based Federation Aviation Agency (FAA) has an organisation which provides air traffic services to all air users of their national ATC system. However, even in this example there are exceptions, in that the military authorities provide air traffic services at most of the military aerodromes. The co-ordination of civil and military air traffic could therefore be regarded as a mixture of: (1) *total integration* in respect of military aircraft which are participating in the national air traffic system, and (2) *procedural co-ordination* in respect of the requirements for co-ordination in regard to operations from military aerodromes, where any conflict may arise between the two types of flying activity. I am making this comment at this stage, for whilst it is necessary for me to explain the systems definitions of how co-ordination can be achieved, it does underline the point that the requirements of military and civil air operations can and do vary, even within a state's own airspace. Therefore a flexible approach towards the solution of these problems is often preferable to the rigid application of a particular system.

'Partial integration', as the above explanation implies, is a compromise solution based upon the willingness of both parties, civil and military, to co-operate in practical terms to achieve the objectives of ICAO, which were set out in the previous chapter. On an international basis it is suggested that partial integration is the solution most likely to appeal to both authorities responsible for this type of flying, for it enables each to retain its autonomy and independence of action away from those areas where co-ordination requires joint action.

The principle of this type of co-ordination is not to try to co-ordinate all types of flying, but to concentrate upon those areas where the two types of flying would otherwise conflict one with the other and, as a result, develop an organisation and procedures which, whilst providing for safe operation, can also minimise interference and delay to both flying operations.

In developing the methods by which this desirable state of affairs can be achieved it is necessary to bear in mind that within a state it may be necessary to adopt differing methods in relation to specific co-ordination problems. For example, in a busily congested terminal area which has a predominant civil activity, or on busy air routes, it may be desirable to physically locate a military controller alongside his civilian counterpart; whereas in a busy military area crossed by air routes of low traffic density such

a physical presence would not be necessary, and co-ordination can be discharged at long range by notification procedures. In other words, examine what the co-ordination problem is, and then apply the most suitable solution.

Before proceeding to examine the methods of co-ordination which can be applied I should like to make the point that no-one has a proprietary right to postulate these solutions but can only offer, from experience, examples of how this can be achieved under a given set of circumstances. In writing internationally it is essential to recognise that military aviation, in particular, varies considerably according to the role it has to adopt in the state of its origin, and also the organisations employed by these states to control aviation activities are equally varied. The concern, however, of all of these states is how to implement the ICAO recommendations in regard to the safe operation of flight, and my purpose in writing this chapter is to explain some of the methods which have been employed by one state, the United Kingdom, to achieve the co-ordination of civil and military air traffic. I have chosen the United Kingdom not as an example of how things should be done, but because it is an area with which I am familiar and for which at one time I was operationally responsible. Before doing so I wish to make the point that although the majority of air traffic services to civil pilots are provided by the Civil Aviation Authority, the military air traffic operations provide some services in certain circumstances to civil aircraft, in addition to their co-ordination responsibilities. I therefore propose to describe the services which they provide and how the military and civil staffs co-ordinate together, and the organisation which has been developed to manage this application of partial integration.

Methods of co-ordination of civil and military air traffic

The United Kingdom has a 'National Air

Traffic Service', the organisation and operation of which is staffed by serving military officers and civilians. For those readers who may have interest in how such an integrated service is organised and administered, I intend to include a detailed explanation in a later chapter. However, for the benefit of those readers who may not be so concerned with this detail, I propose to explain at this stage the physical locations of the military air traffic control officers and then the air traffic services which are provided by them.

Locations of military staff engaged in air traffic operations

Air traffic control centres

The United Kingdom has two ATCCs: the London centre located at West Drayton in Middlesex, and the Scottish and Oceanic centre, located in Prestwick in Scotland. At both of these units civil and military staff are functionally co-located for duties where military flying activities impinge upon the civil route structure. Equally military control officers also operate independently within the same building using common facilities to provide an off-route service both to military and civil aircraft.

The term 'off-route' is used in this context as a generalisation to indicate a service to those aircraft which are flying in airspace other than airways terminal areas, control zones, special rules airspace, and aerodrome traffic zones, where they would be receiving a control service from either civil or military personnel.

Joint air traffic control radar units

To assist in the provision of area radar cover pending the installation of additional radars to increase the present coverage provided by the air traffic control centres, there are three joint air traffic control radar units (JATCRU) in the United Kingdom. Manned predominantly by military personnel they nevertheless have a significant element of civilian control staff. They operate using common sources of radar and flight plan data, and have access to at least two long-range radars either 'on site' or remotely connected by narrow-band links for primary and secondary radar. Currently the JATCRU's are an integral part of the overall air traffic control organisation within the United Kingdom. In addition there are three exclusively military manned air traffic control radar units, which are also an integral part of the NATS organisation; two sited in predominantly military training areas and one which provides a radar service to civil helicopters engaged in the support of oil operations in the North Sea.

Research and development flights

Research and development is a continuing activity which is essential both to civil and military prospects. The future designs of aircraft, and their degree of aerodynamics and avionic sophistication, depend directly upon the ability of new aircraft to operate safely and expeditiously within the United Kingdom's congested airspace. The aerodromes involved are owned and operated either by the aircraft manufacturer or the Ministry of Defence (PE). To assist in such development the military provide area radar services from 'special tasks' sections, and perhaps an appropriate example of such work was the test flying of 'Concorde', which was a military responsibility in terms of traffic control services.

Military aerodromes

These aerodromes are staffed by military personnel and controlled by military command formations. However, the National Air Traffic Service has the responsibility of declaring the agreed overall policy for operations and HQ military air traffic operations (MATO) have the mandate to co-ordinate aerodrome patterns and procedures where necessary and to authorise the agreed procedures. Provision is made for civil aircraft to receive an air traffic control service, on request from these aerodromes, in the lower air space below flight level 100.

Distress and diversion

At each air traffic control centre the military staff provide distress and diversion facilities both to civil and military aircraft, in conjuction with the rescue co-ordination centres, HM Coastguard and mountain rescue units. They operate a 24-hour service monitoring the military and civil emergency R/T frequencies (243.0 MHz and 121.5 MHz) and are supported by a comprehensive and immediate telephone network.

Services provided by military air traffic operations

The services provided by military air traffic operations are as follows:

Emergencies

By virtue of the radar and R/T cover they have available through co-location, the military controllers at the air traffic control centres and joint radar units are in an excellent position to provide initial response in respect of aircraft emergencies.

Upper airspace

The upper airspace in the United Kingdom commences at flight level 245 and in the airspace above this level all military aircraft with the exception of those operating in military training areas, are required to receive a mandatory service from the military controllers within the coverage of the respective radars. The

radar cover equates to that available to the civil controller.

Airways crossing

Military controllers provide an airways crossing service to military aircraft using either radar or a negotiated procedural clearance.

Middle airspace service

Military controllers provide an advisory radar service within the coverage of their equipment to military and civil aircraft flying outside the airways and terminal areas.

Lower airspace

Military controllers located at aerodromes provide a radar penetration service to aircraft in the lower airspace who wish to transit their traffic patterns en-route to destination.

Research and development flights

Military controllers provide a service as required to research and development flights within the coverage of their radar equipments.

Figure 41 provides a diagrammatic representation of these services.

The co-ordination methods employed in the application of military air traffic operations

Where the application of the services listed in the previous paragraph may affect the flight of an aircraft which is being provided with a civilian air traffic control service it is essential that co-ordination is carried out between the concerned military and civil controllers or ATS units, to ensure the safe and flexible operation of both types of flying. I therefore propose, under the headings of the services previously

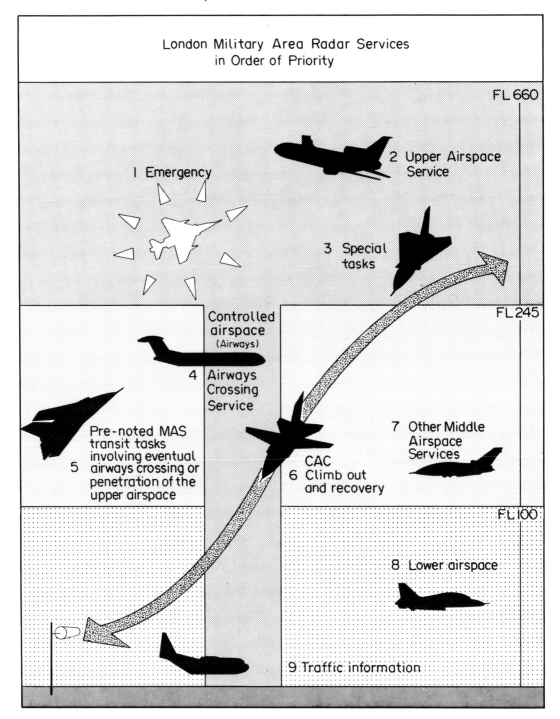

FIGURE 41. Diagram of the services provided by military air traffic operations

given, to explain how this co-ordination is affected, although it must be appreciated that in doing so my explanations are in general terms, and I trust readers will appreciate that each action in itself may be complex and the subject of detailed operating procedures. However, to assist in an understanding of these co-ordination procedures I intend to describe, in the next chapter, details of the flight of a military aircraft from one aerodrome to another and in that chapter I shall endeavour to involve as many of these services as is possible.

Emergencies

Emergencies occurring to military aircraft are handled exclusively by military personnel other than the possible exception of a military aircraft operating on the airways system where initial action would be taken by the concerned civilian controllers. However, in regard to an emergency being handled by a military controller, co-ordination would take place on a direct speech circuit between the military and civil controller responsible for the specific airspace, if the action in respect of the emergency should require deviation of an aircraft under civil control. Military controllers also provide a service to civil aircraft flying 'off-route' in the flight information region, who may require navigational assistance or diversion facilities in an emergency. Co-ordination would take place between the military and civil ATC supervisors to provide the most expeditious solution to the emergency.

The upper air space

Within the United Kingdom a special rules airspace has been established from flight level 245 up to and including flight level 660. The rules governing this airspace are somewhat complex but the main difference between this airspace and that below flight level 245 is that throughout the entire airspace aircraft, both civil and military, are required to operate on a 'known' and co-ordinated basis. Within the upper airspace is contained a network of upper air routes used primarily by civil aircraft, and to which the same rules and procedures apply as for aircraft operating on the airways system immediately below, and which are usually contiguous with the upper air routes. Within this airspace there are also military training areas (MTA) which are designated for specific military activity. They are marked on the international charts and the upper air routes are aligned to avoid these areas. A large part of this airspace is covered by the National Air Traffic Service's radar installations, and within this cover it is mandatory for military aircraft to receive a radar/procedural service from NATS military controllers. Co-ordination between civil and military controllers takes the following form:

(1) Upper air routes. At the present time the major part of the upper air space cover is provided from a variety of radars both on site and remoted and joint air traffic control radar units (JATCRUs) have been established at some of these sites. At these JATCRUs military and civil controllers operate from the same operations room and use a common traffic display upon which details of all traffic in their concerned areas of responsibility is displayed. To avoid unnecessary re-routing of passenger-carrying aircraft the standard procedure is for the military controller to initiate co-ordination with his civil colleague. If avoiding action is necessary, it is normally the military aircraft which will give way. Co-ordination can and does take place whenever this would result in advantage to the military controller such as the use of height separation.

(2) Special flights. There are special categories of military flights of a non-deviating status where co-ordination between both controllers must take place where a conflict of flight

paths is evident. Normally in these circumstances the civil controller will deviate his aircraft to avoid disrupting a critical and perhaps expensive military flight profile.

(3) Military training and exercises. To assist in the co-ordination of air traffic in regard to military training and operational exercises in the upper air space, special co-ordination centres have been established which are staffed by both military and civilian personnel.

All civil traffic movements affecting the concerned areas are passed to these cells and the flight plan data is thereafter continuously updated. Additionally, arrangements can be made for the temporary closure of air routes where a specific exercise would warrant such action. In this event prior co-ordination would take place through the airspace utilisation section (AUS), whose task is to ensure that all air users are aware of the closure of the airspace, who the controlling authority for the exercise will be, and also what procedures exist for avoidance and/or penetration of the exercise area. An explanation of the airspace utilisation section is given later in this chapter but briefly it exists to try to ensure, as far as possible, the flexible and economic use of air space, in respect of these special tasks. In fact so successful has this section been in this co-ordination task, that these co-ordination centres are being phased out and the entire task discharged by the AUS.

Airways crossings

The co-ordination procedures for crossing the United Kingdom's network of airways and terminal areas vary, dependent upon the traffic densities and problems associated with specific areas. The service is provided by NATS military controllers located jointly with their civil colleagues either at the air traffic control centres or joint radar units, and co-ordination takes the following form:

(1) Radar crossings. The civil and military controllers use the same radar source for their displays and have the same traffic data and the military controller can, on his initiative, provide a radar crossing, using the same standards of separation as his civil colleague, or if the airway is busy and radar penetration not possible he can, through co-ordination with the civil controller in charge of the concerned airways sector, obtain a procedural clearance to cross the airway at a specific height, time and position and relay this to the aircraft.

(2) Radar corridors. On some very busy airways where a requirement also exists for a military crossing service, radar corridors have been established to ease the task of both controllers and to facilitate the movement of both types of traffic.

Co-ordination takes place in advance at staffing level, to provide a shallow corridor across the airways, usually approximately 3000 feet deep, through which the military controller can pass his aircraft without co-ordinating with the civil controller. In this instance it is the responsibility of the civil controller to avoid this corridor by employing vertical separation either above or below the corridor's vertical limits. This is termed 'negative' co-ordination. Should the corridor, of course, not be required by the military controller he can by prior co-ordination release the airspace for civil use.

(3) Terminal areas. In general, a combination of the airways crossing procedures apply to the penetration of terminal areas. However, in a busy terminal area such as London, which has a high density of traffic in the climb and descent phase of flight, penetration of the airspace takes place either under the control of the civil controller or by making special arrangements, usually procedural, well in advance through the airspace utilisation section. In exceptional circumstances, where short no-

tice only is possible, these arrangements can be made directly with the supervisor of the ATCC operations room.

(4) Airways sectors. It has been found that the best solution to the co-ordination of civil and military air traffic on busy airways sectors, is to include the military controller as part of the team of controllers operating the concerned sector. Thus the military controller is fully conversant with the up-to-date traffic situation and can co-ordinate directly with his civil colleague to obtain the most expeditious service for his aircraft.

Middle airspace

Outside controlled airspace, in the height band between FL 100 and FL 245, the military controllers provide a radar advisory service to all aircraft, both military and civil. The service depends upon the radar cover and the capability of the unit in terms of control capacity. As the nature of the service is advisory, and as the civilian controllers do not normally provide a similar type of service, co-ordination is not necessary, other than in specific cases, which would be covered by local operating instructions.

Lower airspace

In the lower airspace, namely that below FL 100, special procedures have been introduced to provide a radar service to both civil and military aircraft flying between approximately 3000 feet and FL 100. In this airspace there can be considerable activity generated by training airfields both civil and military, and co-ordination for the provision of this service is primarily direct between the civil aircraft operator and the concerned military controller. Also within this lower airspace a radar service has been introduced to permit penetration by

civil aircraft of the traffic zones surrounding airfields and, as in the previous case, co-ordination is direct between the operator and the military controller.

Co-ordination with defence organisations

One of the major tasks of a defence organisation is that of constantly identifying those aircraft targets (radar responses) which are observed in the particular areas allocated to specific units. This task is known as 'filtering' and, as its name implies, this process when completed may leave a residue of unknown or unfriendly targets. It is, of course, these latter targets which are of concern and which may require further investigation dependent upon circumstances. To assist this process of filtering it is therefore of importance to defence commanders that the identities of aircraft which are operating in their areas, and upon which either military ATC or civil ATC have knowledge, should also be identified to the defence organisations.

From previous reading of Chapter 5 you will be aware of the requirement of aircraft to file a flight plan as a prerequisite to the receipt of an air traffic control service, and you will be equally aware that no distinction was made between civil and military aircraft. In fact in the next chapter describing the flight of a Phantom aircraft you will be aware that a flight plan is indeed filed for its flight from one military aerodrome to another. It is appreciated that all flights of military aircraft may not be amenable to the procedure of a full ICAO flight plan but even for this category of flight an 'air movement' is filed. It will, I trust, be clear, however, that the military and civil ATC organisations are in possession of information which is being continuously updated from aircraft in flight, and which is vitally important to the defence filtering process.

The methods in which this information is

FIGURE 42.   A view of a middle airspace operations room (London ATCC–military)

relayed to the defence units and thereafter continuously updated vary dependent upon the facilities which are available at each operational unit. For example at a location such as the London air traffic control centre which is co-located with a military unit, and which has a computer-assisted flight data base, the computer itself could be programmed to provide the essential information required for a specific defence area and presumably in future could relay this information through computer terminals on a geographical basis. At present, however, methods vary not only in the United Kingdom but throughout the world. One of these methods is to provide at the defence units a 'co-ordination cell' into which flight plan details which are of concern to that specific area, are passed either by telephone or telex. The responsibility for keeping the information contained in the original flight plan up to date

rests with the originator, usually the air traffic control centre. In some parts of the world where air traffic may not be so heavy it is quite practical to provide a military position at the concerned air traffic control centre for the specific purpose of relaying flight data to defence units. Whatever methods or combination of methods are used, it is, however, this co-ordination of air movements which not only assists the defence commander in the difficult task of filtering but also helps to minimise, if not prevent, the expensive and, on occasions, disturbing exercise of airborne interception.

The airspace utilisation section

You will recall that in the 'Introduction' to Chapter 13 ('The civil/military air traffic problem') I quoted from Annex II of ICAO their statements on 'Co-ordination of activities po-

FIGURE 43. The distress and diversion cell (London ATCC) Manned by military Controllers each Air Traffic Control Centre in the United Kingdom has a Distress and Diversion Cell, which provide a 24 hour service to both military and civil aircraft.

(Photo Courtesy UK/MATO)

169

tentially hazardous to civil aircraft', and summarised that this referred to such matters as military training areas, danger areas (i.e. air-to-air firing ranges or tanker-refuelling areas), special military exercises, air displays, fly-pasts, etc.

It has to be accepted not only that some of these special activities are essential for military aviation, but that some are also of interest to the general public, such as air displays and public fly-pasts. What they have in common, however, is that they do not conform to the same category of flight to which the rules, regulations and procedures described in this book can be readily applied; in other words they are indeed 'special activities', and as such the airspace which they are occupying must be sterilised for their use and procedures must be adopted to ensure that aircraft not engaged in these activities are safely separated from them.

Therefore an organisation must exist to ensure not only that the military and civil ATC authorities are fully aware in advance of the special activities, but also that, on an international basis, pilots are also informed of the areas of restricted flight. In this regard ICAO makes provision for this and an international method of promulgation has been adopted on a world-wide basis known as an international NOTAM (notice to airmen). Some of these areas, such as danger areas, are on a permanent basis and routeings of air traffic are specifically designed to avoid such areas. However, a great many of these special activities are semi-permanent and unless an organisation exists to co-ordinate these activities the result can be, and often is, the sterilisation of airspace which could be used for other purposes, for much longer periods than was essential for the activity.

To assist in co-ordinating these activities and the flexible use of the airspace the United Kingdom has established, under the National Air Traffic Services, the *Airspace Utilisation Section.* The section is manned by a mixed staff of Royal Air Force, Royal Navy and civilian personnel who are air traffic control specialists familiar not only with the ATC system but also with the requirements of the three services. Any of these services who require to initiate a special activity are required to give advance notice (sufficient if necessary to provide time for international notification) to the AUS and to obtain from them an authority to proceed. The purpose of this action is two-fold. Firstly it is not unusual, for example, for two aerodromes within flying distance of each other to wish to hold a flying display on the same day, or for the originator of a military exercise not to be fully conversant with possible infringement of controlled airspace; the task of the AUS staff is to propose a rearrangement of activities so that they do not clash, and to advise upon airspace requirements and thus prevent embarrassment to the exercise-controlling authorities.

Secondly because they are aware of the detailed requirements and timings of special activities they are able to use their professional knowledge to limit the interference to other airspace users and also ensure that the airspace which has been allocated is returned to its normal use as soon as possible.

In describing this service, provided by the *Airspace Utilisation Section,* I am not propounding its use on a world-wide basis, but indicating that it is one example not only of how the use of these special activities can be co-ordinated to the benefit of the originators, but also of how the airspace can be used in a more flexible and economic manner.

15

Detailed Description of the Control of the Flight of a Military Aircraft

In the previous chapter I explained how civil and military air traffic is co-ordinated and the air traffic services which are provided by military air traffic operations (MATO) to achieve this objective.

Chapter 10 provides a description of the air traffic control functions associated with a civil passenger-carrying aircraft, and it is now intended to describe the manner in which the flight of a military aircraft is co-ordinated with civil air traffic and how the military air traffic services as detailed in Chapter 14 operate.

To illustrate, as clearly as possible, the co-ordination that takes place between civilian and military controllers, I intend to use as an example the flight of a Phantom (at the time of writing a front-line fighter aircraft of the Royal Air Force) from its base in East Anglia, which is situated in eastern England, to RAF aerodrome St Mawgan in Cornwall, in south-west England.

Reference to Figure 5, 'Airways in the United Kingdom's airspace', will show that the track the aircraft has to follow will cross the busy airways and upper air routes between the London and Manchester terminal areas, also Green Airway One and Amber Airway Twenty-Five. Readers of Chapter 10 will recognise that the track of the Phantom will thus take it across the track being followed by our example passenger-carrying aircraft, on its flight from London's Heathrow airport to Manchester airport.

The flight plan

A military flight of the type being described carries out flight-planning in much the same manner as a civil passenger-carrying aircraft; that is, at least 30 minutes prior to the intended departure of the Phantom a flight plan is filed giving the details as listed in Chapter 6. This flight plan is then transmitted to all of the air traffic control agencies who will be concerned with providing a service to the aircraft throughout the course of its flight. These agencies are:

(1) *Eastern radar-joint air traffic control radar unit (JATCRU)* Eastern radar provides a centralised approach control (CAC) service, in regard to the initial departure phase of the flight and thereafter are responsible for its conduct until the aircraft is handed over to the London joint area organisation.

(2) *London joint area organisation (LJAO)* The LJAO is responsible for providing the aircraft with a safe flight path to cross the busy airways and upper air routes which lie on its track between the London and Manchester terminal areas until the aircraft is handed over to the military area services.

(3) *Military area services (MAS)* Following transfer of control from LJAO, MAS are responsible for providing the aircraft with an ATC service on its track to its destination, which may include crossing clearances for Airways Green One and Amber Twenty-Five. Also in the final stages of its flight MAS provide a centralised approach control (CAC) service, until handing over control to the destination aerodrome, St Mawgan, when the aircraft is approximately 30 nautical miles away from the aerodrome.

(4) *RAF aerodrome St Mawgan* Following handover of control from the MAS (CAC service) ATC at St Mawgan are responsible for the final approach and landing phase of flight.

These then are the ATC agencies who are concerned with the conduct of the flight of the Phantom and to whom the flight plan has been addressed prior to the departure of the flight from its base aerodrome.

It is now intended to follow the flight of the Phantom from the aerodrome of departure to the destination aerodrome, and in doing so, to explain how the concerned military air traffic services operate and how the co-ordination of civil and military air traffic is accomplished.

The conduct of the flight

As the Phantom taxies out to the runway in use, at its base aerodrome in East Anglia, the ground controller who is situated in the control tower advises eastern radar, by a direct telephone circuit, that the flight will shortly become active.

Eastern radar, who already have the Phantom's flight plan details, will handle the aircraft on the dedicated combined approach control (CAC) console and allocate to the aircraft a secondary radar code (SSR) which will discretely identify the aircraft as being controlled from this CAC position, and the R/T frequency, to be selected for use, following hand-off to them.

Shortly after the aircraft is airborne, the approach controller at the base aerodrome contacts eastern radar on the direct telephone circuit and identifies it to them by reference to the position of the radar response and the SSR code, which the pilot will have selected either whilst taxiing or immediately after becoming airborne. When identification has taken place the aircraft is instructed to change his R/T frequency and to call the eastern radar controller.

The eastern radar controller continues the climb of the aircraft and provides a radar advisory service. This involves passing the position, by clock code, and range, and the flight level, if known, of all conflicting traffic, and giving avoiding action. The pilot will usually accept the avoiding action unless he is in visual contact with the conflicting aircraft and content to continue. There is no distinction in the service given between flight in IMC or VMC, but clearly the pilot is more likely to follow the avoiding action in IMC. As the flight progresses the eastern radar controller contacts the LJAO military controller, who is positioned on the Daventry sector alongside his civilian colleagues. The Daventy sector is responsible for the control of the airspace through which the track of the aircraft will pass, and the military controller will already be in possession of flight progress strips, giving details of the Phantom's flight. These strips have already been automatically produced by the 'Myriad' computer, upon receipt of the flight plan details originated by the departure aerodrome.

It will be the responsibility of the military controller to co-ordinate the flight across the busy airways upper air routes within this sector and, to assist in this task, the chief sector controller, who has overall responsibility for handling the air traffic in this sector, is also provided in advance with copies of the flight progress strip. Thus, he also is aware of a pending penetration of the airspace.

The eastern radar controller continues to update the military LJAO controller with the expected time of arrival of the aircraft at the Daventry sector boundary, its track and cruising flight level. This continuously updated intelligence is compared with the traffic which is being controlled in the civil sector and other traffic which the LJAO military controller may also be handling, thus enabling him to formulate a plan of co-ordination, ahead of the transfer of control of the aircraft.

For example, the flight of the Phantom could conflict with the Manchester outbound aircraft from London (Heathrow) which was described in Chapter 10, and should this be the case a course of action is agreed to resolve this and any other conflicts. This action could involve changing the flight level or the route of the Phantom; indeed during busy periods both actions could be necessary. As referred to in Chapter 14 (Civil/military co-ordination method's) it is normal practice to deviate the more manoeuvrable military aircraft to resolve conflicts rather than the larger passenger-carrying aircraft, unless there is an overriding military operational requirement which has been accorded a 'non-deviating' status, under which circumstances arrangements would be made for the en-route traffic to give way.

Returning to the conduct of the flight, however, as the Phantom approaches the eastern side of the Daventry boundary, the eastern radar controller contacts the LJAO Daventry military controller on a direct telephone circuit and identifies the aircraft to him by reference to the position of radar response and SSR code. The control of the aircraft is then handed over to the Daventry military controller and the pilot instructed to change his R/T frequency and SSR code, now identifying that the aircraft is being handled by the Daventry (military) controller. The aircraft is then vectored in accordance with a course of action agreed between the civilian chief sector controller and the LJAO military controller. The military controller then monitors the Phantom's progress to ensure that the separation standards as detailed in Chapter 2 are maintained.

The military area services operations room is located in the same building as the Daventry sector (the London air traffic control centre) and as the Phantom approaches the western side of the Daventry sector boundary, the LJAO military controller contacts, by telephone, a military area services controller in this adjacent operations room. The airspace within which London military area services is responsible for providing air traffic services to military aircraft, extends from just south of the Scottish border to the French coast. The only exception, at the present time, is the East Anglian and north-eastern airspace, for which, as previously described, eastern and border radar JATCRUs and midland ATCRU respectively, provide a service.

It is then this MAS operation room which will be responsible for the conduct of the flight of the Phantom from the point at which it leaves the western boundary of the Daventry sector's airspace until it is handed over to ATC at its destination aerodrome. Before proceeding, however, with the narrative of the control of the flight, it is worth mentioning that to carry out the MAS task, throughout this area of responsibility, there are 17 radar consoles and extensive use is made of advanced computer and electronic technology, to assist the military controllers in their task. In fact this unit is possibly the first to use electronic data displays (EDD) for traffic purposes, in an operational environment. Instead of using the commonly accepted principle of a paper flight progress strip, as portrayed at Figure 7, flight details are manually extracted from the flight plan and entered into a computer and are then presented electronically on a display at the position occupied by the controller concerned with a particular flight. The controller has an input device associated with the computer, known as a touch wire display (TWD) and is therefore able to update the original flight plan data as flights proceed in the live environment. Closed-circuit television is also used extensively for the relay of other data concerned with the conduct of flights.

Returning once again to the flight of the Phantom, the LJAO military controller, as stated earlier, makes contact with the allocated MAS controller as the aircraft approaches the western boundary of the Daventry sector's airspace. The MAS controller will have had details of the Phantom's flight displayed to him on his EDD at least 15 minutes prior to this contact, and is therefore pre-warned of the requirement for his services. The aircraft is identified to the MAS controller by reference to the position of its radar response and SSR code identity. The pilot of the Phantom is then instructed to change his SSR code and R/T frequency to that of the MAS controller and transfer of control is thus completed.

The MAS controller outside of controlled air space, will provide the same radar advisory service as his colleagues at eastern radar gave before the aircraft reached the Daventry sector. He may achieve separation from potentially conflicting traffic by contacting the controller, either civil or military, controlling the other traffic, and agreeing a course of action to ensure separation between the two aircraft. This latter course of action is termed 'co-ordination' and in practice most conflicts within the airspace for which the London air traffic control centre is responsible, are resolved in this manner. As a result it is exceptional for the MAS controller to have to resort to the vectoring of aircraft to achieve separation.

Once the Phantom has cleared Airway Green One, Airway Amber Twenty-Five and any related upper air routes on its track the pilot is instructed to commence descent from his cruising flight level. During the course of the aircraft's descent the MAS controller will provide the centralised approach control service which may be required in regard to any air traffic associated with arrivals and departures from other aerodromes related to the aerodrome of destination (St Mawgan). When the Phantom is within approximately 30 nautical miles of St Mawgan aerodrome the MAS controller contacts, by telephone, the approach controller in the tower at St Mawgan. As the Phantom will now be within range of St Mawgan's own aerodrome radar, the MAS controller identifies the Phantom to the approach controller by reference to the position of the aircraft's radar response. The St Mawgan approach controller is already in possession of the flight plan which was initiated by the aerodrome of departure, and which has since been updated by the military area services controller as the flight proceeded through their airspace. The approach controller is therefore fully aware of this progress of the flight and able to respond to the telephonic contact from the MAS controller. Once identification of the radar target of the Phantom has been accepted by the St Mawgan approach controller the MAS controller instructs the pilot to change his R/T frequency to that of St Mawgan, and it is then the responsibility of that unit to ensure the safe conduct of the flight of the Phantom to landing and final stop engines in its specified dispersal bay.

Thus ends the history of this particular flight plan and of the military air traffic services associated with the conduct of this particular flight.

Figure 44 has been included, to show in diagrammatic form the various functions associated with this narrative.

Having outlined the problems associated with civil/military co-ordination and the methods which are employed to achieve this objective (Chapter 14), and in this chapter demonstrated how some of these methods are put into practice, I now propose in Chapter 16 to provide an explanation of the administrative organisation of the national air traffic service. I hasten to add that my purpose in doing so is not necessarily to advance the philosophy that an 'integrated' civil/military service provides the best solution to civil/military co-ordination, but to demonstrate, to those readers who are interested, the type of organisation which enables this approach to operate in the joint interests of both air users. I ask readers to appreciate that some of the terms of reference and chains of command may vary from the time of writing, but the basic structure of the organisation will, I am certain, not be materially altered.

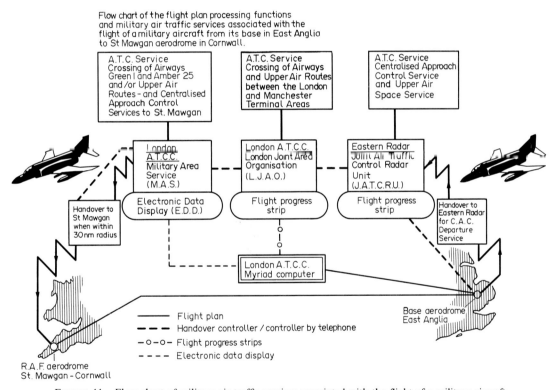

FIGURE 44. Flow chart of military air traffic services associated with the flight of a military aircraft

16

The Organisation of the United Kingdom's National Air Traffic Services (NATS)

Introduction

In the previous chapters I have outlined the problems of civil and military co-ordination and gave examples of how this co-ordination can be achieved in operational practice. I also referred to the fact that one state, the United Kingdom, had adopted a system of 'partial integration' with the objective of providing a National Air Traffic Service common to both civil and military air traffic operations. However, to provide such a service requires the existence not only of highly skilled operational and technical personnel but a sophisticated staffing organisation whose task is to ensure the efficiency of the service being provided by the operational units and to try to anticipate the future demands likely to be placed upon that service. The rapid expansion of the use of the air as a medium of transportation and defence, and the equally rapid extension of technology both in the air and on the ground,

requires for this organisation a combination of technical and administrative skills unique in the history of public and military service. Additionally, it should be remembered that, for all types of air traffic, safety is the paramount feature requiring continuing consultation and standardisation on a national and international basis.

The United Kingdom's National Air Traffic Services organisation came into existence in December 1962, and has as such stood the test of over two decades of expansion and technological change in both civil and military air traffic. It seemed to me, therefore, that it might be of interest, to readers who are not necessarily U.K. citizens, for me to devote a chapter to the manner in which this organisation operates. I must reiterate, however, the statement I made earlier, that I am not suggesting that partial integration of civil and military authorities is necessarily the way to provide for the co-ordination of civil and military air traffic. It is just one way, which has proved successful in the particular environment of the United Kingdom. However it is possible that throughout the world there may be other locations where some of the methods adopted by the United Kingdom could be of assistance to aviation authorities. It is with this objective in mind, and also for those readers who might have an interest in administrative affairs, that I will now proceed to detail the organisation of the U.K. National Air Traffic Services.

Figure 45 shows the present-day (1984) organisation family tree of NATS. However, as with all large organisations it has been subject to change over the years and will doubtless be subject to further changes in the years ahead. I therefore propose to outline the major elements of the organisation which, whilst the chain of command may be subject to minor variation in line with recent changes within the NATS reporting structure, should not detract from the objective of detailing the type of organisation and distribution of duties which are desirable for this type of approach to an integrated air traffic service. The number of directorates which I shall describe may seem somewhat generous to some administrations, but the size of an organisation equates, within reason, to the size of the task to be discharged. In many states with relatively smaller air traffic control commitments the duties and responsibilities would therefore be distributed under a more restricted type of organisation. However, the example which follows has, as one of its primary aims, the detailing of the subjects which require to be covered by an organisation irrespective of its size.

A further point which will become apparent from the detailed description, but which, because of its importance, I wish to draw attention to at this stage, is that the senior appointments within the U.K. National Air Traffic Services are made jointly by the Civil Aviation Authority and the Ministry of De-

fence. Further these posts rotate every 3 or 4 years between a senior-ranking civilian or a senior-serving military Air Force officer. Also the staffing levels are composed of both serving military and civil personnel. This mix of personnel from both services ensures that each understands the problems of the other and assists in a joint approach to the solutions of present-day problems and in planning for future developments.

In regard to the NATS organisation itself, it has three main divisions. Two are located at headquarters, one being headed by the Deputy Controller NATS, and the other by the Director General of Telecommunications. The third division is the Joint Field Headquarters which has responsibility for the day-to-day operation of the NATS units in the field and for short-term planning; it is headed by the Joint Field Commander. Before commencing to explain the organisation of these divisions, however, I wish to make mention of a unique example of organisational democracy, 'The Air Traffic Control Board'.

The Air Traffic Control Board

To safeguard the independence of the National Air Traffic Service and to provide against any unforeseen disagreement arising between the civil and military elements it was decided to set up an Air Traffic Control Board with an independent chairman who would have direct access to the government ministers concerned with aviation affairs. The members of the Board are representative of the major interests in the services provided by NATS, i.e. the Royal Air Force, the Royal Navy, civil aviation, and government. To further indicate its independence in a civil/military sense its joint secretaries are provided by the Ministry of Defence and the Civil Aviation Authority.

The Controller of NATS is not a member of the Board but is present at its meetings to act as a technical adviser. The prime function of

Organisation of the
National Air Traffic Services

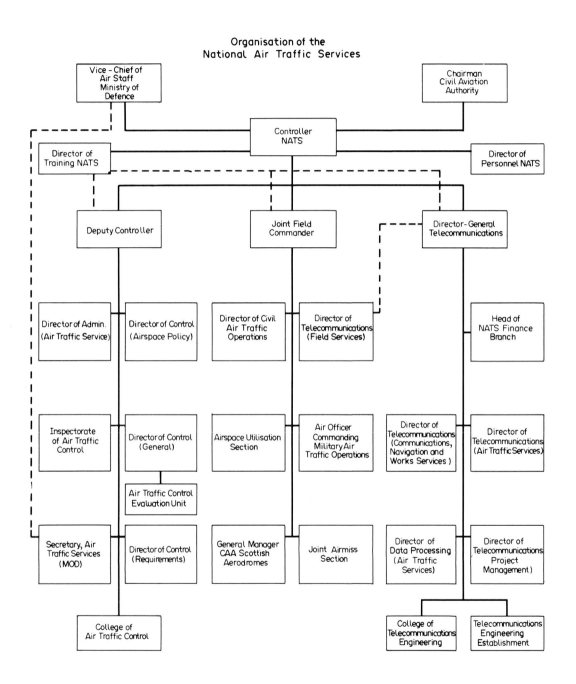

FIGURE 45. The organisation of the National Air Traffic Services

the Board is to act as an advisory and co-ordinating body which reviews and guides the United Kingdom's air traffic control policy and also, as stated earlier, is the forum which would be referred to in the event of a major difficulty arising between the civil and military elements of the National Air Traffic Service. In this latter context it is interesting to note that it has not been necessary to resort to this arbitration machinery since its creation in 1962. It is, however, considered that the existence of the Air Traffic Board for this purpose is an essential democratic element of the United Kingdom's compromise approach to the co-ordination of civil and military air traffic.

Secretary equivalent for a civilian. Occupancy is normally 3 or 4 years for either party, and would only exceptionally be extended beyond this period.

The controller is responsible jointly to the Deputy Chairman of the Civil Aviation Authority and to the Vice Chief of the Air Staff, Ministry of Defence, for the development and operation of a common national system of air traffic control and for ensuring that the system provides for the interests and needs of all branches of aviation, both civil and military. He is, as his title implies, the head, or double head, of the organisation and to assist him to discharge this task he is supported by three Directors General.

the Deputy Controller
the Director General of Telecommunications and
the Joint Field Commander.

All of these Directors General have their own support staffs and it is now intended to explain what their functions are and how these are discharged down to the level of the operational units at airfields, air traffic control centres and remote communication, radar and navigational aid sites.

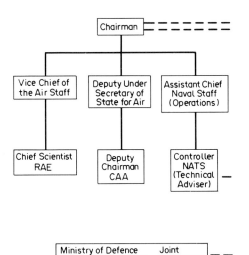

FIGURE 46. The Air Traffic Control Board

The controller of the National Air Traffic Service (C/NATS)

To emphasise the joint nature of the National Air Traffic Service the post of controller rotates between a civil and a military occupant. At the present time the post is graded at Air Marshal level for the Royal Air Force and at Deputy

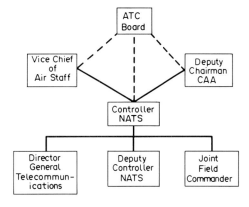

FIGURE 47. The Controller of the National Air Traffic Service (C/NATS).

The deputy controller of the National Air Traffic Service (D/CNATS)

The joint nature of the National Air Traffic Service is again emphasised at the deputy controller level. The post rotates between a civil and a military occupant on the same basis as the controller. At present it is graded at Air Vice Marshal level for a military appointment and Under Secretary status for a civilian. The standard practice adopted since the inception of the service is the counter-balancing of these posts by civil and military occupants. As the title of the post implies the deputy controller acts as deputy head of the organisation and is responsible to the controller for the achievement of the overall objectives of the service.

To assist him to carry out his task he is supported by five Directors whose functions are explained under the sub-heads that follow. It is, however, at this level of the organisation where the close co-ordination between civil and military personnel first becomes apparent, for all of the Directors' support staffs are composed of a mixture of civil and military personnel, working on an integrated basis. They are housed in the same building, often share office accommodation and report equally to either a civilian or military head of section.

The Director of Control – Airspace Policy (DC/AP)

The Director of Control – Airspace Policy is responsible, as his title implies, for the policy and planning of the United Kingdom's airspace. This includes the establishment of controlled or regulated airspace in the vicinity of the busier airports and the continuing review of the en-route or airways network which cater for the safety of aircraft when they are in flight between destinations. He also acts as adviser in these matters to other concerned divisions within the Civil Aviation Authority and to the Ministry of Defence, Air Staff, both for airspace and the related air traffic services. Be-

cause the application of airspace policy affects so many aviation interests, both national and international, he acts as chairman of a number of consultative and executive committees composed of these users. A further requirement is to consider the long-term implications of the developing and changing pattern of aviation movements in regard to airspace requirements and to participate in shorter-term arrangements for air traffic management within the existing capabilities of the ATC system. It is of interest to note that these commitments cover not only the airspace contiguous with the United Kingdom's European neighbouring states but also the area out to the mid-Atlantic essential to protect the traffic flying to and from the North American continent. Additionally, he is responsible for ensuring the existence of an efficient aeronautical information service to pilots and other aviation interests, and its operation on an internationally agreed basis.

The Director of Control – General (DC/G)

The United Kingdom is a member of the International Civil Aviation Organisation (ICAO) which, as stated earlier in the introduction, was formed as a world-wide organisation to lay down international standards for the safe operation of aircraft and it is the Director of Control – General, whose responsibility it is to co-ordinate the National Air Traffic Service's responses to written enquiries or briefing and representation at meetings. The only exception is in respect of the Telecommunications Branch which, due to the highly technical nature of their subjects, prepare their own responses, for co-ordination at the controllers level. Other responsibilities of this Director cover such subjects as the consideration of navigation and communications systems including satellites, the planning for supersonic transport operations and the future use of secondary surveillance radar systems. Additionally, he is responsible for the operation of the

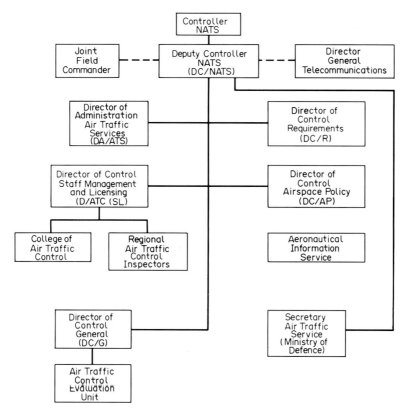

FIGURE 48. The deputy controller of the National Air Traffic Service (D/CNATS)

air traffic control evaluation unit (ATCEU) which is located at Bournemouth (Hurn) airport and has been established to evaluate proposed new air traffic control systems including techniques of operation and associated equipments and also in this regard to liaise with the Research and Development Establishment of the Ministry of Defence.

Director of Control – Requirements (DC/R)

Because of the complex nature of air traffic control, the accommodation, furniture and operational layouts of aerodromes and air traffic control centres is a highly specialised task and it is the responsibility of the Director of Control – Requirements to plan and progress both

modifications to existing locations and, where necessary, entirely new environments in accordance with the overall policy of the service. He is also responsible in this regard, in conjunction with other concerned directorates, for the formulation of any new procedures associated with changes in design, planning or location. He also ensures that any major changes are first evaluated by the air traffic control evaluation unit. In this respect he coordinates with the Director of Control – General. Similarly, in regard to the relatively new techniques of the use of computers, to progress aircraft flight data, he will co-ordinate any proposed new procedures with the Director of Data Processing whose responsibilities are described later.

Director of Control – Staff Management and Licensing (D/ATC(SL)

Air traffic control officers are required by law to be in the possession of a valid licence as a condition for providing a control service to aircraft and, as with a pilot's licence, it must state on the licence what particular service the individual is permitted to exercise. In addition the 'ratings', a term used to describe a particular ATC service, such as aerodrome control, approach control, or radar control, must be kept valid. The terms applying to the granting and renewal of a licence are stringent and accord with the standards set out by the International Civil Aviation Authority (ICAO). Their purpose is to ensure the best possible service to aviation. To assist in the discharge of this responsibility the Director of Control – Staff Management and Licensing has under his authority a College of Air Traffic Control located at Bournemouth (Hurn) airport where air traffic control staff receive basic training on recruitment, thereafter returning throughout their careers for post-course instruction in the additional ratings required as they progress through the ATC service. The certification or validation of a licence can only result from on-the-job training at an operational unit. To assist in discharging this task, and that of a continuing review of the efficiency of individuals to discharge the conditions of their licence, the Director has available to him a team of regional inspectors.

He is also responsible for the issue and amendment of a *Manual of Air Traffic Services* and a *Training Manual*. These manuals ensure that although instructions may have to be supplemented dependent upon varying local conditions, there is only one set of standards and practices throughout the service.

There has been a recent revision in the distribution of these duties between the two headquarters directorates resulting from a recent reorganisation of NATS, but the responsibilities quoted under this heading and allied responsibilities quoted later under the DG of Tels Directorate remain as a total overall NATS responsibility.

Director of Administration – Air Traffic Services (DA/ATS)

The Director of Administration – Air Traffic Services (DA/ATS) is responsible for providing the National Air Traffic Service with the essential administrative and secretarial assistance necessary to ensure the business management functioning of the service. Additionally he is responsible for assisting the controller in discharging the United Kingdom's obligations under the Eurocontrol Convention. Eurocontrol is an organisation of seven European states which was set up in 1958 with the object of achieving a unity of purpose between these states in the provision of services to aviation. As one of the means of obtaining revenue towards the cost of the provision of an air traffic service a charge is levied against aircraft using the system and is known as an 'en-route charge'. It is the responsibility of this Director to collect the data on the air traffic using the United Kingdom's element of the ATC system and to transmit this to a central office for collection purposes. He also acts as a focal point for general correspondence with outside bodies and organisations and for dealing with Parliamentary Questions and with Ministers of the Crown.

The Director General of Telecommunications of the National Air Traffic Services

To provide a service to aviation, air traffic control is dependent upon a highly complex and complicated network of communications both ground-to-air for relaying instructions to pilots and ground-to-ground for the co-ordination and control of these flights; on radar and its associated electronic displays and, in recent years, to further assist them in their tasks, computer installations. Similarly pilots, in addition to the provision of an air traffic control service, require the assistance of ground-based navigational aids and instrument landing systems at airports. It should be appreciated that it is not possible to detail all of the facilities necessary to safeguard the flight of a modern aircraft but the foregoing will give some idea at least of the highly technical nature of some of these facilities.

It is the Director General of Telecommunications who is responsible for the efficient day-to-day operation and maintenance of this branch of the National Air Traffic Service and for the planning procurement and installation of new equipments; also for ensuring that there are available technical staffs with the necessary skills to provide and maintain this service.

Additionally, as these items of equipment are required to conform to international as well as national standards and plans, he is responsible for the policy in respect of the use of existing and proposed telecommunications equipments.

To assist him in the discharge of these tasks he is supported by five directors each with their own staffs who are responsible directly to him for a specific function of the telecommunications service. It is intended to set out the main functions of these directors which illustrate how the Director General's responsibilities are divided to provide him with a comprehensive support organisation. Before doing so, however, attention is drawn to the fact that the Telecommunications Branch is staffed entirely by civilians, co-ordination and liaison being carried out with the Signals Command, Ministry of Defence, where necessary, at the appropriate director level.

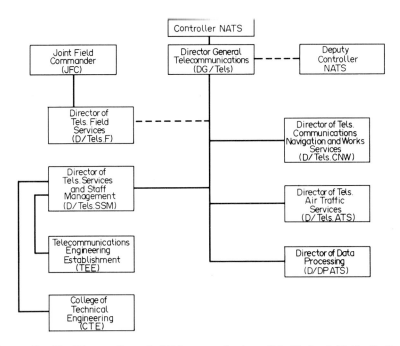

FIGURE 49. The Director General of Telecommunications of the National Air Traffic Services

The Director of Telecommunications Field Services (D of Tels. F)

The Director of Telecommunications Field Services is responsible for the control and co-ordination of all telecommunications facilities at the operational units such as air traffic control centres and airports, and for installation at off-airport sites such as remote radar installations, navigational aid sites and instrument landing systems. Responsibility is exercised through Chief Telecommunications Officers (CTO) who are normally located with their technical staffs at the major operational units such as Heathrow airport and the London air traffic control centre or at a sub-headquarters formation such as the Civil Aviation Office for Scotland.

His major role is to provide advice and guidance to the Joint Field Commander (JFC) whose function is explained later.

Under the recent NATS reorganisation D of Tels. F reports directly to JFC.

The Director of Telecommunications Services and Staff Management (D of Tels. SSM)

The Director of Telecommunications Services and Staff Management is responsible, as his title implies, for the management of staff within the telecommunications branch. This includes recruitment, training, career development, manpower planning and the deployment of staff. He is also responsible for the policy and planning in respect of these staffs, for liaison with the Civil Aviation Authority's staff management and for control of the telecommunications financial budget for manpower requirements.

Two of his further responsibilities are the Telecommunications Engineering Establishment (TEE), which is located at Gatwick Airport, and the College of Technical Engineering which is located at Bletchley, Hertfordshire. The Telecommunications Engineering Estab-

lishment provides engineering services for the installation, maintenance and repair of installations in the field. It has workshop facilities for the test inspection and development of equipment associated with these installations, and provides the air traffic services with the highly technical furniture required by them at operating positions. The College of Technical Engineering provides the Director with the essential specialised training facilities required by him to maintain a high level of skills both at recruitment and post-course. Under the recent NATS reorganisation some of these duties, and those referred to earlier under D/ATC(SL), have been redistributed under a Director of Personnel and a Director of Training, but the totality of responsibilities remain the same.

The Director of Telecommunications, Communications, Navigation and Works Services (D of Tels. CNW)

The Director of Telecommunications, Communications, Navigation and Works Services is in general terms responsible for the provision, policy and planning of the facilities which form the fundamental basis of the air traffic control system, that is the communications air and ground, the navigational facilities both en-route and at aerodromes, and the work services pertinent to their installation and maintenance. He is also responsible for liaison with other government departments such as the Ministry of Defence and the Department of the Environment, and with aircraft operating agencies. Additionally his responsibilities extend to the preparation of briefs and representation at international meetings and for the budgetary control of both revenue and capital expenditure, representing a considerable investment.

Director of Telecommunications Air Traffic Services (D of Tels. ATS)

The Director of Telecommunications Air Traffic Services is responsible for the policy, planning and the provision of radar facilities for the air traffic services. This includes not only primary radar but also secondary radar and the complex processing displays associated with this equipment. The increasing use of radar, and its future exploitation in association with computer technique, requires him to work closely in liaison with other directorates, in particular that of data processing and additionally, similar to his fellow directors, he has budgetary responsibility within his own functional area.

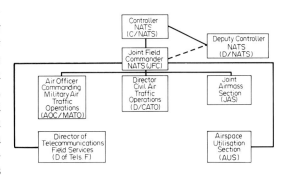

FIGURE 50.   The Joint Field Commander of the National Air Traffic Service

The Director of Data Processing (D/DP)

One of the most significant developments in the air traffic control system since the introduction of radar has been the application of computer techniques to the radar data and to the flight data, both of which form the basic elements upon which 'control' is exercised within the ATC system environment, and it is the Director of Data Processing who is responsible for the policy, the planning, the provision and subsequent support of the data processing system. As many of the techniques are yet to be implemented his responsibility, in this instance, extends to the operational units and continues as such until the various system elements are accepted into operational practice. Additionally, he is required to liaise with international bodies and organisations concerned with this new branch of technology and to manage a budget covering his directorate activities including financial forecasting in respect of the planned implementation of the system.

The Joint Field Commander of the National Air Traffic Service

The Joint Field Commander is responsible to the Controller for the efficient day-to-day oper-

ation of all units throughout the United Kingdom at which the National Air Traffic Service is responsible for providing a service. His title has been specially chosen to reflect the fact that his responsibility extends to both civil and military air traffic operations. To further emphasise this dual responsibility the post is similar to that of the controller and deputy controller, in that it can be occupied either by a civilian or a serving RAF officer. The post is graded at Air Vice Marshal level for a military occupant and at the equivalent status for a civilian; that is at Under Secretary/Director General level.

His responsibilities also include the investigation and analysis of air-misses and for taking immediate action where safety requires amendments to procedures. He is required to ensure the efficient utilisation of United Kingdom airspace in regard to special civil or military requirements such as air displays and tactical exercises, and further to provide a link between practical field experience and the concerned headquarters forward planning sections as described earlier. Additionally, in regard to the civil element of his organisation he is responsible for financial control of the overall budget delegated to him by headquarters to maintain air traffic control operations at all units in the field.

185

To assist him in the discharge of these tasks he has a civil director responsible to him for civil air traffic operations and an RAF officer of 'air' rank responsible to him for military air traffic operations. Both of these officers have support staffs composed of civil and military personnel which, whilst not integrated as at headquarters, are located in the same building. He also has a Joint Air-miss Section with integrated civil/military staff under a serving RAF Group Captain and a similar integrated airspace utilisation sector under a serving RAF Wing Commander.

The Director of Civil Air Traffic Operations (D/CATO)

The Director of Civil Air Traffic Operations is responsible for the operational efficiency of the air traffic services provided at aerodromes, air traffic control centres and the civil element of the joint air traffic control radar units. The area of his responsibility in this regard covers the airspace over the North Atlantic to 30°W as well as the designated controlled airspace over the United Kingdom. He is required to keep under review the procedures related to the control of this airspace, to take short-term action where he considers it necessary and to keep the concerned headquarters section informed of any requirements for longer-term indications reflecting a need for a change in national procedures or planning. This principle can apply equally to technical equipment, furniture and accommodation. He is also responsible for the budgetary control of staff levels and manpower planning and for advising the Joint Field Commander on other aspects of budgetary control.

As many of his duties affect military as well as civil operations he is required to co-ordinate those aspects with the Air Officer Commanding Military Air Traffic Operations.

The Air Officer Commanding Military Air Traffic Operations (AOC/MATO)

The Air Officer Commanding Military Air Traffic Operations is a serving RAF Air Commodore responsible for the provision of air traffic services not only to the Royal Air Force but also to all military users of the United Kingdom's airspace such as the Royal Navy, the Army and the United States Air Force stationed in the United Kingdom.

He differs somewhat from his civilian counterpart (D/CATO) in that whilst he is responsible for operational matters to the controller through the Joint Field Commander, administratively he commands a functionally independent group within RAF Strike Command. This arrangement preserves the military chain of command without in any way inhibiting the service and co-ordination required within the air traffic service organisation. It is possibly a typical example of 'British compromise' which has worked well in practice since the establishment of the organisation in 1962.

He is required to co-ordinate with the Director of Civil Air Traffic Operations (D/CATO) on operational matters affecting the differing requirement of civil/military traffic and it is at this level and the formations supporting the AOC/MATO where co-ordination of these two types of aviation activity is put into practical terms. As civil/military co-ordination is fundamental to the existence of the national air traffic service, the facilities available to AOC/MATO, and the manner in which they are used in operational terms to achieve this objective, are described in Chapters 14 and 15 earlier in the book.

The Joint Air-miss Section (JAS)

Regrettably no system yet devised is 100 per cent foolproof; errors can occur either in the system itself or by the human operator or by equipment malfunction, and as the first requirement in aviation is that of safety, such errors must be thoroughly investigated to permit immediate steps to be taken to try to prevent any repetition of the circumstances which lead to a particular error. It is the responsibility of the Officer Commanding the Joint Air-miss Section to receive all air-miss reports, co-ordinate investigations into their cause and prepare reports on his findings for consideration by an independent working group whose task it is to try to assess the cause and propose remedial action where this is considered pertinent. He is also responsible for advising the Joint Field Commander of any 'trend' in the pattern of errors which would indicate the need to examine specific aspects of the operation of aircraft, the application of procedures or deficiencies of the air traffic control systems.

The Airspace Utilisation Section (AUS)

The Airspace Utilisation Section is one of the more recent additions to the responsibilities of the Joint Field Commander. It was set up in January 1975 to achieve the most safe, efficient and economical use of the United Kingdom's airspace in respect of those aircraft who wished to participate in what is termed 'unusual aerial activity'. That is such things as flying displays, military exercises, parachute dropping, low flying, crop spraying and a host of other activities which are unable for one reason or another to conform to the standard rules. Prior to the establishment of the unit these activities often clashed one with the other in respect of the airspace they wished to use, or alternatively sterilised the use of airspace for periods of time when it could well have been used for other purposes. It is the responsibility of the officer commanding this unit to co-ordinate these requirements and notify other air users where and when the activity is taking place, thus achieving the flexible use of airspace and increasing safety by informing all air users. Since its inception the unit has been singularly successful in achieving its objective in both these regards. A more detailed explanation of the work of this section is given in Chapter 15.

Appendix

Communications Technique and International Standard Radio Telephony Phraseology

Introduction

The International Civil Aviation Organisation (ICAO) has decided, in the interests of safety, to revise the recommended international standard radio telephone phraseologies. This work, which has now been completed, brings the R/T phraseologies up to date with the changes which have occurred in the performance characteristics of aircraft, the introduction of new technical equipment and the air traffic control practices which have been adopted in recent years to incorporate these changes.

The changes will be incorporated in ICAO Annex 10 Volume 2 (*International Standards Recommended Practices and Procedures for Air Navigation Services - Aeronautical Telecommunications*) and ICAO Doc. 4444 (*Procedures for Air Navigation Services, Rules of the Air and Air Traffic Services* - PANS/RAC). Additionally it is the practice of a number of the member states of ICAO to reproduce changes of this nature in the relevant documents of the concerned state. The United Kingdom is one such state and, due to the importance of the use of standard radio telephony phraseologies to any international user or student of the world's airspace, the United Kingdom's Civil Aviation Authority has kindly given me permission to reproduce their Appendix to the *Manual of Air Traffic Services,* which deals with communications technique and standard phraseology.

The Appendix incorporates the amendments recommended by ICAO and came into force in the United Kingdom in June 1984. To ensure uniformity in cross-referencing by readers to the relevant documents, I have had the appendix reproduced in its original format (UK/MATS Part 1, Appendix 'E').

Finally may I add that, due to the lengthy

process which is understandably necessary in revising material and obtaining agreement on a world-wide basis, it is likely to be several years hence before any further revision of standard phraseologies will be conducted; therefore the information contained in this Appendix should remain substantially correct for some considerable time. Users of radio telephony should, however, be aware, as stated in the 'Introduction' to the Appendix, that occasions may arise where it may be necessary to extend or modify the standard phraseologies; but when this does occur both pilots and controllers should take care not to confuse or prejudice the basic meanings of their intentions.

APPENDIX E

COMMUNICATIONS TECHNIQUE AND STANDARD PHRASEOLOGY

SUMMARY OF CONTENTS

1   INTRODUCTION

The procedures and phraseology in this appendix have been laid down with the object of ensuring uniformity in telephone and RTF communications with persons of diverse nationalities and languages.

The importance of the correct use of accurate and precise phraseology cannot be overemphasised. Controllers will find, however, that it may be necessary to extend or modify the phraseology but should take care not to confuse or prejudice basic meanings or intentions.

2   SPEECH TECHNIQUE

Correct enunciation of words, spoken at a uniform rate in a voice pitched somewhat higher than normal but preserving the rhythm of ordinary conversation will do much to assist satisfactory reception of mechanically reproduced speech. Microphones are directionally functioning and controllers should therefore speak directly into them. To avoid clipped transmissions, particularly where the transmitter is remote from the microphone, it is important to depress the transmit switch fully before speech is commenced and to avoid returning it before the transmission is completed. Controllers should endeavour to use clear concise sentences and to eradicate such obvious faults as hesitation sounds, verbosity, lowering of voice, blurring of consonants, etc. This will ensure maximum efficiency and prevent irritating repetitions.

It is correct procedure for controllers to announce identity on all telephone calls: with incoming calls it is the opening remark and with outgoing calls the reply to the recipient's announcement of identity.

It is just as important that this procedure is not relaxed for direct telephone lines because mistaken identity can occur when another line has been inadvertently left open from a previous call.

The identity to be used is that of the function relative to the telephone extension being used. On outside calls the identity should be given in full, for example 'This is London Control Clacton Eastbound Sector' but on direct lines, where it will require no further amplification, it may be abbreviated to 'Clacton Eastbound'.

Appendix E

WORD SPELLING ALPHABET

The ICAO word spelling alphabet is given below with the pronunciation in parentheses for each letter; the syllables requiring emphasis being underlined. This alphabet is to be used at all times when it is required to indicate letters except for particular letter groups which by every-day use have become unmistakable, eg ILS, QFE, ETA, etc.

A	ALPHA	(AL FAH)	N	NOVEMBER	(NO VEM BER)
B	BRAVO	(BRAH VOH)	O	OSCAR	(OSS CAH)
C	CHARLIE	(CHAR LEE)	P	PAPA	(PAH PAH)
D	DELTA	(DELL TAH)	Q	QUEBEC	(KEH BECK)
E	ECHO	(ECK OH)	R	ROMEO	(ROW ME OH)
F	FOXTROT	(FOKS TROT)	S	SIERRA	(SEE AIRRAH)
G	GOLF	(GOLF)	T	TANGO	(TANG GO)
H	HOTEL	(HOH TELL)	U	UNIFORM	(YOU NEE FORM)
I	INDIA	(IN DEE AH)	V	VICTOR	(VIK TAH)
J	JULIETT	(JEW LEE ETT)	W	WHISKEY	(WISS KEY)
K	KILO	(KEY LOH)	X	XRAY	(ECKS RAY)
L	LIMA	(LEE MAH)	Y	YANKEE	(YANG KEY)
M	MIKE	(MIKE)	Z	ZULU	(ZOO LOO)

NUMERALS

The phonetic representations of figures and associated words are given below.

0	ZE-RO		5	FIFE
1	WUN		6	SIX
2	TOO		7	SEVEN
3	TREE		8	AIT
4	FOWER		9	NINER

Thousand – TOU SAND

Decimal – DAY SEE MAL

All numbers, except those which are whole thousands, are to be spoken by pronouncing each figure separately. Decimals will be indicated where necessary.

TIME

GMT and the 24-hour clock will be used at all times.

When speaking a time value, normally only the minutes of the hour are required; each figure being pronounced separately. However, if there is any possibility of confusion the full four-figure group will be spoken.

STANDARD SPEECH ABBREVIATIONS

The words and phrases shown in the table below are to be used whenever applicable.

Phrase	Meaning
ACKNOWLEDGE	Let me know that you have received and understand this message.
AFFIRM	Yes
APPROVED	Permission for proposed action granted.
BREAK	I hereby indicate the separation between portions of the message. *To be used where there is no clear distinction between the text and other portions of the message.*
CHECK	Examine a system or procedure. *No answer is normally expected.*
CORRECT	That is correct.
CORRECTION	An error has been made in this transmission (or message indicated). The correct version is ....
HOW DO YOU READ	What is the readability of my transmission?
I SAY AGAIN	I repeat for clarity and emphasis.
NEGATIVE	No, or permission not granted, or that is not correct.
OVER	My transmission is ended and I expect a response from you.
OUT	This conversation is ended and no response is expected.
PASS YOUR MESSAGE	Proceed with your message.
READ BACK	Repeat all, or the specified part, of this message back to me exactly as received.
REPORT	Pass me the following information.
ROGER	I have received all of your last transmission. *Under no circumstances to be used as an affirmative.*
SAY AGAIN	Repeat all, or the following part, of your last transmission.
SPEAK SLOWER	Reduce your rate of speech.
STAND BY	Wait: I will call you back.
VERIFY	Check and confirm with the originator.

Appendix E

Standard Speech Abbreviations (continued)

Phrase	Meaning
WILCO	Your last message (or message indicated) received, understood and will be complied with.
WORDS TWICE	*As a request:* Communication is difficult. Please send every word twice. *As information:* Since communication is difficult, every word in this message will be sent twice.

RTF CALLSIGNS OF AIR TRAFFIC CONTROL UNITS

The RTF callsign of a ground station is normally the place name of that station to which a suffix is added to indicate the appropriate air traffic control service provided:

Air Traffic Control Service	Suffix
Aerodrome Control	Tower
Ground Movement Control	Ground
Approach Control	Approach
Radar (in general)	Radar
Approach Radar Control	Arrival/Departure
	(Radar when tasks combined)
Precision Approach Radar Control	Precision
Area Control	Control
Flight Information	Information

3 COMMUNICATION WITH AIRCRAFT

AIRCRAFT CALLSIGNS

Aircraft are identified by one of the following types of callsigns:

(a) the registration of the aircraft, eg GBFRM, N753DA;

(b) the registration of the aircraft preceded by the approved telephony designator of the operating company, eg Speedbird GBGDC;

(c) the flight identification or trip number, eg Clipper 100.

Once satisfactory two way communication with an aircraft has been established controllers are permitted to abbreviate the callsign but only to the extent shown in the table below.

Full callsign	GBFRM	Speedbird GBGDC	N31029	N753DA	PA100
Abbreviation	GRM	Speedbird DC	N029	N3DA	No abbreviation

Callsign Confusion

Controllers should be aware that the similarity of some aircraft callsigns can cause confusion which could lead to incidents. In many cases strict R/T discipline can alleviate the problem. Callsigns which contain three or more common digits are particularly liable to be confused.

When there is a likelihood that callsigns will be confused, the pilots of the aircraft concerned should be warned, especially when the flight numbers are identical, eg AI 515 and SK 515.

Callsign abbreviation must not be used when two aircraft on the same frequency have similar registrations eg GASSB and GATSB. In this situation both aircraft are to be instructed to use full callsign.

Where an incident is caused by callsign confusion (or would have been caused if not averted) a mandatory occurrence report must be submitted.

The omission of the company designator when it is an integral part of a callsign can lead to confusion with other numerical and literal information; eg levels, headings, reporting point designations etc. It may also negate the 'alerting' effect on the pilot of hearing his own company designator. Therefore, company designators must always be used when they are part of a callsign.

ESTABLISHMENT OF CONTACT

The initial call made to establish RTF contact should take the following form:

(a) the full RTF callsign of the station being called;

(b) the full RTF callsign of the station calling,
eg 'Speedbird 501 — Stansted Tower — Over'

The phrase 'continue as cleared' should not be used when replying to an initial call made by an aircraft which has been transferred from another frequency.

READABILITY OF TRANSMISSION

When the checks are made the following readability scale is to be used to indicate the quality of the transmission:

Quality	Scale
Unreadable	1
Readable now and then	2
Readable but with difficulty	3
Readable	4
Perfectly readable	5

CONTINUATION OF COMMUNICATIONS

Once satisfactory two-way contact with an aircraft has been established, controllers are permitted to shorten the procedures providing no mistaken identity or confusion is likely to arise.

(a) It can be assumed that the aircraft is listening out and controllers may transmit messages without waiting for a reply from the aircraft.

(b) Continuous two-way conversation with the aircraft may be held without further identification until the end of the conversation.

(c) Phrases such as 'over', 'roger', 'out', may be omitted.

ACKNOWLEDGEMENT AND READ BACK OF MESSAGES

As a general principle, all messages should be acknowledged by the use of the aircraft callsign.

Executive instructions will be acknowledged by an abbreviated read back of the instructions, eg:
    'G-ABCD aircraft landing runway 23, hold position'
    Reply 'G-CD holding'

A full read back will be made to messages containing any of the following:

    Level instructions
    Heading instructions
    Speed instructions
    Airways or route clearances
    Runway-in-use
    Clearance to enter, land on, take-off on, backtrack or cross an active runway
    SSR operating instructions
    Altimeter settings
    VDF information
    Frequency changes

An acknowledgement only should not be accepted when a complete read back is required.

TRANSFER OF COMMUNICATIONS

To transfer communication with an aircraft to another unit, controllers shall pass instructions giving:

(a) the identity of the unit to be contacted;
(b) the frequency to be used for contact.

When the frequency of an aeronautical mobile service station is an intermediate 25 kHz the full figure will comprise 6 digits. However, controllers transferring aircraft to these frequencies are to use only the first 5 digits, eg:

Frequency	Spoken
124.725 MHz	124.72
119.775 MHz	119.77

If no further communication is received after acknowledgement, satisfactory transfer of communication may be assumed.

TRANSMISSION OF COMPANY MESSAGES BY CONTROLLERS

When requested by a company representative controllers may transmit specific operational messages to aircraft subject to normal air traffic service requirements and shall prefix the transmission 'Company advise/request . . .'

Where messages of a technical and complicated nature are involved it may be found advisable to permit direct speech between the originator of the message and the pilot. In such cases the company's representative may be permitted to use the RTF himself provided that his identity is announced before the message is passed and that the controller continues to monitor the frequency.

A message affecting the safety of an aircraft in flight (eg bomb warning, suspected damage to the aircraft, etc) is to be passed to the commander immediately using the company representative's precise wording. An abbreviation or precis could be misunderstood and lead to a wasteful operation or even a dangerous situation.

4 TELEPHONE PHRASEOLOGY

	Phraseology
FLIGHT PLAN DETAILS	...... (direction of flight) ETD ...... flight level requested ...... aircraft identification ...... type ...... crusing TAS ...... (departure aerodrome) ...... (route) ...... (destination) .... (flight plan number).
CLEARANCE REQUEST	...... (aerodrome) request clearance for ...... (a/c identity).
AIRWAYS CLEARANCE	Clearance ...... (a/c identity) cleared to ...... (clearance limit) ...... (level) ...... (SID) SSR code ......
	Clearance ...... (a/c identity) cleared to ...... (clearance limit, eg point of first intended landing) via ...... (route) cross ...... (reporting point(s)) at ...... (altitude(s) or level(s) for reporting point(s)) ...... (climbing instructions) ...... (cruising level) SSR code ......
	Clearance ...... (a/c identity) cleared to ...... (clearance limit, eg point of first intended landing) via ...... (route) cross ...... (reporting point(s)) at ...... (altitude(s) or level(s) for reporting point(s)) to climb when instructed by radar ...... (cruising level) SSR code ......
RESTRICTIONS TO CLEARANCE	...... (a/c identity) unable to clear ...... (item not approved). Released subject to your discretion with regard to ...... (a/c identity) ...... (aerodrome) ...... (direction of flight) departing/landing at ...... (time).
	Clearance expires ...... (time). Release not before ...... (time). Release not before ...... (a/c identity). Release not before ...... (a/c identity) plus ...... (number of minutes). Release not before ...... (a/c identity) has left ...... (level). Release not before ...... (a/c identity) has reported ...... (place). Release to maintain ...... ft below ...... (a/c identity).
DEPARTURE	...... (aerodrome) departure ...... (a/c identity) departed at ...... (time).
APPROVAL REQUEST	Approval request ...... (a/c identity) ...... (type) expected departure from ...... (aerodrome) at ...... (time) requests ...... (level) ...... (filed TAS) via ...... (route) ...... (point of first intended landing).

Appendix E

	Phraseology
ESTIMATES MESSAGE AND REVISION	...... (direction of flight) estimate ...... (a/c identity) SSR code .... (type) estimated over ...... (place) at ...... (time) ...... (level) speed ...... (filed TAS) ...... (route) ...... (clearance limit if other than destination). Revision ...... (a/c identity) now estimated over ...... (place) at ...... (time) or other revisions, eg a different level.
RELEASE TO APPROACH CONTROL	Inbound release ...... (a/c identity) SSR code .... (type) from ...... (point of departure) released at ...... (place, time or level) cleared to and estimating ...... (clearance limit) at ...... (time) at ...... (level) expected approach time ...... (or no delay expected) contact at ......
RADAR HANDOVER MESSAGE	Radar handover ...... (a/c identity) ...... (position, SSR code and heading/observed track, if own navigation) ...... (level) ...... (additional information). *Additional information shall include transfer of control details if not coincident with transfer of communication.*

Appendix E

5　RTF PHRASEOLOGY COMMON TO ALL ATS UNITS

	Phraseology
ROUTE CLEARANCE	You are cleared, or ...... (ATSU callsign) clears, or ...... (a/c identity) cleared. From ...... (place) to ...... (place), or through ...... (place) to ...... (place), or ...... (place) direct. Via ...... (reporting point /AWY/ADR) and ...... (reporting point/AWY/ADR), or to leave Control Area ...... miles ...... (direction) of ...... (reporting point).
LEVEL INSTRUCTIONS	Maintain ...... (level). Maintain ...... (level) to ...... (reporting point). Maintain ...... (level) until past ...... (reporting point). Maintain ...... (level) until ...... (time). Maintain ...... (level) until advised by ...... (ATSU callsign). Maintain ...... (level) until further advised. Maintain ...... (level) whilst in control area/on airway. Maintain ...... ft above/below ...... (a/c identity). Cross ...... (reporting point) at ...... (level). Cross ...... (reporting point) not above/not below ...... (level). Cross ...... (reporting point) at ...... (level) or below/or above. Cross ...... (reporting point) above/below ...... (level). Maintain ...... (level) ...... or below. Report your level. Report leaving/passing/reaching ...... (level). Climb/descend to ...... (level). Climb/descend now to ...... (level). Climb/descend immediately to ...... (level). *NOTE:　This phraseology will only be used to resolve an urgent situation.* Climb/descend to ...... (level) immediately after passing ...... (reporting point)/at ...... (time)/at ...... ft per minute. Climb/descend to reach ...... (level) at ...... (time/reporting point). Climb/descend maintaining own separation and VMC to ...... (level). Stop climb/descent at ...... (level). Expedite climb/descent. Climb when instructed by radar to ...... (level).
HOLDING INSTRUCTIONS When a pilot requests details of a holding procedure	...... (a/c identity) hold ...... (fix) ...... (level) inbound track ...... turns right/left ...... (time of leg).

	Phraseology
GENERAL	Expect onward clearance at ...... (time). Delay not determined ...... (reason for delay). No delay expected. Contact ...... (ATSU callsign) on ...... (frequency) at ...... (reporting point or time). Monitor ...... (ATSU callsign) on ...... (frequency). IMC reported/forecast in the vicinity of ...... (locality). Unable to clear ...... (level/route etc). Report crossing ...... (reporting point). Next report at ...... (location/time/level). Traffic is ...... (essential traffic information).
Initial clearance to inbound a/c	...... (a/c identity) cleared to ...... (destination) via ...... (routeing) maintain ...... (level). Time check ......
Clearance into a Control Zone	...... (a/c identity) cleared from ...... (position) ...... to ...... (holding point) via ...... (routeing). Enter zone at ...... (level) descend ...... (descent instructions) contact ...... (Approach control) at ...... (contact point) expected approach time ..... (time)/no delay.
Crossing Clearance	...... (a/c identity) cleared to cross ...... (AWY/ADR) at ...... (reporting point) maintain ...... (level) whilst in control area/on ADR. Report crossing/cross not later than ...... (time). Time check ......
Joining Clearance (to be used in conjunction with route clearance)	...... (a/c identity) enter controlled airspace ......(direction) of ...... (reporting point) level at ...... (level). Time check ...... *NOTE: Direction may be specified as SW, NNE, etc, or more precisely as a VOR radial, eg 'Enter controlled airspace on the 225 radial of Brecon VOR level at flight level 150'.*
Time Adjustment	Cross ...... (position) not later than ...... (time). Lose time by reducing speed/circling over to arrive over (reporting point) at ...... (time). Arrange your flight to arrive over ...... (reporting point) at ...... (time).
Special VFR Clearance	...... (a/c identity) cleared ...... (route) Special VFR, not above ...... feet.
URGENCY AND DISTRESS Imposition of silence in a distress situation	All stations ...... (ATSU callsign) Stop transmitting – Mayday.
Acknowledgement of Distress	(a/c identity) ...... (ATSU callsign) Roger Mayday.
Cancellation of Urgency	All stations ...... (ATSU callsign) ...... (time) – Urgency traffic ...... (a/c identity) ended out.
Cancellation of Distress	Mayday all stations ...... (ATSU callsign) ...... (time) – Distress traffic ...... (a/c identity) ended out.
Transfer of other Aircraft to another frequency	Mayday ...... (a/c identity) – all other aircraft contact ...... (station) on ...... (frequency) out.

AMENDMENT 30   IMPLEMENTATION DATE 7.6.84   9.3.84

	Phraseology
Emergency Descent	Emergency to all concerned — Emergency descent at ...... (aerodrome/holding facility/location) all aircraft below ...... FL/ft within ...... miles of ...... (aerodrome/holding point/ location) leave ...... (location or locality) immediately. *NOTE: Where standard routes for leaving the area are not published routeing instructions will be given according to the circumstances.*

6 RTF PHRASEOLOGY FOR GROUND MOVEMENT AND TAKE-OFF

	Phraseology
At apron or parking area, aircraft ready to start	Stand by for start up, temperature ...... OR Start up approved, temperature ...... OR Expect departure at ...... (time). Start up at your discretion.
Aircraft requests push back from stand	Push back approved OR Stand by. Expect ...... mins delay due ...... (reason).
Aircraft ready to taxi	Taxi to holding point. Runway ...... Aerodrome QNH ...... Transition Level ...... (on request). OR Hold position. (When necessary, detailed taxying instructions — eg Turn left from apron and take first intersection right.)
At or before holding point	...... (routeing instructions and airways clearance where applicable). OR Leave the control zone, VFR.
When aircraft or vehicles request permission to cross a runway in use	...... (a/c identity) cross, Report vacated; OR ...... (a/c identity) cross runway ...... (runway designator) at ...... (point of crossing) — Report vacated. ...... (a/c identity) after the landing ...... (aircraft type) cross runway ...... (runway designator) at ...... (point of crossing) — Report vacated; OR ...... (a/c identity) after the landing ...... (aircraft type) cross and report vacated. ...... (a/c identity) after the departing ...... (aircraft type) cross runway ...... (runway designator) at ...... (point of crossing) — Report vacated; OR ...... (a/c identity) after the departing ...... (aircraft type) cross and report vacated.
To refuse a request for crossing clearance	...... (a/c identity) negative — I will call you.
When a vehicle requests permission to move on the manoeuvring area	...... (vehicle identity) proceed to ......

	Phraseology
When a tug requests permission to tow an aircraft	...... (tug identity) tow approved via ......
When ready for take-off	(Any special local instructions) ...... Cleared take-off OR ...... (aircraft type) ...... miles on final approach, cleared immediate take-off *The wording 'immediate' shall not be used in the take-off clearance unless there is actual urgency.* OR Line-up OR Hold position OR After the landing ...... (aircraft type) line up.
When take-off clearance has not been complied with	Take-off immediately or hold short of runway. OR Take-off immediately or vacate runway.
To cancel a take-off clearance (aircraft stationary)	...... (a/c identity) hold position, Cancel — I say again Cancel take-off — acknowledge.
To cancel a take-off clearance (aircraft commenced take-off roll)	...... (a/c identity) Stop immediately — I say again ...... (a/c identity) Stop immediately — acknowledge.
When airborne	Report at/over ...... (altitude/reporting point). OR Contact ...... (ATSU callsign) on ...... (frequency).
There is reason to believe that the flight will endanger life. (a) Information received from an outside agency. (b) Observed by the controller.	 I am informed that ...... (details of hazardous condition) It appears that your planned flight is liable to endanger life, acknowledge. You are advised that ...... (details of hazardous condition) It appears that your planned flight is liable to endanger life, acknowledge.
There is reason to believe that a breach of legislation is likely.	Your planned flight appears to contravene legislation because ...... (details of apparent breach if flight takes place) If you take-off I shall be required to report the facts, acknowledge.

	Phraseology
It is known that an aircraft has been detained by police or customs officer or a person authorised under civil aviation legislation to prohibit flight.	Your aircraft has been detained by ...... (authority issuing detention order) I am unable to issue taxi instructions/ take-off clearance.
Marked temperature inversion warning	A marked temperature inversion is present from the surface to ...... feet and the temperature difference between the bottom and the top of the layer is likely to be 10°C or more.

7 RTF PHRASEOLOGY FOR INBOUND AIRCRAFT − VFR
(including IFR traffic which has been cleared to approach maintaining VMC)

	Phraseology

Aircraft requesting straight-in approach	Cleared straight-in approach.
	 Runway ......
	 Surface wind ......
	 QNH ...... Aerodrome/Threshold Elevation ...... ft.
	                OR
	 QFE/QFE Threshold ......
	 Report long final/final
	                     OR
	 Join circuit ...... (then as below).

OR If aircraft is not cleared to make straight-in approach:	
Aircraft requesting circuit joining instructions.	Join circuit. (Where necessary) Left/Right hand traffic pattern (where necessary) At ...... (altitude/height). Runway ...... Surface wind ...... QNH ...... Aerodrome/Threshold Elevation ...... ft. OR QFE/QFE Threshold ...... Report downwind − Over. (Add any special information − eg traffic information, etc.)
Preceding aircraft is in a higher weight category.	Caution vortex wake. The recommended spacing is ...... miles.

At commencement of downwind leg (ie when abeam the up-wind end of the runway in use).	Number ...... follow ...... (aircraft type and position)
	           OR
	 Report final.
	           OR
	 Orbit right/left and report again downwind.
	           OR
	 Report base leg.

Straight-in approach at 'long final' position (ie 4 to 8 miles from touchdown).	Continue approach
	           OR
	 Land after ...... (aircraft type)
	           OR
	 Report final.

On final	Cleared to land. Runway ......
	 Surface wind ...... (if required).
	           OR
	 Continue approach
	           OR
	 Land after ...... (aircraft type)
	           OR
	 Go around − I say again, go around (and appropriate instructions) − acknowledge.

	Phraseology
Circuit training aircraft on final	Cleared touch and go.
After touchdown	...... (appropriate taxying instructions)
When clear of runway in use	Roger ...... (any further taxying instructions)

Appendix E

8 RTF PHRASEOLOGY FOR APPROACH AND LANDING — IFR

	Phraseology
INITIAL APPROACH	Cleared to ...... (fix) via ...... (or direct) at ...... (level) (appropriate initial approach or homing altitude).
When no delay is expected	No delay expected. Runway ...... (and final approach direction where different from runway in use). Surface wind ...... Visibility and weather ...... Cloud amount and height ...... Aerodrome QNH ...... — (if necessary). Where applicable:— Contact ...... (Radar/Arrival) on ...... (frequency).
When it is necessary to delay an aircraft	Roger, cleared to ...... (fix) via ...... (or direct) at ...... (level) and hold. Expected approach time ...... (time). Surface wind ...... Visibility and weather ...... Cloud amount and height ...... Aerodrome QNH ...... (as necessary). <div align="center">OR</div>
When a straight-in approach is practicable	Roger, cleared straight-in approach on ...... (aid). Runway ...... Surface wind ...... Visibility and weather ...... Cloud amount and height ...... Report at ...... (altitude/Marker, etc.) Aerodrome QNH ...... (QNH ...... Aerodrome/Threshold Elevation ......, or QFE/QFE Threshold ...... will be passed at a suitable altitude or position on the straight-in approach.) *In order to avoid lengthy transmissions it may be preferable at times, to pass weather information in a second transmission. The words Surface wind, visibility, weather, cloud amount and height may be omitted at the discretion of the Approach Controller. The appropriate title of the barometric pressure must always be given.*
INTERMEDIATE APPROACH When ATC has advised 'No Delay Expected'	Cleared for ...... (type of approach). Runway ...... Report starting final Procedure Turn. <div align="center">OR</div>Report Procedure Turn complete. QFE/QFE Threshold ...... <div align="center">OR</div>QNH ...... Aerodrome/Threshold Elevation ...... ft. *Where necessary, Approach will request position reports at intermediate points.*

	Phraseology
At commencement of final procedure turn, or procedure turn completed	Cleared to land. Runway ...... OR Continue approach. Report at Outer Marker OR Report visual } (if necessary)
FINAL APPROACH At Outer Marker on final approach (when ATC has instructed aircraft to report at this position)	Cleared to land. Runway ...... Surface wind ...... (if required). OR Continue approach. OR (if necessary) ...... (instructions to discontinue approach).
When visual reference to the surface has been established (having requested this report).	Runway ...... Surface wind ...... Cleared to land. OR Report downwind/final.
MISSED APPROACH Initiated by pilot Initiated by controller	...... (appropriate instructions). Go around — I say again, go around (followed immediately by appropriate instructions) — acknowledge.
After touchdown	As for 'Inbound Aircraft — VFR'

MISCELLANEOUS EXAMPLES

To acknowledge cancellation of an IFR flight plan.	IFR plan cancelled at ...... (time).
Holding for weather improvement: To the first aircraft To subsequent aircraft	No traffic delay expected. Delay not determined ...... (number) aircraft holding for weather improvement.
Depletion of rescue services	...... (a/c identity) message from airport authority; fire service depleted. Take-offs and landings of aircraft operating for the public transport of passengers are restricted to aircraft under ...... metres in length, except in emergency.
Windshear	At ...... (time) a departing/arriving ...... (a/c type) reported windshear at ...... (altitude). Airspeed loss/gain ...... knots, strong left/right drift (if applicable).

	Phraseology
To pass aerodrome operating minima for non-public transport aircraft.	*See Section 3, Chapter 1*
To pass RVR values	*See Section 3, Chapter 3*
To pass runway braking action	*See Section 3, Chapters 3 and 4*
Governmental refusal of an ATC clearance to enter UK airspace	*See Section 5, Chapter 5*

9 RTF PHRASEOLOGY FOR RADAR CONTROLLERS

	Phraseology
To request an aircraft's heading	Report heading.
Turn an aircraft for identification	For identification, turn left/right heading ...... (for ...... time*). *If considered necessary.*
On identification	Identified ...... (position) OR Identified (further instructions as necessary).
If the aircraft is not identified after a turn	Not identified. For identification, turn left/right heading ...... OR Not identified. Resume own navigation.
To inform the pilot that radar control applied	Under radar control. OR Radar control service.
To inform pilot that radar advisory service is being applied.	Under radar advisory service. OR Radar advisory servcice.
Vectoring instructions (except avoiding action)	Continue present heading OR Continue heading ...... OR Turn left/right heading ...... OR Stop turn heading ...... OR Stop turn now OR Continue the turn heading ...... OR Leave ...... (fix) heading ......
Unknown traffic information	Unknown traffic ...... o'clock ...... miles ...... (opposite direction/crossing left/right) ......, if not sighted turn left/right heading ...... (if appropriate).
Avoiding action	Avoiding action, turn left/right immediately heading ...... traffic at ...... (position).
When all collision risk has passed	Clear of traffic. Turn left/right heading ...... (or, resume own navigation).

Appendix E

	Phraseology
Delaying action	Delaying action. Turn left/right heading ...... OR Delaying action. Make a 360 degree turn left/right. OR Delaying action. Orbit left/right.
When vectoring is completed	Resume own navigation ...... (followed by position or magnetic track and distance to next reporting point). *This transmission may be prefaced by the phrase.'Radar control/service terminated' if necessary*
When speed adjustments are necessary to maintain separation in the traffic pattern	Increase speed to ...... (number) knots. OR Reduce speed by/to ...... (number) knots. OR Maintain present speed. OR Resume normal speed. OR Reduce to minimum approach speed.
Instruct an aircraft to disregard a speed restriction contained in an ATC procedure	No ATC speed restriction.
Prior to a direct handover to another radar unit.	...... miles N/E/S/W of ...... (destination or reporting point). Continue heading ...... and contact ...... (ATSU callsign) on ...... (frequency).
Not yet within radar cover	No radar contact. I will keep you advised.
Prior to passing out of radar cover	Will shortly be leaving radar cover.
Loss of radar contact	I have lost radar contact due to ...... (reason). I will advise you when contact regained ...... (alternative instructions). OR Radar contact will be broken for ...... minutes due ...... (reason). I will advise you when contact regained ...... (alternative instructions).
To inform the pilot that radar services are being terminated.	Radar service terminated.
Giving navigational assistance to aircraft lost, or off track	Magnetic track to ...... (place) is ...... (degrees), distance ...... miles.
Giving navigational assistance to aircraft when gyro and compass unserviceable	Make all turns rate one. Execute instructions immediately on receipt.

Appendix E

	Phraseology
To give gyro check	Check your gyro heading. Magnetic track made good appears to be ...... *A gyro check need only be given if the radar controller suspects significant error.*
Aircraft radio failure	Reply not received. If you read ...... (ATSU callsign) turn left/right heading ....., I say again turn left/right heading ..... OR If you read (ATSU callsign) Squawk ......
If, after the above transmission has been made, the aircraft is seen to follow instructions	Turn observed. I will continue to pass instructions. OR Squawk observed, I will continue to pass instructions.
To instruct aircraft to omit position reports	Omit position reports. OR Next report at ...... (reporting point). OR Reports required only at ...... (reporting point(s)).
To instruct an aircraft to continue position reporting	Resume position reporting.
Operate transponder.	Squawk.
Select the mode and code, as applicable	Squawk ...... (code).
Confirm mode and code selected	Confirm squawk.
Reselect assigned mode and code	Recycle ...... (mode) ...... (code)
Use IDENT or SPI feature, retaining present code	Squawk Ident.
Select Emergency	Squawk Mayday.
Switch to Standby, retaining present code	Squawk Standby.
Switch on altitude reporting facility	Squawk Charlie
To confirm altimeter setting and aircraft level	Check altimeter setting and confirm level.
Stop altitude reporting, incorrect level readout.	Stop squawk Charlie. Wrong indication.
Switch off altitude reporting facility	Stop squawk Charlie
Switch off Mode A	Stop squawk Alpha
Switch off transponder	Stop squawk
When verifying Mode C data for accuracy	Verify ...... (level)
To verify that selection of special code 7500 is intentional	Confirm your are squawking assigned code ...... (code assigned to the aircraft by air traffic control).

10   RTF PHRASEOLOGY EXCLUSIVE TO APPROACH RADAR CONTROLLERS

	Phraseology
When a radar approach can probably be completed, but there is a possibility of the aircraft response being lost in clutter:— (a) When ILS is usable (b) When ILS is not usable	 ...... (type) approach may be affected by clutter, advise you check the approach with ILS. ...... (type) approach may be affected by clutter. Missed Approach instructions will be passed in good time if necessary.
When a radar approach is impracticable or not available	...... (type) approach not available due to ...... (reason).
Radar vectoring for surveillance radar approach	Vectoring for a surveillance radar approach; Runway ......
Radar vectoring for ILS approach	Vectoring for an ILS approach; Runway ......
Radar vectoring for an ILS approach with glidepath inoperative.	Vectoring for a localiser only approach; Runway ......
Before reaching Base Leg	(a) Descend to ...... ft. (Intermediate approach altitude) QNH ...... (b) This is a left/right hand circuit for runway ...... (c) On downwind leg ...... miles N/E/S/W of ...... (aerodrome). (Where applicable.)
On Base Leg When the radio failure procedure to be adopted is not published	On left/right base leg ...... miles N/E/S/W of ...... (aerodrome). If you lose radio contact on this approach ...... (instructions) and contact ...... (ATSU callsign) on ...... (frequency).
On the closing leg — at approach radar controller's discretion.	Closing final approach track from the left/right ...... miles from touchdown. *(The aircraft may be asked for a level check if applicable.)*
Circuit adjustment when spacing aircraft on final approach	Expect vector across ...... (aid) ...... (reason). OR This turn will take you through ...... (aid) ...... (reason) OR Taking you through ...... (aid) ...... (reason).

	Phraseology
Radar vectoring for ILS final approach.	
(i) Turns on to localiser.	
Radar controller to make final turn on	Turn left/right heading ......, report established on the localiser.
Aircraft to make final turn on	Closing the localiser from the left/right; report established.
Aircraft using automatic coupling (at pilot's request only).	Closing the localiser from the left/right; report established.
(ii) Pilot reports established on the localiser.	Continue descent on the ILS. (QFE ...... contact ...... tower on ...... frequency.)
(iii) Pilot reports established on the localiser. (Glidepath inoperative.)	...... (distance) ...... miles from touchdown, cleared for a localiser only approach, contact ...... tower on ...... (frequency).
At the controller's discretion (Glidepath inoperative)	Advisory height and distance from tochdown information is available if required.

NOTES:

1   Where radar vectoring is carried out as a standard procedure for arriving flights, certain of these phrases may be omitted at the discretion of the approach radar controller.

2   Indication of distance from touchdown should be added to the above phraseology as appropriate.

11   SURVEILLANCE RADAR APPROACHES

Example phraseology

The following phraseology and advisory heights indicated, assume a glidepath of approximately 3° with the aircraft at a height of 2000 ft. If commencing at other heights, descent should begin at the appropriate range (eg 1500 ft–4¾ miles, 1100 ft–3½ miles). Advisory heights and distances from touchdown at which descent is commenced will be adjusted for non-standard glidepaths and detailed in unit instructions.

Pressure datum

It is assumed that the aircraft is flying on QFE datum, and this shall be emphasised by inserting the words, 'on QFE', after the advisory heights at intervals during the approach. If the pilot advises that he is using QNH, the aerodrome/threshold elevation shall be added to these advisory heights and rounded up to the next 25 ft and 'altitude' shall be used in place of 'height' wherever applicable.

SRA Terminating at ½ mile from touchdown

	Phraseology
During the Intermediate Procedure.	This will be a surveillance radar approach, terminating at ½ mile from touchdown. Obstacle Clearance Limit ...... ft (above aerodrome/threshold elevation). Check your minima.
If a change of frequency is required for final approach.	Contact ...... on ...... (frequency) for final approach. After landing contact ...... on ...... (frequency).
Before commencing final descent.	Check wheels.
To alter course of aircraft.	Turn left/right (...... degrees) heading ......
At any convenient point during the approach.	Report runway (approach lights) in sight. After landing contact ...... on ...... (frequency).
Azimuth information.	Closing (final approach) track from the left/right. Heading (of ......) is good. On track. Slightly left/right of track.
Approaching 6½ miles from touchdown.	Approaching 6½ miles from touchdown — commence descent now to maintain a 3° glidepath.
At 6 miles from touchdown.	6 miles from touchdown — height should be 1850 ft.
At 5½ miles from touchdown.	5½ miles from touchdown — height should be 1700 ft.
At 5 miles from touchdown.	5 miles from touchdown — height should be 1550 ft.
At 4½ miles from touchdown.	4½ miles from touchdown — height should be 1400 ft.
At 4 miles from touchdown.	4 miles from touchdown — height should be 1250 ft — do not reply to further instructions.

	Phraseology
Landing Clearance. (Normally passed between 4 and 2 miles from touch-down.)	Cleared to land Runway ...... (Surface wind also given if necessary.)
At 3½ miles from touchdown.	3½ miles from touchdown – height should be 1100 ft.
At 3 miles from touchdown.	3 miles from touchdown – height should be 950 ft.
At 2½ miles from touchdown.	2½ miles from touchdown – height should be 800 ft.
At 2 miles from touchdown.	2 miles from touchdown – height should be 650 ft. Check Decision Height.
At 1½ miles from touchdown.	1½ miles from touchdown – height should be 500 ft.
At 1 mile from touchdown.	1 mile from touchdown – height should be 350 ft.
At ½ mile from touchdown.	½ mile from touchdown – Approach completed out.
Avoiding action or breaking off approach on instructions from Approach/Aerodrome Control.	Turn left/right ...... degrees, heading ...... climb to ...... ft (further instructions) – acknowledge.
No landing clearance received by 2 miles from touchdown, or other range agreed with Aerodrome Control.	Go around – I say again, go around – (missed approach or further instructions) – acknowledge. *The reason for the missed approach shall be given as soon as convenient.*
If during the latter stages of the the approach an aircraft reaches a position from which it appears to the controller that a successful instrument approach cannot be completed.	Continue visually or go around – (missed approach or further instructions) – Over. OR Go around – I say again, go around – (missed approach or further instructions) – acknowledge. OR Climb immediately, I say again climb immediately on heading ...... to ...... ft (further instructions) – acknowledge. *According to circumstances.*

SRA Terminating at 2 miles from touchdown

	Phraseology
During the Intermediate Approach.	This will be a surveillance radar approach, terminating at 2 miles from touchdown. Obstacle Clearance Limit ...... ft (above aerodrome/threshold elevation). Check your minima.
If a change of frequency is required for final approach.	Contact ...... on ...... (frequency) for final approach.
Before commencing final descent.	Check wheels.
To alter course of aircraft.	Turn left/right (...... degrees) heading ......
At any convenient point during the approach.	Report runway (approach lights) in sight. After landing contact ...... on ...... (frequency).
Azimuth information.	Closing (final approach) track from the left/right. Heading (of ......) is good. On track. Slightly left/right of track.
Approaching 6½ miles from touch-down.	Approaching 6½ miles from touchdown — commence descent now to maintain a 3° glidepath.
At 6 miles from touchdown.	6 miles from touchdown — height should be 1850 ft.
At 5 miles from touchdown.	5 miles from touchdown — height should be 1550 ft.
At 4 miles from touchdown.	4 miles from touchdown — height should be 1250 ft.
Landing Clearance. (Normally passed between 4 and 2 miles from touch-down.)	Cleared to land Runway ...... (Surface wind also given if necessary.)
At 3 miles from touchdown.	3 miles from touchdown — height should be 950 ft. Check Decision Height.
At 2 miles from touchdown.	2 miles from touchdown — height should be 650 ft. Approach completed out.
Avoiding action or breaking off approach on instructions from Approach/Aerodrome Control.	Turn left/right ...... degrees, heading ...... climb to ...... ft (further instructions).
No landing clearance received by 2 miles from touchdown, or other range agreed with Aerodrome Control.	Go around — I say again, go around — (missed approach or further instructions) — acknowledge. *The reason for the missed approach shall be given as soon as convenient.*

	Phraseology
If during the latter stages of the approach an aircraft reaches a position from which it appears to the controller that a successful instrument approach cannot be completed.	Continue visually or go around − (missed approach or further instructions) − Over. <div align="center">OR</div>Go around − I say again, go around − (missed approach or further instructions) − acknowledge. <div align="center">OR</div>Climb immediately, I say again climb immediately on heading ...... to ...... ft (further instructions) − acknowledge. *According to circumstances.*

12   RTF PHRASEOLOGY FOR QGH LETDOWN PROCEDURE

	Phraseology
INITIAL APPROACH	(a/c identity) transmit for D/F Make your heading ...... degrees, report steady.
Essential information	(a/c identity) this will be a QGH procedure. Aerodrome QNH is ...... The runway in use is ...... Obstacle clearance limit/visual manoeuvring height ...... ft Check decision height.
Weather Information	The (time) weather; Surface wind ...... (direction and speed). Visibility ...... km. Cloud ...... (amounts and heights). Weather ......
Homing	Transmit for D/F, turn left/right heading ...... degrees. *Repeated as necessary to overhead the VDF aerial.*
INTERMEDIATE APPROACH Overhead turn	(a/c identity) D/F indicates that you have passed overhead, turn left/right heading ...... degrees, report steady.
Outbound descent	(a/c identity) QFE/QFE threshold ...... Acknowledge. Descend to ...... ft. Report level. Transmit for D/F (repeated as necessary). Turn left/right heading ...... degrees.
Inbound turn	Standby for inbound turn, (pause) turn left/right heading ...... degrees, report steady.
FINAL APPROACH Inbound descent	In the event of a missed approach (appropriate instructions) Report QFE set. Descend to decision height, report field in sight. Transmit for D/F. Turn left/right heading ...... degrees OR continue heading ...... degrees. (Landing or circuit instructions as required).
Aircraft reports aerodrome in sight.	Contact tower on ...... (frequency).
If the aircraft indicates passing overhead the VDF aerial but has NOT reported 'visual'.	(a/c identity) go around, I say again go around (followed by the appropriate instructions) – acknowledge.

Glossary of Terms

This glossary is limited to terms which have a specific meaning in civil aviation.

Aerodrome Any area on land or water set apart or commonly used for affording facilities for the landing and departure of aircraft.

Aerodrome traffic zone The airspace extending from the surface to a height of 2000 ft above the level of the aerodrome and within a distance of $1\frac{1}{2}$ nm of its boundaries, except any part of that airspace which is within the aerodrome traffic zone of another aerodrome which is notified as being the controlling aerodrome.

Air-ground communications Two-way communications between aircraft and stations or locations on the surface of the earth.

Air traffic control centre A term used in the United Kingdom to describe a unit combining the functions of an area control centre and a flight information centre.

Air traffic control clearance Authorisation for an aircraft to proceed under conditions specified by an air traffic control unit.

Airway A control area or part of a control area established in the form of a corridor equipped with radio navigational aids.

Alternate aerodrome An aerodrome specified in the flight plan to which a flight may proceed when a landing at the intended destination becomes inadvisable.

Altitude The vertical distance of a level, a point or object considered as a point, measured from mean sea level.

Apron The part of an aerodrome provided for the stationing of aircraft for the embarkation and disembarkation of passengers, the loading and unloading of cargo, refuelling and for parking.

ATS route A specified route designed for channelling the flow of traffic as necessary for the provision of air traffic services.

Clearance limit The point to which an aircraft is granted an air traffic control clearance.

Code (SSR code) The number assigned to a particular multiple pulse reply signal transmitted by a transponder.

Control area (CTA) A controlled airspace extending upwards from a specified limit above the surface of the earth.

Control zone (CTR) A controlled airspace extending upwards from the surface of the earth to a specified limit.

Controlled airspace An airspace of defined dimensions within which air traffic control service is provided to IFR flights.

Cruising level A level maintained during a significant portion of a flight.

Data processing A systematic sequence of operations performed on data.

Decision height A specified height at which a missed approach must be initiated if the required visual reference to continue the approach to land has not been established.

Elevation The vertical distance of a point or level on, or affixed to the surface of, the earth, measured from mean sea level.

Entry point The first airways reporting point over which a flight passes on entering an FIR.

Estimated time of arrival The time at which the pilot estimates that the aircraft will be over a specified location.

Exit point The last airways reporting point over which a flight passes before leaving the FIR.

Flight information service A service provided for the purpose of giving information useful for the safe and efficient conduct of flights.

Flight levels (FL) Surfaces of constant atmospheric pressure which are related to a specific pressure datum 1013.2 millibars and are separated by specific pressure intervals.

Flight plan (FPL) Specified information provided to air traffic services units relative to an intended flight or portion of a flight of an aircraft.

Flow control Measures designed to adjust the flow of traffic into a given airspace, along a given route or bound for a given aerodrome, so as to ensure the most effective utilisation of the airspace.

Glide path A descent profile determined for vertical guidance during a final approach.

Height The vertical distance of a level, a point, or an object considered as a point measured from a specified datum.

Holding point A specified location, identified by visual or other means, in the vicinity of which the position of an aircraft in flight is maintained in accordance with air traffic control clearances; or a location on the manoeuvring area of an aerodrome at which an aircraft carries out an engine run-up or is held before entering a runway for take-off.

Holding procedure A predetermined manoeuvre which keeps an aircraft within a specified airspace whilst awaiting further clearance.

IFR The symbol used to designate the Instrument Flight Rules.

IFR flight A flight conducted in accordance with the Instrument Flight Rules.

Instrument approach procedure A series of predetermined manoeuvres for the orderly transfer of an aircraft under instrument flight conditions from the beginning of an initial approach to a landing, or to a point from which a landing may be made visually.

Instrument meteorological conditions Meteorological conditions expressed in terms of visibility, horizontal and vertical distance from cloud, less than the minima specified for visual meteorological conditions.

Known traffic Traffic, the current flight details and intentions of which are known to the controller concerned through direct communication or co-ordination.

Level A generic term relating to the vertical position of an aircraft in flight and meaning variously, height, altitude or flight level.

Location indicator A four-letter code group formulated in accordance with rules prescribed by ICAO and assigned to the location of an aeronautical fixed station.

Manoeuvring area The part of an aerodrome provided for the movement of aircraft, excluding the apron and the maintenance area.

Mode (SSR mode) The letter or number assigned to a specific pulse spacing of the interrogation signals transmitted by an interrogator.

Night The time between half an hour after sunset and half an hour before sunrise; sunset and sunrise being determined at surface level.

Non-radar separation The separation used when aircraft position information is derived from sources other than radar.

Primary radar A radar system which uses reflected radio signals.

Profile The orthogonal projection of a flight path or portion thereof on the vertical surface containing the nominal track.

Quadrantal cruising level Specified cruising

levels determined in relation to magnetic track within quadrants of the compass.

Radar A radio detection device which provides information on range, azimuth and/or elevation of objects.

Radar approach An approach executed by an aircraft under the direction of a radar controller.

Radar control A term used to indicate that radar-derived information is employed directly in the provision of air traffic control service.

Radar departure A term used where the control of departing traffic is subject to the use of surveillance radar to assist them to leave the vicinity of an aerodrome safely and expeditiously.

Radar display An electronic display of radar-derived information depicting the position and movement of an aircraft.

Radar handover The transfer of responsibility for the control of an aircraft between two controllers using radar, following the identification of the aircraft by both controllers.

Radar identification The process of correlating a particular radar blip or radar position symbol with a specified aircraft.

Radar monitoring The use of radar for the purpose of providing aircraft with information and advice relevant to significant deviations from nominal flight path.

Radar separation The separation used when aircraft position information is derived from radar sources.

Radar unit That element of an air traffic service unit which uses radar equipment to provide one or more services.

Radar vectoring Provision of navigational guidance to aircraft in the form of specific headings, based on the use of radar.

Radial A magnetic bearing extending from a VOR/VORTAC/TACAN, or NDB

Release point The position, time or level at which an arriving aircraft comes under the jurisdiction of either:

(a) approach/zone control *or*
(b) approach/zone radar control in accordance with published procedures.

Reporting point A specified geographical location in relation to which the position of an aircraft can be reported.

Rescue Co-ordination Centre (RCC) A centre established within an assigned search and rescue area to promote efficient organisation of search and rescue.

Runway A rectangular area on a land aerodrome prepared for the landing and take-off of aircraft.

Secondary Surveillance Radar (SSR) A system of secondary radar using ground interrogators and airborne transponders to determine the position of an aircraft in range and azimuth and when agreed modes and codes are used, height and identity as well.

Special VFR flight A controlled VFR flight authorised by air traffic control to operate within a control zone under meteorological conditions below the visual meteorological conditions.

Surveillance radar Radar equipment used to determine the position of an aircraft in range and azimuth angle.

Terminal Control Area (TMA) A control area normally established at the confluence of airways in the vicinity of one or more major aerodromes.

Threshold The beginning of that portion of the runway usable for landing.

Touchdown The point where the predetermined glide path intercepts the runway.

Transfer of control point A defined point located along the flight path of an aircraft, at which the responsibility for providing air traffic control service to the aircraft is transferred from one control unit or control position to the next.

VFR The symbol used to designate the Visual Flight Rules.

Visibility The ability, determined by atmospheric conditions and expressed in units of distance, to see and identify prominent un-lighted objects by day and prominent lighted objects by night.

(a) Flight visibility: the visibility forward from the flight deck of an aircraft in flight.
(b) Ground visibility: the horizontal visibility at ground level.

(c) Runway visual range (RVR): horizontal visibility along a runway.

Visual Meteorological Conditions (VMC) Me-teorological conditions expressed in terms of visibility, horizontal and vertical distance from cloud, equal to or better than specified minima.

List of Abbreviations

ACC—Area Control Centre

or

Area Control

ADC—Aerodrome Control

ADF—Automatic Direction Finding Equipment

ADIZ—Air Defence Identification Zone

ADR—Advisory Route

AFIS—Aerodrome Flight Information Service

AFS—Aeronautical Fixed Service

AFTN—Aeronautical Fixed Telecommunications Network

a/g—Air-to-ground

AIP—Aeronautical Information Publication

AIRAC—Aeronautical Information Regulation and Control

AIREP—Plain language form of air report

AIS—Aeronautical Information Service

alt—Altitude

altn—Alternate

APC—Approach Control

ASMI—Aerodrome Surface Movement Indicator

ATA—Actual Time of Arrival

ATC—Air Traffic Control

ATCC—Air Traffic Control Centre

ATCO—Air Traffic Control Officer

ATD—Actual Time of Departure

ATS—Air Traffic Service

ATSU—Air Traffic Service Unit

awy—Airway

bcn—Beacon

BOH—Break-off height

C—Degrees Celsius (Centigrade)

CAC—Combined Approach Control Services

CDN—Co-ordination Message

com—Communications

cor—Correction

CRT—Cathode ray tube

c/s—Callsign

CTA—Control Area

CTR—Control Zone

CW—Continuous wave

cwy—Clearway

D—Danger area

deg—Degrees

dep—Departure

dest—Destination

DFTI—Distance from Touchdown Indicator

dist—Distance

DME—Distance Measuring Equipment

DVOR—Doppler Very High Frequency Omni-directional Radio Range

E—East or eastern longitude

EAT—Expected Approach Time

elev—Elevation

ETA—Estimated Time of Arrival

ETD—Estimated Time of Departure

Abbreviations

fac—Facilities
FDPS—Flight Data Processing System
FIC—Flight Information Centre
FIR—Flight Information Region
FIS—Flight Information Service
FL—Flight Level
flt—Flight
FPL—Filed Flight Plan Message
fpm—Feet per minute
FPPS—Flight Plan Processing System
freq—Frequency
ft—Feet

GAT—General Air Traffic
GCA—Ground Controlled Approach
GMC—Ground Movement Control
GMT—Greenwich Mean Time
gnd—Ground
GP—Glide Path
g/s—Ground speed

hel—helicopter
H/F—High Frequency (3MHz – 30MHz)
hgt—Height
hr—Hour
hvy—Heavy
Hz—Hertz (cycles per second)

IAL—Instrument Approach and Landing Chart
IAS—Indicated Air Speed
IBN—Identification beacon
ICAO—International Civil Aviation Organisation
IFF—Identification friend/foe
IFR—Instrument Flight Rules
ILS—Instrument Landing System
IM—Inner marker
IMC—Instrument Meteorological Conditions
IMI—Interrogation sign (.. – ..)
int—Intersection
intl—International

JATCRU—Joint Air Traffic Control Radar Unit

kg—kilogrammes
kHz—kiloHertz
km—kilometres
kmh—Kilometres per hour
kt—Knots
kW—Kilowatts

Lat—Latitude
LCN—Load Classification Number
ldg—Landing
LF—Low Frequency (30 – 300 kHz)
lgt—Light or lighting
LMT—Local Mean Time
Long—Longitude
LRG—Long range
ltd—Limited

m—Metres
Mag—Magnetic
maint—Maintenance
max—maximum
mb—millibars
MEA—Minimum En-route Altitude
met—Meteorology
MF—Medium Frequency (300kHz – 3 MHz)
MHz—MegaHertz
Mil—Military
min—Minutes
mKR—Marker radio beacon
MLS—Microwave Landing System
MM—Middle Marker
MOTNE—Meteorological Operational Tele-communications Network Europe
mph—Statute miles per hour
mps—Metres per second
msl—Mean Sea Level
MTA—Military Training Area
mtu—Metric units

N—North or northern latitude
nav—Navigation
NDB—Non-directional Radio Beacon
NE—North East
nm—Nautical miles

NOTAM—A Notice containing information concerning the establishment, condition or change, in any aeronautical facility, service, procedure or hazard.

NW—North West

OAC—Oceanic Area Control Centre
obst—Obstruction
OCA—Oceanic Control Area
occ—Occulting
OCL—Obstacle Clearance Limit
OM—Outer marker
ops—Operations
OSV—Ocean Station Vessel

P—Prohibited area
PANS—Procedure for Air Navigation Services
PAR—Precision Approach Radar
PLN—Flight plan
PNR—Point of No Return
POB—Persons on Board
PPI—Plan Position Indicator

QAM—Latest meteorological observation
QBI—Compulsory IFR flight
QDM—Magnetic heading (zero wind)
QDR—Magnetic bearing
QFE—Atmospheric pressure at aerodrome elevation (or at runway threshold)
QFF—Atmospheric pressure converted to mean sea level (millibars)
QFU—Magnetic orientation of runway
QNE—Indicated height on landing, with altimeter sub-scale set to 1013.2 millibars (29.92 inches)
QNH—Altimeter sub-scale setting to obtain elevation when on the ground
QTE—True bearing

RAC—Rules of the air and air traffic services
RCC—Rescue Co-ordination Centre
RCF—Radio communication failure message
RDPS—Radar Data Processing System
Rec—Receiver
ref—Reference

REP—Repointing point
RNG—Radio range
ROC—Rate of climb
RSP—Responder beacon
RSR—En-route Surveillance Radar
RTF—Radiotelephone
RTT—Radioteletypewriter
RVR—Runway Visual Range
rwy—Runway

S—South or southern latitude
SAR—Search and Rescue
SE—South East
sec—Seconds
SIA—Standard Instrument Approach
SID—Standard Instrument Departure
SIGMET—Information in plain language issued by the meteorological office
SMC—Surface Movement Control
SMR—Surface Movement Radar (ASMI)
SPL—Supplementary flight plan message
SRA—Surveillance Radar Approach
SRE—Surveillance radar element of GCA
SSR—Secondary Surveillance Radar
SST—Supersonic transport
STOL—Short Take-off and Landing
SUPPS—Regional Supplementary Procedures
SVFR—Special Visual Flight Rules
SW—South West
swy—Stop way

T—Temperature
TAF—Aerodrome forecast in abbreviated form
TAR—Terminal Area Surveillance Radar
TAS—True Airspeed
TDZ—Touchdown
TFC—Traffic
thr—Threshold
TMA—Terminal Control Area
TR—Track
TVOR—Terminal VOR
twr—Aerodrome control tower
twy—Taxiway

Abbreviations

UAC—Upper Area Control Centre
UAR—Upper Air Route
UHF—Ultra High Frequency (300–3000 MHz)
UIC—Upper Information Centre
UIR—Upper Flight Information Region
unl—Unlimited
UTA—Upper Control Area

Var—Magnetic variation
VASIS—Visual Approach Slope Indicator System
VDF—Very High Frequency Direction Finding Station
ver—Vertical
VFR—Visual Flight Rules

VHF—Very High Frequency (30 MHz – 300 MHz)
vis—Visibility
VLF—Very Low Frequency (3 – 30 kHz)
VLR—Very Long Range
VMC—Visual Meteorological Conditions
VOLMET—Meteorological information for aircraft in flight
VOR—VHF Omni-directional Radio Range
VTOL—Vertical Take-off and Landing

W—West or western longitude
WIP—Work in progress
WX—Weather

Index

Index